Industrial Studies 2
the bargaining context

Trade Union Industrial Studies

This series makes two new types of provision in the
area of industrial relations: first it is specifically
directed to the needs of active trade unionists who
want to equip themselves to be more effective, and
second, the books are linked together in a series
related to the requirements of existing training and
education courses.

The books have been designed by a Curriculum
Development Group drawn from the Society of
Industrial Tutors: Michael Barratt Brown, Ed Coker,
Jim Fyrth, Bob Houlton and Geoffrey Stuttard,
together with Charles Clark and Francis Bennett of
the Hutchinson Publishing Group. The Curriculum
Development Group has prepared the guide lines for
the texts and edited them so that they form a
complete set of teaching material for tutors and
students primarily for use on trade union courses.

The texts are issued in sets of four, together with
an accompanying resource book which provides
additional background material for tutors and
students.

Trade Union Industrial Studies

This series is published in three sets, each consisting of
four student texts and an accompanying resource book like
this one. This book includes additional teaching material for
tutors and students, a recommended list of books and a
further exploration of the subject.

Already published

The Activist's Handbook   *Bob Houlton*
Statistics for Bargainers   *Karl Hedderwick*
Calculating   *Joyce & Bill Hutton*
The Organized Worker   *Tony Topham*
Industrial Studies 1: the key skills   *Eds. Ed Coker &*
   Geoffrey Stuttard

Industrial Action   *Ernie Johnston*
Pay at Work   *Bill Conboy*
Work Study   *Jim Powell*
Workers' Rights   *Paul O'Higgins*
Industrial Studies 2: the bargaining context   *Eds.*
   Ed Coker & Geoffrey Stuttard

In preparation

The Trade Union Rule Book   *Richard Fletcher*
Information at Work   *Michael Barratt Brown*
Trade Unions and Government   *Ann Taylor*
Now You're the Manager
Industrial Studies 3: understanding industrial society
   Eds. Ed Coker & Geoffrey Stuttard

Industrial Studies 2
the bargaining context

Edited by Ed Coker & Geoffrey Stuttard

Arrow Books in association with the
Society of Industrial Tutors

Arrow Books Ltd
3 Fitzroy Square, London W1

An imprint of the Hutchinson Publishing Group

London Melbourne Sydney Auckland
Wellington Johannesburg and agencies
throughout the world

Set in Monotype Times
Printed in Great Britain by
The Anchor Press Ltd, and bound by
Wm Brendon & Son Ltd, both
of Tiptree, Essex

ISBN 0 09 912250 2

Contents

A Note about the Contributors

Eric Batstone: Research Fellow, Industrial Relations Research Unit, University of Warwick

Ron Bean: Senior Lecturer in Economics, Dept of Economics and Commerce, University of Liverpool

Ian Boraston: Lecturer, Dept of Management Studies, Lanchester Polytechnic

Stephen Frenkel: Lecturer in Industrial Relations, Dept of Economics, University of New South Wales

Doug Gowan: Assistant Secretary, Training College, Trades Union Congress

John McIlroy: Staff Tutor in Industrial Relations, Dept of Extra-Mural Studies, University of Manchester

J. E. Mortimer: Chairman, Advisory, Conciliation and Arbitration Service

Paul O'Higgins: Lecturer in Law and Fellow of Christ's College, Cambridge

Mike Pedler: Senior Lecturer, Dept of Management Studies, Sheffield Polytechnic

Geoffrey Woodcock: Lecturer in Sociology, Institute of Extension Studies, University of Liverpool

Section I

Introduction

'Collective bargaining is the best method of conducting industrial relations...'
(Report of the Donovan Commission, p. 50, para. 203(1)).

As one trade union official said, 'The difficulty is that you're often trying to apply logic to illogical situations; sitting back and analysing what happens – we rarely have time to do this.' (See also p. 52.)

The bargaining process is so familiar to trade unionists that it is often taken for granted. There is little opportunity for 'sitting back and analysing what happens'. There is, too, a surprising scarcity of reading material to which active trade unionists may refer. As one trade union negotiator (see p. 67) reminded us, 'It's not just a game you're engaged in.' Bargaining, after all, is at the centre of industrial, social, political and economic arguments; it is subject to local, national and international pressures; it is important in the short term and the long term, both to those in industry and to others outside.

Furthermore, effective collective bargaining is the activity that many other elements in industrial relations are designed to support: the disclosure of information, communication systems, union organization, procedure agreements, to mention but a few. In fact, considering that bargaining is the basic element of our 'system' of industrial relations it is remarkable that so little has been written about it for the practitioner and teacher. We hope that this book will go some way to remedying that.

The subject of this resource book, therefore, is bargaining. It has been written for active trade unionists and tutors who teach bargaining skills. It is concerned with the practice and theory of bargaining, with its nature and scope, the skills involved and the ways in which these may be learnt, taught and practised.

This book follows the pattern of *Industrial Studies 1* in presenting material to accompany the four books in the same set. However, it differs from it in that it concentrates on one theme only, albeit a very wide one.

Like *Industrial Studies 1*, this book's first aim is to help students – if necessary through their tutors – in their search for greater understanding of the industry and society in which they work and live. Also, as in the rest of the Trade Union Industrial Studies series, the book starts from the assumption that in the development of self-confidence, greater knowledge and understanding are as important as the acquisition of skills such as chairmanship and negotiating techniques.

THE TRADE UNION INDUSTRIAL STUDIES SERIES

The series makes two new types of provision. Firstly, it is specifically directed towards the needs of active trade unionists who want to equip themselves through study to be more effective. Secondly, the books of the series are linked together for use in existing training and education courses or for individual study at home.

These are the twelve books in the series: *The Activist's Handbook*; *The Organized Worker*; *Statistics for Bargainers*; *Calculating*; *Pay at Work*; *Industrial Action*; *Work Study*; *Workers' Rights*; *Information at Work*; *Trade Unions and Government*; *The Trade Union Rule Book*; *The Job of the Manager*.

These texts are issued in sets of four, each of which is accompanied by a resource book (*Industrial Studies 1, 2* and *3*) which provides additional material for tutors and students.

Many active trade unionists come into adult study by way of day release or other such courses. The fifteen books in the series provide a reserve of knowledge and ideas from the field of industrial relations. Both tutors and students will find the series valuable for use in organized courses.

For those who cannot attend an organized course or who have completed a course and wish to study at home the series also provides essential material. Most books in the series have exercises for use either in class or when studying at home and the three accompanying resource books provide advice on how to study and give extensive reading lists and other references.

The twelve books and the sections on teaching and learning in the supplementary resource books cover very many industrial relations topics and the necessary advice about both learning and teaching the subject to others. Thus the series is a complete learning package which also contains much that is new for the reader who is interested in industrial relations.

The series has been designed by a Curriculum Development Group drawn from the Society of Industrial Tutors: Michael Barratt Brown, Ed Coker, Jim Fyrth, Bob Houlton and Geoffrey Stuttard, in association with Charles Clark and Francis Bennett, of the publishers, Hutchinson, with the editorial assistance of Penny Butler. Over three years, this Curriculum Development Group has produced the guide lines for the series and shaped the three resource books to ensure they form an integrated set of teaching and learning material for tutors, students and the general reader.

Several assumptions have guided this work:

1. Most students have considerable potential learning capacity.
2. Any limitations due to age or inadequate schooling *can* be overcome.
3. Experience is the adult learner's 'hidden asset' providing it can be developed.
4. Books grounded in experience, and linking theory and experience, are essential to adult intellectual development.
5. Adult learning is enhanced when the student's experience of *skills* and *contexts* is related to theories and *concepts*.

The authors of the twelve books were asked to follow this progression: starting from the *skills* needed by students, and then analysing the *context* within which these skills are relevant, and finally considering the *concepts* which relate to these processes in an industrial society. The three resource books follow in the same progression. *Industrial Studies 1* concentrates on basic teaching and learning skills; *Industrial Studies 2* is centred round negotiating, which is the context within which trade union students operate; *Industrial Studies 3* moves into a wider, more theoretical and conceptual examination of industrial studies generally and of teaching and learning in an industrial context.

A review of these assumptions, and of other theories, possible biases and blind spots in the project is planned for the end of the series.

HOW TO USE *Industrial Studies 2*

Industrial Studies 1 in this series dealt with much basic material and carried reading matter suitable for 'first time' and advanced students as well as tutors. This volume stands, as it were, on the shoulders of *Industrial Studies 1* and the first eight books in the series. It therefore carries much more material suitable for tutors and more advanced students. But each of Sections III, IV and V carries at least one essay which is aimed at students. (The one essay in Section II is for students too.) These essays are listed below, but we would emphasize that the tutor should decide whether he thinks an essay is appropriate for a group or a particular student to tackle on their own. For those who have no tutor, however, we suggest that the following essays are suitable for students who have done some work on the books accompanying this volume and *Industrial Studies 1*:

'Principles in Work-Place Bargaining' (Section II, pp. 19–39): The single essay in this section is a good basic thesis which many students might look at and which should provoke much thought and discussion.

'Bargaining in Practice and Theory' (Section III): 'Trade Union Negotiators' (pp. 43–67), a transcript of statements by practitioners, gives much matter-of-fact advice which students might examine and discuss further.

'The Framework of Collective Bargaining' (Section IV): In this section the essay 'The Bargaining System' (pp. 142–59) outlines the main trends in the development of the bargaining framework from an institutional viewpoint. It may be supplemented by some of the references given on pp. 261–82 in Section VI, 'Reading Guide and Useful Sources'.

'Bargaining and Workers' Rights' (Section V): The essay 'Bargaining for Rights' (pp. 211–45) is aimed at students who have done some previous study, in particular those who have read *Workers' Rights* by Paul O'Higgins in this series.

'Reading Guide and Useful Sources' (Section VI, pp. 261–82): will be useful both to those who have worked on the accompanying books and to those who have read the essays in this volume.

Finally, we think that all the essays in this volume will have something to offer the tutor, because they add either to the contents of the four accompanying books or to the body of literature on collective bargaining.

MICHAEL BARRATT BROWN   ED COKER
JIM FYRTH   BOB HOULTON
GEOFFREY STUTTARD   CHARLES CLARK
FRANCIS BENNETT

The Bargaining Context
by Geoffrey Stuttard

You learn negotiating skills by experience and observation. You know how far they will go, they know how far you will go and there are certain steps which both sides can take to resolve the problem. But the two sides can misjudge each other. You can't be 100 per cent sure that you've judged your case rightly or you've judged their reactions rightly. You may hear certain statements and think, 'Ah, they've gone as far as they're going to go on this issue and there's no point in pressing them any further.' You agree and find you're wrong, and you could have got more if you'd pursued it. That teaches you you can't always be right in your judgements, though most of the time you are right if you have years of experience. (A trade union official: see p. 58.)

The essays in this book are about bargaining because that is one of the main pursuits of active trade unionists; it is also the central theme of the four books in this batch of the Trade Union Industrial Studies series. Bargaining is not the only pursuit of trade unionists, but it is a necessary one, and always has been. It has grown out of the historical development of unions in their role of protecting workers regarded as instruments of production, it is linked to their role of changing industrial society, and it is essential to their role today.

Tony Topham in *The Organized Worker* in this series has described unions as 'organized for bargaining', and when George Woodcock as General Secretary of the TUC said that trade union structure should depend on purpose, it was clear that bargaining was part of that purpose. In the nineteenth century, unions had to take collective action to bargain on behalf of the isolated individual worker. In the twentieth century, they still need to take this action, especially now when work is being broken up into individual or small group units. This is emphasized in the books in this batch. In *Work Study*, Jim Powell describes how bargaining is central to work-place control of jobs; in *Pay at Work* Bill Conboy demonstrates the importance of bargaining in the settlement of wages, and in *Workers' Rights* Paul O'Higgins sums up by stating that workers get their rights by negotiation and action, a view mirrored in *Industrial Action* by Ernie Johnston.

The more recent developments in national incomes policies, redundancies and increased unemployment, rapidly changing technology, the growth in the power of international companies, and moves towards increased worker participation are signs that the context of bargaining is constantly changing.

There are various participants in the bargaining arena, for example:

1. Trade unions: the Trades Union Congress; international union federations; industrial trade secretariats; national federations; unions at national, regional, district, area and local levels; trades councils; and work-place organization, especially work groups, works councils, shop stewards' committees and combine committees.

2. Employers: the Confederation of British Industry; confederations and federations; multi-plant companies; multi- and international companies; regional and local associations; single-industry and multi-industry firms; cartels, monopolies, oligopolies; family, private, public, nationalized and semi-nationalized firms.

3. Joint organizations: national joint councils for a firm or industry; district joint councils; joint works councils; the National Economic Development Council.

4. Government: Ministries, especially the Treasury, the Departments of Industry and Employment; agencies, especially the Manpower Services Commission and the Health and Safety Commission.

5. The Courts: High Court and Appeal Courts; tribunals and arbitration bodies; the Advisory, Conciliation and Arbitration Service.

6. Local authorities.

7. Consumers, customers, individuals, voters, the media.

8. Academic specialists, consultants, researchers.

The scope of bargaining has grown out of all recognition since early industrial days. It now includes:

1. Wages and salaries, rates and differentials, incentive schemes, prices and incomes policy.

2. Hours, holidays, special working arrangements; shifts, overtime, weekends.

3. Job evaluation, work and method study.

4. Technical and organizational change, productivity.

5. Sickness, accidents, health and safety.

6. Job security, pensions, retirement schemes.

7. Discipline, redundancy, dismissals.

8. Job and work satisfaction, work groups and working conditions.
9. Human relations, welfare, social activities.
10. Education, promotion, training.
11. Policy-making, investment, accounts.
12. Power-sharing and participation.
13. Union recognition, facilities, closed shops, check-off systems.

The essays in this book relate to the context of bargaining, moving through the following stages, outlined below, each of which is the title of a section:

1. Principles in work-place bargaining.
2. Bargaining in practice and theory.
3. The framework of collective bargaining.
4. Bargaining and workers' rights.

Principles in Work-Place Bargaining

The first question for an active trade unionist, as well as for an employer, for the T U C, or for a government, is what is the purpose of bargaining. A book or an essay in the Trade Union Industrial Studies series often starts with a practical example of its main theme which will connect it with work-place experience. In this book we have deliberately put an essay on strategy first, before examples of bargaining in practice, in order to underline the importance of what the three authors of the essay call 'directions in bargaining'. They indicate that some of the conditions away from the bargaining table are crucial, and that the most valuable of these is a widespread knowledge and understanding of trade union principles.

This thesis, that the work-place trade unionist needs to look further than the immediate problem and to judge issues in the long term, can be extended to the need to look more widely still, perhaps nationally and internationally, and over a time scale longer than the year or so of a collective agreement. Industrial tutors' knowledge of this need leads them to press for continuity of study, for longer courses, for the extension of the areas of study, and to counter the inevitable lure of their particular work-place and industry for trade union students.

Bargaining in Practice and Theory

Some people are engaged in bargaining, and others write about it and teach it. But there is not always a link between the practice and the theories, which is essential if all those involved are to learn from each other.

We have included a long section on trade union negotiators to illustrate the thought and actions of practitioners, sometimes contradictory, sometimes untidy, but based on their day-to-day experience of the bargaining context as they see it and feel it. This matches material in Jim Powell's *Work Study*, in which, for instance (p. 77), he claims that a good negotiator has to be something of a prophet. It also underlines other material set out at length in Ernie Johnston's book *Industrial Action*.

Ron Bean's essay, 'Industrial Reactions', contains a more formal description of the actions and reactions which the bargaining context causes trade unionists to take, bridging theory and practice. This essay suggests that many of the sanctions described are normal and to be expected in British industrial relations, arising from understood and intelligible conflicts of interest and values.

Trade unionists recognize, of course, that much negotiation and discussion with management is not over matters in which interests conflict, but over those where agreements can be reached that are to the advantage of both parties. In these cases, the importance of negotiation is that it allows the unions to exercise some influence and power over the decisions. But the essays in this section suggest that the essential relationship between unions and management is one of conflict, and that bargaining is about matters where interests are opposed, or are seen as opposed, either in the short or long run. They also stress, incidentally, the importance of trust and confidence between the bargaining partners, in spite of the underlying conflict.

Then there is the question of how to teach and learn about bargaining, whether this can be done at all, or whether it is a matter of experience and temperament. The essay in two parts by Mike Pedler sets out some of the ways in which the bargaining process can be analysed and some of the ways in which it may be taught and learned. Tutors and students have different ways of approaching the subject, which have grown out of experience in work-places and industries, and which are very disparate – economic, political, social, institutional, or a mixture. Mike Pedler's behavioural approach may be new to some tutors and students, and has been included for that reason.

The Framework of Collective Bargaining

In the work-place the bargaining 'opponent' of the trade union representative is often the supervisor or local manager. However, in industrial bargaining the parties can be much more varied. Doug Gowan's essay, 'The Bargaining System', describes the different forms of bargaining machinery developed over the years to cover a mixture of interests and levels – work-place, company, industry, federal, national. The list extends to future international bargaining.

Employers, like trade unionists, have had to adapt *their* organizations to suit the bargaining context. Geoffrey Woodcock's essay, 'Key Management Institutions', sets out for trade unionists some of the forms, mainly at national and industrial levels, that have grown out of this pressure.

There is another interest at the bargaining table which has in the past either been unrecognized or seen as secondary – the Government. J. E. Mortimer's essay, 'The Government and Collective Bargaining', demonstrates the present impossibility of ignoring this factor. This situation is developed at length in the book in this series, *Trade Unions and Government*. The essay indicates a growing trend towards a form of 'national' bargaining between Government, the TUC and the CBI, seen in the joint statement of intent of 1964, ten years later in the social contract of 1974, and the pay and prices policies of the years between and since. Shall we see the emergence of a fourth major party, the consumer, demanding a place at the bargaining table?

But institutions should be the servants of the active trade unionists' needs: they must serve a realistic purpose. If not, then new ones will be created and old ones discarded. This is one of the reasons for the emergence of the 'informal system' described in the Donovan Commission *Report*, for the pattern, for example, of shop stewards' local and national combine committees which cut across the institutions of unions, employers and government, and present such an enigma to the courts. The various factors and pressures in the work-place which can affect the practitioners constantly cause them to challenge neatly set out patterns: technologies, social rules, political power manoeuvring, custom and practice, ever-changing rules, regulations and laws.

Bargaining and Workers' Rights

The extensive changes in the scope of bargaining are described in detail in John McIlroy's essay, 'Bargaining for Rights'. He feels that these rights depend not so much on the law as on union strength in the work-place or industry. Paul O'Higgins' essay, 'Picketing and the Law', demonstrates the theme of this book, *Workers' Rights*, the law's difficulties in its attempts to deal fairly with what seem to be simple questions of union needs.

The move away from mere wage negotiations, from limited 'terms and conditions of employment' into discussions about many other topics (see pp. 232 ff.), illustrates a major change in the bargaining context, a new and wider-angled attitude to work and jobs, a social concern for health and safety, a moral concern for fairness, a political concern for power-sharing, and a psychological concern for involvement, which are some of the pressures behind the trend towards industrial democracy, whatever shape it may eventually take.

For the active trade unionist and for the tutor who is sharing in learning and teaching about bargaining, the context is a rich one. It can range from the smallest work-place to the international scene, Governments, EEC, OPEC and multi-national companies. Its richness and variety can be used positively as a valuable area for study, only a small part of which has been covered in this book. Some of the other parts are dealt with in *Industrial Studies 3: understanding industrial society.*

Section II
Principles in Work-Place Bargaining
by Eric Batstone, Ian Boraston and Stephen Frenkel

This section, consisting of a single essay, has been placed first in the book because it analyses for the work-place trade unionist some of the crucial conditions, circumstances and relationships which can lead to local bargaining success, which may be judged in terms of maintaining and advancing union members' interests. The essay is based upon some years of research in a variety of firms.

The main topic is *work-place* bargaining, although the authors recognize that their analysis has to be seen within a larger context: 'In the face of major changes in industrial techniques and industrial reorganization, and with a greater state involvement in industrial relations, stewards will face both opportunities and obstacles.' (p. 38)

It is through work-place bargaining that most trade unionists first become involved in the bargaining context, and thence can begin to look outwards at wider bargaining circles, regional, national and international, as well as across the industrial network through contact with other shop stewards, unions, firms and industries.

It is interesting to consider whether this work-place view, organic and somewhat opportunist, can suit or be fitted into the developing bargaining interdependence of the national framework of industrial relations. Does the analysis fit, for example, the 1975/6 national bargaining context? Are trade union principles, bargaining awareness, the favourable balance of power, and bargaining relationships just as important at the national level? What light does the analysis throw on emerging forms of industrial democracy and workers' participation?

Whatever the answers to these questions, the essay provides a helpful starting point for the active work-place trade unionist within the bargaining context. (Eds.)

Introduction

Shop stewards employ a wide range of methods in their attempts to protect and promote the interests of their members. Through their unions, stewards may attempt to influence government policy; to improve the benefits provided by the union, and to develop rules of behaviour among their members without involving management. But for most stewards bargaining is the most important way in which they can maintain and advance their members' interests. It is bargaining that we focus upon in this essay.

Stewards, when bargaining, seek to win certain concessions and rights from management. Success in bargaining is often thought to depend upon good arguments and debating skills at the bargaining table itself. This is true in part, but success does depend much more on a number of conditions which exist away from the bargaining table. These conditions are our main interest here. In summary, our argument is that effective trade union bargaining requires an understanding of the following four fundamental, though complex, areas of knowledge:

1. Trade union principles.
2. Bargaining awareness.
3. Power.
4. Bargaining relationships.

An understanding of *trade union principles* is required to give trade union bargaining effort a sense of direction; *bargaining awareness* is the ability to identify issues for bargaining; a knowledge of the realities of industrial *power* is necessary, as is also an awareness of the nature of *bargaining relationships* between unions and management. But clearly, in practice, knowledge and understanding are not sufficient conditions for effective bargaining. A favourable balance of power and favourable bargaining relationships are necessary. Each of these four elements is set out in Figure 1 opposite. Obviously each in turn raises a number of subsidiary issues, some of which are also indicated in Figure 1. These are dealt with in the text.

UNION PRINCIPLES

If the aim of bargaining is the promotion of members' interests, then the steward requires some sense of direction. He needs to know pretty clearly what he is trying to do. Union principles are important for this reason: that they give the steward a sense of perspective. Our first section (pp. 23 ff.) considers union principles and the importance of an 'educated' mem-

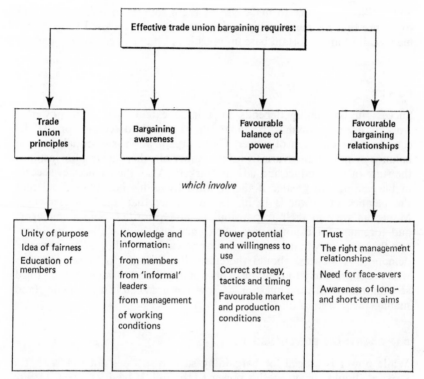

Figure 1

bership as a precondition for successful bargaining. The section is there-fore concerned with what we will call 'principled bargaining', or bargaining based on union principles.

BARGAINING AWARENESS

Our second section (pp. 25 ff.) looks at bargaining awareness: the ability to identify bargainable issues. We consider the bargaining opportunities provided in written agreements, and also the development of 'custom and practice'. Familiarity with agreements is not sufficient on its own, however, as the steward needs to know what is happening. He has to keep a close check on events on his 'patch'. In this, his members and good general steward organization can help. Management and groups outside the plant such as union members, full-time officials and journalists, can also be important sources of information. The steward requires freedom and facilities in order to make use of these sources of information and to ensure that his membership is educated. Similarly, closed shop agreements can be an important base upon which to build an educated membership.

POWER

Success in bargaining depends to a large extent upon how powerful workers are compared with management; our third section (pp. 31 ff.) considers the question of power. Good organization is essential, but the balance of power also varies with a number of other factors, for instance the state of the product and labour markets. Also, the chances of success in bargaining are greater if the steward times his negotiations so that the balance of power is in his favour rather than the management's. Managers vary in their responsibilities and priorities. Senior managers and foremen, for example, are often concerned with different problems and therefore vary in how sympathetic and vulnerable they are to stewards' demands. A steward should therefore direct issues to those managers who are more likely to concede. This point will be considered in the third section, along with the question of how stewards can learn to understand management organization.

BARGAINING RELATIONSHIPS

While power is crucial for bargaining success, it does not follow that a steward should always use his power to the full. If he does, open warfare may develop, with management similarly exploiting its position when the balance of power turns in its favour. Moreover, there are areas of common interest between management and unions. Thus some trust between manager and steward can make bargaining both easier and more successful. In the fourth section (pp. 35 ff.), we therefore consider the advantages and dangers of bargaining relationships which are based upon a degree of mutual trust.

Before going on to discuss these aspects of bargaining more fully, we must emphasize one point. The nature of steward bargaining varies enormously. Reasons for the variations are many. They include, for example, the nature of agreements; the level at which agreements are made; management organization; union strength and organization; the individual skills of managers and stewards; the nature of the product and its market, and the historical and present conditions within the plant. Given these variations, we should emphasize from the start that the preconditions for successful bargaining are likely to vary among plants as well as among stewards. The steward who attempts to adopt a pattern of bargaining behaviour which does not fit easily with his personality or the strength of his members is quite likely to find himself in difficulties so that his success in bargaining may deteriorate. In other words, a steward has to work out his own methods of bargaining. It is wrong to believe that an outsider can provide all the answers; he cannot, for there are so many factors to be taken into account that generalizations are both difficult and very conditional. All that an outsider can do is to provide ideas and suggestions, drawing upon theoretical discussions of bargaining and the practice of other stewards.[1] The aim of this essay is, therefore, a very limited one and the steward who believes that it will provide all the answers – or even many answers – will be disappointed. Our aim is merely to suggest some of the considerations which are often important in bargaining in practice. It is for each steward along with his colleagues to work out what is the most successful pattern of bargaining within his own plant.

Union Principles: A Sense of Direction

It is quite possible for a steward to be a successful bargainer and yet achieve little for his members. He may bargain only over trivial issues, or the agreements he makes may contradict each other. In other words he may just be running round in circles. For this reason union principles are important for stewards and members. A trade unionist committed to union principles is not merely someone who pays union dues or is willing to strike with his immediate workmates; he is also committed to goals and ideas, and even ideals which have been central to trade unionism for over a century.

One of the most important of these principles is the idea of unity. 'Unity is strength' is still a valid principle, and groups of workers who pursue their own selfish interests to the detriment of their fellows may sap the strength that unity gives. Such union activity is little better than the activity of an individual worker trying to make his own little deal with the management. Unity means that workers define their interests collectively. Within any one plant, a steward should not merely be concerned with his own members but also with the interests of other workers in the plant and, indeed, of workers elsewhere. If stewards and their members fail to take notice of this wider viewpoint, union strength may decline. As groups pursue their particular interests, organization will be fragmented and fighting will break out. Lack of unity means lack of strength and lack of coherent action.

The idea of unity also implies a concern with justice, fairness, equality and the protection of the less fortunate. Trade unionism is not, or should not be, solely about helping the relatively well-off become even better off. Groups lacking bargaining skill or strength should be protected; individual workers who for a variety of reasons find themselves in difficulties should be helped too. Unless this is done not only is unity endangered but also the traditional cries of 'brotherhood' become meaningless.

Lack of concern with union principles can weaken union organization not only through this fragmentation of groups but also through the way individual members may come to view the union. For them it may simply become a means whereby they can more easily get their own way. These members may find it easy to spurn the union when they believe they can get what they want by individual means. If the steward, on the other hand, bargains from union principles the union becomes more than a mere channel comparable to an individual member's right to approach his own foreman. Union principles, which members themselves formulate, become the means by which members understand and realize their interests. This is not to imply that a steward should not be concerned with individual grievances. He should, as long as the case is consistent with union principles. For full effectiveness, then, trade unionism cannot be just a bureaucratic channel. It must be a set of principles by which goals and action should be determined. These should provide the sense of direction which is so important for successful bargaining.

If this is accepted, then the steward should continually be asking whether what happens in the plant or in his section is fair. He is not merely concerned with increasing earnings – although that is obviously important – but also with other questions. For example, should overtime be permitted? Would it be to the advantage of members? How would refusal affect other groups? Would too much overtime create more unemployment?

But the steward is the representative of his members who democratically elect him. Without their support he has little power. At the extreme, if he fails to settle a crucial issue by negotiation, calls for strike action and does not get it, he is a failure to both members and management. If a steward is to follow union principles successfully, then his members must also be committed to those principles. The number of members who are committed in this sense clearly varies, but it is a vital precondition of a steward's success that he educates his members in the real meaning of trade unionism.

Educating members in this way is certainly not easy. In particular, it cannot be done quickly when a crisis occurs but must be done continuously. Chatting to members, encouraging them to be involved in the trade union movement, explaining the meaning of their work experiences and showing the validity of trade union principles: these are the ways to win their commitment. Members educated in this sense provide the power base for successful bargaining, because their commitment to union principles means that they will both understand and support what the steward is trying to do.

In this section we have stressed the importance of union principles in providing a sense of direction in bargaining. We have also argued that if the steward is to be successful he must ensure that his members accept a similar definition of trade unionism. He has therefore to continually educate his members.

Bargaining Awareness

Given a sense of direction a steward still has to spot the issues which give him an opportunity to bargain; he needs 'bargaining awareness'. Some stewards more readily pick up bargaining issues than others; they continually negotiate over changes in work content and allocation, overtime, working conditions, and so on. Others do not bother to bargain over what appear, at the time, to be small changes in work conditions. Our research showed that members whose stewards had more bargaining awareness were less subject to managerial whim and were more highly paid. A steward, therefore, must have bargaining awareness if he is to get the best possible conditions for his members. In this section we first consider the importance of agreements, and then go on to consider how a steward collects the information essential for bargaining awareness.

BARGAINING AWARENESS AND AGREEMENTS

Collective agreements generally lay down rules which regulate when bargaining is permissible. For example, often under piecework agreements new prices can be negotiated when there are changes in methods or materials or work. Bargaining awareness clearly means that the steward should take up issues which are formally permissible under such agreements. But in one case we studied, a steward failed to negotiate over a change in work because, as he explained, 'it didn't seem to matter' when it first occurred since it had little immediate impact on his members. A year or so later much more of his members' time was taken up with the job, and only then did he try to negotiate a new price. By then it was too late, for management argued that the change was now part of custom and practice. Because the steward failed to identify the initial change as important and had not bargained over it, his members suffered,

A crucial aspect of bargaining awareness is, then, the grasping of the opportunities provided in agreements. But bargaining awareness does not stop there. In many companies, particularly those in which shop steward organization is strong, bargaining is about a much wider range of issues than the written agreements suggest. Unwritten agreements and custom and practice cover many areas. When stewards are strong, management will prefer to bargain about issues and reach informal agreements than to face the possibility of opposition to its plans when it tries to implement them. This informal activity also provides opportunities for bargaining.

New written agreements are often made because of these pressures from strong stewards. On occasion, it is true, new written agreements have been made on the initiative of management, and some commentators have suggested that management should do this more often.[2] But in the past agreements covering new subjects have come about primarily through pressure from workers. In principle, therefore, if workers are powerful enough they can increase the range of issues over which they bargain. In practice, the problem the steward faces is whether he and his members are powerful enough and whether he can afford to take the risk of finding out.

Other considerations are also involved. One is, as we have already noted, that bargaining is not the only means of pursuing members' interests. The level at which demands are expressed is also important. Many issues can be handled at the level of the work-group, but some may need to be handled plant-wide, and some may have to be dealt with at national level. For example, in the coal industry, workers wanted a representative of their own to check the output which determined their pay. The issue might appear to be a local one, and relatively easy to solve. But employers were opposed to it. However, the demand was one common to many pits. Finally, the miners achieved their aim by raising the issue nationally and getting an Act passed in Parliament. What was unsuccessful at one level by one means, was achieved by changing both the level at which the issue was pursued and the means by which it was pursued.

But there may be issues which it is inadvisable to pursue at all. Demands which have little hope of success because of a strong management and/or poorly organized work force may be defeated. The defeat may have wider effects. First, it may encourage management to adopt a harder line because the union is proved weak. Secondly, the defeat may affect members' attitudes towards the union. If expectations have been built up and then dashed, members may become more hesitant and less committed to the union. We observed this effect in one factory where the stewards raised a number of issues and were defeated. The union membership fell dramatically to a level that would take several years to build up again.

KNOWLEDGE AND INFORMATION

To identify issues for bargaining the steward obviously has to know what is happening, to be aware of any change in work or working conditions. He has to know in detail what the 'proper' working practices are, as embodied in written agreements and custom and practice. He has to understand the nature of his members' work and its problems. For many stewards this is no problem, but for some it is. A steward covering a variety of jobs, but who has worked on only one of them, may lack knowledge of potential problems and opportunities. This can lead to difficulties. In one case we examined, the steward could handle problems relating to his own job, but failed to notice those on other jobs. As a consequence, workers on the other jobs became critical of him, particularly when he reached an unsatisfactory agreement with management. Clearly he had failed to pursue fully the interests of his members. He had also encouraged division among his members by being more alert to problems in certain areas, and he had lost the confidence of many members because he had been 'conned' by the company. Eventually he was forced to resign. This situation derived from the steward's ignorance.

A steward can improve his ability to identify changes which require bargaining. Here we will consider three ways in which he can do so. The first of these is what he himself can do; the second concerns the way in which he can make use of his own contacts; and the third is reference to publicly available information from outside the company. We will look at each of these in turn.

The steward can improve his knowledge of what is going on by learning from his members. By chatting to them he can learn to identify what are their most common problems. This sort of information will enable him to predict what circumstances will lead to problems, which he may thus raise with management before they actually happen.

The steward can also regularly check his members' work and conditions. A checklist might include:

Actual levels of wages received and deductions made.
Changes in work content, no matter how small.
Problems in work.
Changes in job allocation.
Changes in overtime allocation.
Machine maintenance.
Stocks of materials.
Orders for work.
Changes in management behaviour.

Safety of machines and working practices.
Working conditions.
Relations between members.
Absenteeism and sickness.

Many more items could be included for, in effect, the steward needs to be aware of virtually every aspect of the work-place. His job is therefore a difficult one, but he can be helped considerably by others.

This brings us to our second way of getting information necessary for bargaining awareness. This is the steward's contact with his own members, other stewards, the union and management. Within most work-groups there are members who are more committed to union principles and are respected by their workmates. They are informal leaders. It is important for the steward to have close contact with informal leaders, for they are in a position to reaffirm union principles among their fellow members on the one hand, and bring issues to the steward on the other. This is crucially important because the steward cannot possibly identify all the issues, particularly if he covers many members. Informal leaders may highlight not only changes in work, but also situations like possible victimization by a foreman, or the fact that a particular member seems to be ill.

Stewards are not the only people who bargain. Often individual members may attempt to do so in pursuit of their own interests. Sometimes managers encourage this; it appears to happen particularly in small establishments and among white-collar workers. Most procedure agreements explicitly state that individual workers should take their grievances in the first instance to the foreman. This may save the steward a great deal of work, but individual processing of problems may not be a good thing in terms of collectivity. First, it makes the union less central and important to members. Secondly, it may mean that the steward is later expected to bargain about something which he may believe is really a non-runner or should not have been raised in the first place. Thirdly, it may mean that he is stuck with the wrong sorts of arguments which have been put forward in support of an issue. It should be noted, however, that many stewards see this first stage, the worker going direct to the foreman, as useful. It enables them to fend off difficult or impossible demands from members by asking them to go first of all to the foreman. Often this is enough to deter unreasonable and 'unprincipled' demands. Some also argue that it encourages members to be good trade unionists on their own behalf, and helps to bring on potential negotiators and shop stewards. In some factories there is clear evidence of the emergence of 'assistant' shop stewards who need practice and responsibility. Whatever the pros and cons of this question, it is important that the steward himself controls bargaining. At the least, it means that members should seek the advice of the steward before they themselves take problems to the foreman. In practice this is usually done. If not, unity and success may be endangered; also it may mean that the steward is unaware of what problems exist.

Managers may also be an important source of information for bargaining. Management provides information by direct consultation or the offer of opportunities for negotiation. Trade unionists have often argued that the extent is insufficient, and that managers should be made to open the books to stewards and unions. Of course the amount of information about potential issues for bargaining from management is generally significantly less than most stewards would like. Nevertheless, consultation may show that bargaining is necessary over an issue which management may wish to consult about; or discussions on one issue may provide information which prompts the steward to seek to bargain on others. While discussing company performance, for example, a steward may learn things which suggest he should be prepared to bargain over redundancy or rationalization.

Individual managers may also provide information which gives clues about opportunities for bargaining. The manager's reasons for this will be discussed more fully below, but they might include his political views, or be part of a strategy in a managerial power struggle; or they might reflect the dependence of a manager upon stewards and workers – their support is necessary to achieve his goals. For any of these reasons he may slip pieces of information and warnings to stewards he trusts. Information of this kind obviously has to be treated with caution. Some managers may attempt to develop close contacts with stewards specifically in order to impart misleading information. However, a steward is normally able to distinguish truth and falsehood. In one case we studied, for example, a steward knew that management was in a weak position and that a strike would be successful precisely because a manager had told him the opposite. The steward's assessment proved correct; the manager, by trying to mislead, had given the steward the information he wanted. Clearly games of bluff and counter-bluff can be played; good judgement is a prerequisite of survival.

Another source of information for stewards is published material. Here we only have space to note the wide variety of this information, for instance press comments about trends and prospects in one's industry and articles about the company and its performance. There are many published studies of companies which can be of great use to stewards.[3] Economic prospects will affect industries in different ways, but few will escape the impact of general trends. It is helpful, therefore, to know about these. Finally, with government's increasing involvement in industrial relations, knowledge of new legislation and new or possible government policies may also be useful to stewards in pointing to issues and providing arguments.

Probably the most important sources of information are the shop steward organization itself and the union. In many plants, a great deal of information is exchanged at joint shop stewards' committees. Convenors often relay information from managements and discuss their assessment of present and future possibilities. Stewards raise their own problems and thereby provide background information. In many plants less formal contacts between stewards are very helpful. In one case we studied, for example, groups of stewards regularly discussed what was going on in the plant; they collected odd pieces of information from their members and management, and tried to build up a coherent picture of events. In doing so, they highlighted problems and worked out common strategies. In another plant, stewards have put this exchange of information on a more routine and organized basis. Every steward enters in one book everything that happens in his area, including what he has negotiated, what arguments he used, and the outcome. Other stewards are able to learn about what is happening in the plant by simply referring to this book.

The trade unions outside the plant can also provide much useful information. Many unions have research departments which collect the publicly available information discussed above. They are also able to supplement this through knowledge derived from the unions' involvement with the company. Similarly, full-time union officials are continually in touch with stewards and many managers. They therefore often have a good general knowledge and understanding of what is happening. In some unions, officials attempt systematically to collect basic information, notably on wages and conditions. Close contacts with full-time officials can therefore be useful. Convenors, particularly, are often able to check rumours and find out information relevant to their own problems by phoning their full-time officials or other convenors. Finally, mention should be made of new statutory rights to information. The Industry Act, the Employment Protection Act and the Health and Safety at Work Act could make much more information available to stewards than hitherto.

If stewards are to ensure that they collect and exchange basic information, they should also ensure that they have the proper facilities to do so. These include easy access to their members and other stewards; a room to meet and somewhere to store information safely, and telephones to contact their full-time officials. Consequently, stewards need to be careful that they have agreements with management which protect their rights and facilities. In the same way, the task of the steward can be made easier if he can rely on his members. Closed-shop agreements are therefore important. In other words, stewards need to be concerned with maintaining strong organization both in terms of commitment to union principles and ensuring union security and rights through collective agreements. Such good organization is the basis of union power.[4]

Bargaining and the Balance of Power

The balance of power between company and union often varies. When it changes in favour of one side, then two things may happen. First, new agreements may be made which are more in one side's interests than previous ones. Secondly, existing agreements are more likely to be ignored or reinterpreted to the advantage of the more powerful side. Perhaps we should explain what we mean by reinterpretation. An agreement has to be implemented in order to affect what happens; it does not affect industrial relations simply by being signed. An agreement must be interpreted if it is to be implemented, and most agreements can be interpreted in a variety of ways. Stewards are often involved in bargaining over what an agreement means. The disagreement rests upon whether the letter of the agreement should be followed, or its 'spirit and intention'. It often takes some time for the interpretation of a new agreement to be agreed between managers and stewards. And that interpretation may then change as one side realizes its power and attempts to gain a more favourable interpretation. In one company we examined, for example, it took nearly two years for a common interpretation of an agreement on job mobility to be worked out. But then, because of a change in market conditions, management became considerably more powerful. The result was that management sought a new interpretation of the job mobility agreement, placing very strong emphasis upon a clause which until then had been virtually ignored. In another plant, what was defined as new work, permitting renegotiation of piecework values, varied considerably according to the balance of power.

The chances of success in bargaining are, then, dependent to a large degree upon the balance of power. We therefore need to ask what exactly makes up that balance. This is a notoriously difficult question to answer. Having power is not merely having the potential to win, but also a willingness to use that potential. The common understandings between company and union often limit the use of 'potential' power. In addition, as we have already noted, the steward's power rests upon the commitment of his members.

The balance of power may fluctuate considerably. Workers' power depends not merely upon the ability to disrupt production, although that is important, but also upon how badly management wants production to go on. When sales are booming, then worker power is likely to be considerable because management is keen to exploit its markets. But in slump periods, or when production is impossible due to lack of supplies or breakdowns, worker power is likely to be limited. Most obviously, workers' power is low when men are being laid off. This is particularly true of many plants since lay-off pay agreements have been introduced. Generally, these agreements state that no lay-off pay is given if an internal dispute has interfered with production. These clauses are often interpreted so that virtually any strike means that no lay-off money is paid. Consequently, strikes aimed at hurting management in fact help it by saving it lay-off pay.

The impact of workers' pressure on managers varies. Moreover, in many companies there are conflicts between departments. For example, factory accountants are concerned to ensure that managers do not exceed their budgets. Industrial relations managers want to protect agreements. Both groups of managers may consequently disagree with production managers who consider that their primary task is to ensure that output continues. They may therefore want to exceed their financial budgets or to break certain collective agreements so as to achieve their production targets.

Success in bargaining is related to both these aspects of the power balance. The relative power of workers and management generally suggests the importance of the timing of bargaining. The conflicts between managers with different priorities and objectives suggest that success will vary according to which managers are involved in bargaining. We will consider each of these points in turn.

WHEN TO BARGAIN

The main point can be made briefly. Whenever possible, bargain when you are strong and not when you are weak. To raise issues when the market is poor, or when the company does not want or cannot achieve output, is to stack the chances against success.

The speed at which the balance of power changes varies considerably, so that opportunities to time bargaining will vary too. The most dramatic changes appear to occur in a company where sales vary considerably, the stages of production are highly integrated and there is a dependency upon a large number of suppliers. In some companies all it needs is a lorry to break down and work stops because of a shortage of supplies. In such a situation the balance of power changes rapidly. One minute the stewards may be strong, but as soon as supplies run short and production is impossible, their power evaporates. What the exact power balance is in this sort of situation depends also upon what management attempts to do. If in the face of a shortage of one component management tries to switch production to something else, then the steward remains strong. But if they do not, or find such a switch impossible, then the steward is weak.

The extent to which issues can be timed also depends upon two other points. First, there are certain issues which cannot, or should not, be delayed. A steward should not delay bargaining over a safety hazard, or over issues which are of a perishable or temporary nature. The second point which may make timing more difficult is that management will probably be trying to do the same thing. When workers are weak, then generally management will be strong (although this is not always the case). Consequently, a sensible management will be trying to implement certain policies or raise issues for bargaining when the steward is least able to resist.

One important strategy for management is divide-and-rule, that is, by dividing workers management can reduce their power. So, for example, when management wants to lay workers off, it may purposely raise issues with certain groups in the hope that they will strike, thus ensuring that their fellow-workers receive no lay-off pay. Defence against this sort of managerial strategy requires commitment to union principles, good contact with other stewards and information on the balance of power and managerial strategy generally.

DIRECTING AN ISSUE

The extent to which stewards have the freedom to direct issues to certain managers clearly varies. Some companies maintain very tight control over their managers and, many stewards argue, force them to follow procedure strictly. But often there is quite a wide choice. In one company we examined, for example, some stewards could choose from over ten managers with whom they could raise issues. This choice covered many levels and sections of management.

One reason for the choice was that the stewards were strong because their members supported them and were committed to union principles. Moreover, the stewards were able to argue cases in various ways. Take, for example, a problem of promoting workers in a particular section from unskilled to semi-skilled jobs. The steward often has the choice between arguing that the problem exists solely in that particular area, and so he

B

should bargain over it with the departmental manager; or that promotion rules are a plant-wide matter and hence must be negotiated with an industrial relations manager. In piecework systems stewards can often choose a manager to deal with if there are problems about the ability to earn bonus. If the problem is technical, the steward may try to deal with production management, stressing the difficulties over meeting output targets. Or he may take the issue to work study management in the hope of achieving a total renegotiation of the job.

Even when the ability to direct issues to any particular section of management is severely limited because of the company's control, there still remains a choice of level of management. Most obviously, the use of procedure may be accelerated or slowed down, so that bargaining is focused at a more senior or a more junior level of management. Many companies, particularly in the mid-1960s, attempted to reduce stewards' choices because it was thought that they were bargaining too successfully with foremen. Often the foremen's powers were reduced in an attempt to limit bargaining at shop-floor level. But the effectiveness of this strategy can be questioned for three reasons. First, the pressures upon foremen are often strong enough to make them ignore the controls. In some plants, therefore, foremen bargain over issues which they should not, and hide their activities from their superiors. Secondly, foremen make deals with stewards in order to ensure continuity of work. If the company wants output and foremen's powers are limited, then it is likely that more senior managers will make similar deals. Hence, in some companies major deals are made with quite senior managers rather than with foremen. The third reason is related to the conflicts between different kinds of management which we mentioned earlier. In some companies, these conflicts between managers are very great, and more experienced stewards exploit them. This is made easier because of the way managers act in these conflicts. They often try to hide information from each other and will make decisions which should be made by others. This managerial in-fighting can make a steward's bargaining easier. He can choose between managers. He can inform a manager not directly involved about what is happening, emphasizing the implications for him and his own objectives. The manager may then bring pressure to bear in support of the steward's claim.

Finally, it is not necessary for one steward alone to be involved in bargaining over an issue. As different levels of the management hierarchy may be simultaneously involved in implementing a company policy, so may different levels of the steward organization be employed in pursuit of an issue. Hence, in one plant we observed it was common for the stewards to 'have a word' with the convenor before negotiating with the junior management. What then happened was that while the steward negotiated, the convenor would have 'a quiet word' with the manager's superior and impose pressure through him.

If the above is accepted, then some managers, given their differing priorities, are clearly more sympathetic to particular union demands than others. It is wrong, therefore, to think of management as necessarily a totally united group. Also the power of managers varies according to the state of management politics; as well, the impact of market trends and of shop-floor organization is likely to differ among managers. Thus, success in bargaining can be influenced by which manager handles the issue. A corollary of this is that arguments which are effective with one manager are not necessarily effective with another.

Our discussion of timing and directing issues stresses the need for a steward to know and understand clearly what is happening in the plant. He therefore requires information. This can be derived from the same sources as described above in connection with bargaining issues, that is, members, stewards and managers. Contacts with other stewards are especially important in order to acquire an intimate knowledge of the power politics in a plant, and so need to be frequent. Production problems and management conflicts may change frequently, and with them both the balance of power and the weak links in management. Unless stewards keep up to date, and have the opportunity to plan and discuss strategy with other stewards, their timing and direction of issues can be misjudged.

In concluding this section, it is useful to stress that timing and directing issues and collecting the information upon which such strategies are based is not the preserve of stewards. Many managements also keep their ear to the ground. What this suggests is that success in bargaining is related not merely to collecting one's own information, but also to preventing management from learning about conflicts within the steward organization. Better still, of course, is to make sure that there are no conflicts or weak links. Commitment to union principles, an educated membership and strong shop steward organization reduce such dangers.

The Bargaining Relationship

In industrial relations there are often limits to unions' and managers' use of power. First, given the broad balance of power, each side believes the other is there to stay. Few managers really believe they can get rid of unions. Most union members do not believe they can get rid of employers, although this may be changing. In other words, both sides generally accept that in day-to-day terms they have to live with each other. There is, therefore, some attraction in limiting the aggressiveness of conflict.

Secondly, there is an awareness that to exploit one's own power advantage when strong is to encourage similar action on the part of the opponent. There is no guarantee which party will win in such open conflict.

The pursuit of union principles is therefore complex, for it has to occur within what is often a hostile environment. The steward has to think not only of short-term advantage, but also of maintaining organization in the longer term. He needs success in the short term and continued strength for the longer term. For this reason a steward's relationship with management may be important to him. If management believes that the steward is honest, powerful and represents his members, then it will be more ready to deal with him and to trust his word. But why should management be ready to develop special relations with stewards? The answer is simply that many managers are subject to pressures similar to stewards'. Individual managers are also representatives – of the company – and a condition of their success is often a good relationship with the steward who can lead and control his members. Both steward and manager, therefore, are in a way dependent upon the other for the general achievement of their goals. If each sees the other as powerful and important, they tend to develop a relationship of trust which helps each to achieve his respective goals. It should be emphasized that this does not necessarily mean that one or the other sells out, although clearly there is that danger. The trust relationship is one of dependence, and rests upon the existence of conflict combined with a recognition that some sort of accommodation is inevitable and that power, over a period, is more or less evenly balanced. Hence, if the power or representativeness of either party changes dramatically over a period, then the equilibrium is disturbed and the bargaining relationship also tends to deteriorate, since the *mutual* advantages gained from it may disappear.

We have said that the relationship rests upon a conditional degree of trust. This means that the manager and steward have developed a set of working rules for their relationship; these rules reflect the balance of power as discerned over a period of time. The rules will often be different from those formally laid down. One of the most important aspects of the relationship is that the manager will provide the steward with information which he cannot get through formal channels. Along with this, informal chats between the manager and the steward will be common. In these chats the problems are discussed from the steward's and manager's standpoints more openly than is normal in negotiations, and means of overcoming their respective problems are worked out. In other words, informal deals may be made. Or, more commonly, ways in which the steward's demands can be met in a more formal and legitimate manner will be developed. Similarly, the manager will sometimes pursue issues on behalf of the steward with other managers. The informal chat is important to the manager because often it means that a way is agreed whereby he can both meet the steward's demands and prevent sanctions being imposed upon him by his superiors. The significance of agreements is not merely their formal regulation of relations between management and workers. What is often just as important is that agreements serve as guides and controls within management. A manager who blatantly breaks an agreement in favour of workers risks sanctions from his superiors who may see the agreement as a means of controlling *him*. An important aspect of bargaining, therefore, is that stewards should provide good reasons with which managers may convince their superiors that demands should be met. This is similar to the idea of providing face-savers for the other side.

A bargaining relationship like the one described improves the chances of success for the steward since it is based upon a recognition of his power and competence. But it depends upon not abusing the trust upon which it rests. This involves two things. First, it means that each party to the relationship generally attempts to protect, and maintain, the position of the other, simply because in the long term the relationship helps both of them. But, secondly, such mutual protection is dependent upon not betraying the trust, in other words, not purposely telling lies or making the other look a fool. This is one reason why it is important that the steward himself checks any claims that his members put forward.

One of the main ways of making a manager look a fool is to exploit him and the agreements he makes. This often occurs in piecework negotiations. For example, in one case we examined, a steward argued that a certain level of effort could not be exceeded, and finally persuaded the manager to agree. The members then proved him wrong by exploiting the new agreement and achieving very high earnings. This made the manager look a fool, since he had justified the agreement to his superiors. When the workers proved his justification to be false, his position within management was weakened. Accordingly, the manager reduced his trust in the steward, who when he again said the men could not possibly increase their effort was not believed. The trust between manager and steward was gone. Moreover, since trust had once existed, the steward's action was defined as betrayal. The manager attempted to get his own back and weaken the position of the steward.

This discussion serves to emphasize another point. Bargaining is not merely about the immediate, specific issue. In bargaining, both parties may be attempting to influence the politics of the other's organization by influencing levels of success and by increasing conflict within the other's organization. At the extreme, of course, managers may attempt to split the members from the union.

Basic to the bargaining relationship is an understanding of the goals, organization and behaviour of management. Many of the concerns of managers are similar to those of stewards, for example concern with maintaining their organization, and possibly limiting the role of the other party. In addition, managers will be concerned with a balance between a short-term resolution of problems and maintaining their position, rights and the pattern of wages within the plant or company. This problem of compromise between the long term and the short term is often the focus of conflict between production managers and other managers. In the same way, then, that claims have to be negotiated within the union, the answer to those claims has to be negotiated within management. An understanding of these elements is both learnt and used in the bargaining relationship.

Again, however, it is necessary to give notes of caution. Management clearly gains from bargaining relationships. What stewards and their members have to be aware of is that such advantages to management are not at the expense of themselves. In the same way as an over-aggressive approach to management can create problems, so can an over-cooperative one.

Conclusion

In this essay we have tried to look at what we consider to be the major aspects of bargaining. In particular we have stressed the importance of factors which exist away from the bargaining table itself. We have done so because we are convinced that success in bargaining ultimately depends on organization and principled behaviour. If a steward is able to maintain good organization, identify issues and time and direct them properly, and if he has good relations with management, then success at the bargaining table and in the steward's role of promoting members' interests follows. But we must emphasize that successful bargaining does not consist of applying a simple, neat formula. Stewards have to work out for themselves what is likely to be most successful in their own particular situation.

In the face of major changes in industrial techniques and reorganization, and with greater state involvement in industrial relations, stewards will face both opportunities and obstacles. It will become increasingly important for stewards to maintain a good organization and to be effective bargainers, for these assets are vital in promoting and defending the dignity of workers at work. This, after all, is the essence of union principles.

Notes

1. Much of this essay derives from studies of shop stewards we have undertaken and from teaching and talking to shop stewards. We would like to thank all of these stewards who have taught us so much. We hope that this essay will help us pass on what they have taught us.

2. See *Report* of the Royal Commission on Trade Unions and Employers' Associations, 1965–68 (HMSO, 1968) Cmnd. 3623, and McCarthy, W. E. J., and Ellis, N. D., *Management by Agreement* (Hutchinson, 1973).

3. There are many sources of information, not least the various unions. In addition, *Labour Research* is a useful journal. Reviews of public companies can be obtained from such bodies as Extel services.

4. For a full description of this question of knowledge and information, see *Information at Work* by Michael Barratt Brown in this series.

Section III
Bargaining in Practice and Theory

This section describes negotiating in practice, some of the reactions of workers to their industrial environment, a theory of bargaining, and some of the ways in which bargaining skills may be taught. (Eds.)

Trade Union Negotiators
edited by Ed Coker

We have started the section with examples and advice from practitioners which should provide material for learning and teaching about the subject. Practitioners rarely write or comment in detail on what they practise, and material which often emerges in study courses from the experience of the students, visiting specialists and union officials tends to go unrecorded. We *have* recorded some of this experience, both as useful in itself and as an example of the raw material which others might record.

We held long interviews with four experienced trade union negotiators, two full-time officials and two convenors, identified as 'F1', 'F2', 'C1', and 'C2' against the quoted material.

'F1' is the District Organizer for a large general union in the Midlands. He worked and was shop steward in the factory which now takes up much of his negotiating efforts. After attending day release classes he did a full-time course of study and then became a full-time official.

'F2' is the Organizer for London and the South-East for a large general union. He was for some years convenor of shop stewards in a North London engineering works, became a full-time official in 1946, and has moved steadily since then into his present senior position. He now oversees organizational and bargaining issues in South-East England.

'C1' is the senior steward for a large general union in the Midlands. He works in a plant employing about seven thousand which is part of a large multi-national company. He has considerable experience of shop-floor negotiations in the motor industry.

'C2' is the convenor of shop stewards in a South-East London machine-making firm, employing 2800 people, with four plants in Britain, and with overseas connections. He is in the AUEW, and other unions represented in the firm are TASS and APEX. He has worked there for fourteen years, became a steward in 1969, and was elected convenor in 1971. He is also active in local and regional union affairs, in tribunal work and in the Workers' Educational Association. (Eds.)

Why Negotiate?

'Industry . . . is a conflict of interest.'

Much of the theorizing about negotiations takes conflict in industry as its starting point. But little is said of the ideologies of the individuals concerned with negotiating.[1] The union negotiators we talked to had firm ideas about the nature of society and industry which gave them good reasons why trade unionists need to negotiate with employers.

TO ENSURE MINIMUM EXPLOITATION

You live in a society where workers have to sell their labour in order to exist. Problems crop up continuously on the shop floor and you've got to discuss them, negotiate them, and resolve them in the best way possible. (C1)

Basically, industry with the work force on one side and the management on the other, is a conflict of interest. Where you have a conflict of interest the work people are going to say, 'Look, what you've got we want; either some of it or all of it.' There's going to be resistance to this and it's accepted that we go through the haggling process to sort out who's going to have what. (F1)

At a given point in time you're concerned with getting an agreement to ensure that exploitation of labour is kept to a minimum. It's a day-to-day battle. (C1)

Are Good Negotiators Born or Created?

'We can learn a lot from education and training courses but there's no substitute for experience of the real thing.'

All of our union negotiators stressed the importance of experience in the training of shop stewards and negotiators. They did not completely discount training but clearly saw it as a supplement and an adjunct only to experience and personal encouragement at shop-floor level.

THE SHOP STEWARDS' COMMITTEE AS TRAINING GROUND

In the work-place, negotiators come up through the shop stewards' committee. Not every steward turns into a good negotiator, but it's the experience of being on the committee itself that does the real training of negotiators. It's true that we can learn a lot from education and training courses: we've gained a great deal from WEA day release courses, especially from role-playing. But no role-playing exercise is exactly right for the things you have to face in reality: they can give you confidence, but there's no substitute for the experience of the real thing.

The shop stewards' committee is a good training ground, because you have to bargain and negotiate on that first. It's often more difficult convincing your fellow stewards than it is to convince management. They are a tough group of realists, and through arguing amongst ourselves, we often rehearse most of the points likely to be brought up later by the employers. And on the committee you have to do more than just produce a party line, or a lot of political theory: you can forget all that, because we all know we have a here-and-now practical problem to settle, and we concentrate on that. Marxist theory won't get you far when you meet the employer.

Though not all stewards make good negotiators, they can all help in training the ones they elect to negotiate for them just by being themselves on the committee. (C2)

CHOOSING STEWARDS AND GETTING THE ATMOSPHERE

But we have another activity which helps this training. We have a monthly stewards' management meeting, for 'running negotiations' on anything, not consultative. This is staffed by the stewards' officers – committee chairman, assistant chairman and secretary – and we meet what is in fact the full factory negotiating management team. And we have an arrangement to bring three other alternating stewards in as members of our team, not as observers, but as participators. We try to choose stewards who have special interest in and knowledge of agenda items, and this is a useful opportunity to get the atmosphere of negotiating with the employers. It's a kind of 'arena of learning', and through this we can try out people and they can test themselves: realistic role-playing. (C2)

OBSERVING SENIOR STEWARDS AT WORK

Stewards also learn and test themselves through representing their members over individual grievances, where, as in most grievance procedures, they are quickly brought in once there is a first failure to agree between member and manager: and in the procedure, at other stages they may be operating alongside other senior stewards and see them at work, often facing some of the same managers who appear in more collective negotiations. (C2)

Trust and Confidence

'There's a certain code which is accepted by both sides.'

All four union negotiators accepted that there is a conflict of interest in industry. Yet they all said they had to maintain a dependable relationship with the managers on the other side of the negotiating table whose politics cover the whole spectrum. In particular all felt that it is necessary to maintain an *goign-on* bargaining relationship.

MUTUAL RESPECT AND TRUST

It's essential there's a certain mutual respect and trust, because in spite of being opposed to the capitalist system and having to negotiate with employers who represent the capitalist system, you often resolve problems by talking and you only know by talking how you're going to pursue a particular problem.

If you know that a particular manager always lies to you well obviously you react differently to him, but if you have a manager who always keeps agreements that he's made and signed, there's a mutual respect. If I was a manager and I had a senior shop steward who always went back on his agreements I wouldn't expect him to respect me. I think they'd be quite entitled to distrust me. (C1)

POLICIES BEFORE PERSONALITIES

I respect some managers even though I know full well we both have different roles to fulfil. I never bear grudges against individuals although they may represent a certain class and I represent my class. Never personalize a problem; that always weakens your case. (C1)

This code of practice holds good while both parties are willing to negotiate realistically. But if the opposing party is intransigent he is likely to create a much more negative response.

NO MERCY TO THE ANTI-UNIONIST

If a manager is so anti-union it hurts him to sit and talk with the union official, and it shows in his actions, I don't show him any mercy. I'll do the best I can to grind him into the ground as quickly as I can. Every deal will be an expensive one and then if somebody more senior comes along to me and says, 'What's with you and this bloke?' I'll say 'Well, I'm afraid we just don't get on. He hates us, and as long as he's in that position there'll be trouble in the firm.' I've got personnel managers sacked from companies where the relationship has been impossible. Other companies have moved managers because it's in their interests to do so. (F1)

Targets for Negotiations

'If you really know what you want . . . it helps to concentrate your mind.'

The conventional wisdom here is that it is crucial for the union negotiator to know exactly what he would like to achieve, that is, an *ideal* settlement; what he can *realistically* hope for in practice; and also where his *fall-back position* is, beyond which there must be a failure to agree.[2] Our negotiators agreed it was certainly essential to have clear objectives, but were less positive about formulating fall-back positions.

KNOW WHAT YOU WANT

I'm absolutely certain about the need to know exactly what you want out of negotiations. I've gone into negotiations where I've been a bit uncertain and I think that has weakened my arguments. If a smart manager detects it you're going to come out of it pretty badly. If you really know what you want and put it on the table it helps to concentrate your mind. (F1)

A DISADVANTAGE OF FALL-BACK POSITIONS

Sometimes you know what you can fall back to because you know your members and maybe they've even said, 'Look, be prepared to settle for this but not less.' I discourage members from doing that because it nearly always gets back to bloody management, and they know what my fall-back position is! (F1)

Preparing a Case

'I rely a great deal on my instinct.'

Some tutors suggest that there are three stages in preparing a case for negotiation: getting all the facts; preparing the arguments in the case; deciding on strategy and tactics. Anyone who has been a shop-floor negotiator or has observed the work-load of full-time union officials knows that these are certainly desirable objectives but they are difficult to attain in practice. Major negotiations obviously require some detailed preparation. Clearly, also, it is easier to talk about getting the facts than actually doing so. But even if it were always possible, not all of the union negotiators accepted that a mass of information is desirable. One mentioned with approval a story in which unions and management abandoned their well-documented 24-page submissions and returned with relief to the usual style of bargaining: 'What will you offer?' 'It's not enough.' When pressures were great and issues small our experienced negotiators sometimes made little preparation:

On the day-to-day run of the mill stuff I suppose I'm like most other people; I'm so busy I just get stuck into the problem and get it sorted out – I haven't reasoned anything to any extent. (F1)

But big and important negotiations are a different matter.

SERIOUS CASES NEED CAREFUL PREPARATION

If there is a major problem or if it is the kind that's going to become a major issue I'll have to prepare myself very carefully right from the beginning. I've got to work for the long-term principle and I want to be consistent all the way. I'll give you an example. I'd gone through the annual salary review for some white-collar people – both men and women – and had agreed that by a certain date the females would have x per cent of the equivalent male grade rate; that was the agreement clearly written and understood. About three or four months later the senior shop steward came to me and said, 'The bastards are robbing our women; they are using their merit money and transferring it over to the grade rate.' They were robbing one part of their wage packets to put it into another. That clearly wasn't the agreement.

I realized the management would fight like hell as they obviously hoped to get away with it throughout their whole, large, multi-plant company. When we met I'd carefully prepared our position. Ultimately it went to arbitration and we won. The arguments we put to the arbitrator were the same as those we put to the manager on the first day. We'd been consistent all through and the manager had kept changing his position. You must analyse each case and if you think it's a serious one you've got to prepare especially carefully. (F1)

The foregoing example illustrates how important it is to sort out the important issues right at the start. Is the case a single grievance or part of a general attack on custom and practice or written agreement? This sort of question clearly concerned one of our convenors.

ASK IF IT IS A CONCERTED ATTACK

When an issue arises you think immediately, ah, who's doing it? Is it just a personal decision or is it a planned attack from the management? You analyse it in those terms right away. If it's a concerted attack on existing conditions and agreements you have to handle the case accordingly. You'd have to have a meeting with members and explain. You'd have to show that if they could do it in one place they could get away with it in every other place; it becomes very important to stop the management right away. (C1)

THE SENIOR STEWARD'S JOB: ANTICIPATION

The ordinary shop steward probably doesn't think in terms of overall policy. The senior steward may see similar problems cropping up in different parts of the factory and suspect a concerted attack. It's the senior's job to anticipate this sort of thing. When a member of lower management says he can't change his decision because he's under instructions you often confirm that it's a concerted attack. (C1)

Plant bargaining in large plants clearly requires, on occasions, a more formal approach to bargaining. All of our negotiators said this. Usually, a negotiating team is elected and pursues larger and more important issues.

THE NEGOTIATING TEAM

In work-place bargaining our team is elected by the shop stewards' committee and consists of the three officers plus one senior steward for each of the day and night shifts. When we are engaged in a very large-scale negotiation we elect a team of eleven but that's unusual. (C2)

DISCUSSING THE CLAIM

Take as an example the annual wage bargain. The matter would come up for first discussion at a shop stewards' meeting. The officers may have discussed it before then and present their tentative ideas. The stewards will collect views from members and the major policy discussion will take place at another meeting. Apart from members' views other things which may have an influence are, say, other groups' gains; the company's trading figures and other plants' negotiations which affect us or could be affected by us. (C2)

CONSULTATION ON THE CLAIM

We have steward contacts across the group of factories but we bargain plant by plant. We do see it very much as a work-place bargain and pay less attention to outside factors than might be thought. Other issues, social contract, comparisons and so on, although they affect us, they are influences rather than prime factors.

We may have had first thoughts, as a kind of policy, to go for a plain wage demand and not for a 'package'. Then, in the process of consultation the message may come back that members want a large package of items. (C2)

Thinking of strategies and tactics may involve considering who is likely to be the chief negotiator on the other side of the table. All four union negotiators agreed it was important to know their opponent in order to assess their chances.

DIFFERENT OPPONENTS NEED DIFFERENT TACTICS

You've got to know your opponent, how he reacts, it's essential. (C1)

I've known and studied some employers closely for a long while. I think I've got them analysed about right. But what kind of tactics I employ will depend very much on *which* person I'm negotiating with. But I've never had any training in bargaining and I'm very much motivated by instinct – I rely a great deal on my instincts. (F1)

One tactic which negotiators are often advised to use is to rate demands in order of importance and so make concessions easy. It is sometimes suggested too that demands can be made with the intention of trading them off during negotiations. Clearly, this is not as straightforward as it looks.

WHAT GOES IN THE CLAIM?

There are some managers who'd just be irritated if I put in demands as padding, to be conceded as part of a final deal. I just wouldn't do it then. Others want to go through the whole process. In fact, some may want to go back to their superiors and say, 'Well, I've got him to drop this and that and in return I've conceded so and so.' I've sometimes put very little in a claim because I don't want to say I've made concessions and got little in return. So the question of what's put into a claim and what isn't depends very much on the circumstances and the character you're going to meet. (F1)

Preparing the Work Force

'The more united you are the better placed you are to resist.'

No description of industrial negotiations is complete without a reference to sanctions (see pp. 61–4). Tactics and strategies may require that the work force and shop stewards are prepared beforehand in order to mobilize the greatest possible show of strength. Our union negotiators – full-time officials and convenors – felt this strongly. Several linked it to the development of company-wide and international bargaining and also to changing power structures brought about by different pay systems.

STEWARDS SHOULD GIVE A LEAD

The most important thing for improvements in conditions is membership pressure. But that pressure is affected by many factors including the lead given by shop stewards. (C1)

If the company's embarked on some general attack on conditions, the more people you convince and the more united you are, the better placed you are to resist. (C1)

PAY SYSTEMS AND NEGOTIATING STRATEGIES

Piecework brings the steward close to the membership and management think a lot more of him too; they respect him because they have to discuss money with him and money always means money from the employer and nobody else. Under measured-day-work all money negotiations are taken away from the steward. It then becomes the function of the senior stewards. They've got to form sub-committees and negotiating committees because the shop-floor stewards are not involved in a direct way any longer. The senior stewards must put all their energy into annual bargaining or whatever the case is to get the wages right for the next twelve months or two years. (C1)

MOBILIZING LARGE NUMBERS IS MORE DIFFICULT

If you're representing say five thousand members it's far more difficult to convince them you've got to get the highest possible wage that you can achieve through negotiations and that they are able to achieve it. When you ask for industrial action it is more difficult to organize masses of people and obviously this assists management. (C1)

MANAGEMENT TACTICS

In big negotiations like this management will always try to get away with the lowest possible offer. They'll use all sorts of methods like distributing clock notices and letters to individual employees to emphasize what they are doing and putting pressure on in other ways. They will even create situations where people won't be able to fight to achieve a higher wage than is being offered. It lessens the militancy and this is exactly why companies want measured-day-work and high day rate systems, because they know it will eventually kill all militancy over wages. (C1)

UNION TACTICS

You have to prepare your members for an annual review. Statistics become important. Leaflets, statistics and facts become important. Managements will use their own propaganda – you never had this under piecework – but now they'll use the local press, the lot. The whole effort will be designed to psychologically weaken the membership. Of course, the conscious shop steward will know this but it's a difficult task to convince the members of what's really going on and what are the best tactics to combat it. The best contact with stewards and members is through meetings. It makes stewards and members conscious. The senior steward and the steward has to explain what is being done and what tactics are being deployed. This is the only way to prepare the membership against management propaganda. These things are increasingly important. (C1)

Strategy and Tactics

'It's difficult talking about tactics in isolation.'

The union negotiators were most unwilling to talk in general principles about the different strategies and tactics they may employ when presenting their arguments in the negotiating room. They stressed that they depend upon the specific occasion. As one said:

It's difficult talking about tactics in isolation; there are some obvious things, like the agreement to have only one spokesman to lead and direct the negotiations. Also to bring other members of the team in only at the appropriate point, when invited by the spokesman; or the need to have negotiating team meetings before the actual meeting with management to agree these and other things. (F1)

THE EMERGENCE OF TACTICS IN 'BUZZ SESSIONS'

At these preparatory meetings we often have a kind of a buzz session pooling ideas, and from this tactics for the meeting emerge. We may be facing a new situation for which previous tactics are no longer suitable. For example, in the past we may have been prepared to 'throw away' some things; we could work out our priorities, our sticking points and minimum and maximum we expected. But this year we are concentrating on a straight money increase, and there's nothing to throw away. It demands a more direct presentation for a 'substantial increase' with a whole range of comparisons drawn in. (F1)

We put to one of the full-time officials the idea that there is a range of strategies for resolving conflicts. We based these on Mike Pedler's analysis (see Figure 3, p. 97). He suggested that the Newmarket stable lads' dispute might contain many of the elements listed by Pedler, that is, avoiding, defusing, confronting (two types), collaborating. But finally his view was:

The difficulty is that you're often trying to apply logic to illogical situations; sitting back and analysing what happens – we rarely have time to do this – but I suppose we might be able to see some kind of pattern. (F2)

Strategy may dictate that early negotiations are purely ritual and that real bargaining is left until the end of the procedural line. One union negotiator said that this was a result of moves in the direction of corporate bargaining where the stakes are invariably higher than in fractional bargaining.

KEEPING BARGAINING AMMUNITION UP YOUR SLEEVE

They wanted to change something that had been in existence for about thirty odd years. Now I knew and the senior stewards knew we were just not going to agree with the management. We went through all the motions, all the stages in procedure, and did our set pieces. At the final conference before we went to York I arrived with our considered reply to the management's case.

It ran to fourteen pages and all I had to do was add a page and a half of notes based on what the company had said that afternoon. It was only when we'd exhausted the procedure and had got into a conflict situation that the real negotiations began. When you know you've got to exhaust the procedure and at the end of it there's going to be a trial of strength you keep all your main bargaining ammunition up your sleeve and just natter to one another through the procedure till it's exhausted. Then, if a battle takes place, the real bargaining begins. I think it's the development of multi-plant and multi-national companies that's bringing this about. Negotiations are on a much bigger scale than they used to be. I mean, at the plant I was talking about when it was an independent company we were negotiating with the local managers. They didn't have to ring up Head Office, but now it's totally different. These multi-plant and multi-nationals are trying to get agreements which operate over a whole group of plants and so the bargaining pressure is different. (F1)

Personalities

'It depends on the individual you're dealing with every time.'

Our union negotiators felt that circumstances often changed the tactics. They also felt that tactics depended on the individuals involved.

I keep qualifying – saying it depends on the character you're involved with and it does constantly come back to that. There are some employers to whom I'll say, 'Well, look, you don't really want the full spiel about the retail price index and so on do you? You only want to know how bloody much we want don't you?' And they'll say, 'Yes, for God's sake spare us the propaganda.' Other employers are exactly the opposite. They expect you to go through all the motions and they'd be heartbroken if you bloody didn't. Likewise, there are some employers who will say, 'Look we don't want to waste time, this is what we've got to offer – will you please tell us whether you want to accept it or not.' (F1)

TAKING NOTES IS TAKING NOTICE

Others want to go through a long spiel and I just let them go on with it because I know that if I cut them off it might even influence their way of thinking when we get down to the nitty-gritty. I let them come out with it all. I usually indicate that I'm not taking much notice by not making notes. That's an important thing in negotiations: you always know when the other man's paying attention to you when he's writing down what you say and not just sitting there listening. It depends on the individual, if he wants to make me sweat then I don't mind him making me sweat providing it's right at the end. (F1)

KNOWING THE MAN OPPOSITE

It depends on the individual you are dealing with every time. I think this is one of the important things about a negotiator, whether he's on the management side or union side: he's got to try and assess as accurately as he can the man opposite him. If you don't do that some of these tactics just won't get you anywhere. If you've got the kind of individual who despite all the facts being obvious to anybody who's got half a grain of sense, is just not taking any notice, you can very easily hurt his pride by saying, 'I simply can't negotiate with you, you haven't got the ability, I shall have to go elsewhere.' Where it's just been a bit of arm-twisting, I've said, 'Look, I'll go away and come back tomorrow and that will give you time to think about what I've said.' That's sometimes produced the goods and the man has been more sensible. (F1)

VARYING TACTICS

If the man opposite me is a rather nice pleasant sort of a person, you know, the perfect English gentleman who doesn't like to think that he's upset somebody, if I'm not winning by one means I'll try it by another. I'll pick up my papers, put them in my briefcase and say, 'Good afternoon, I'm wasting my time here and I'll go back and tell the lads what's going on in here and see what they've got to say about it.' They'll then say, 'Please sit down, we don't want you to leave in such a bad atmosphere, it's not our normal way of doing business you know.' I'll sit down and say, 'Well, of course I've got to make more progress in the next half hour than I've made in the last half hour if I'm going to stay here.' That very often extracts a bit more. But you might have a character in front of you who is not impressed by that sort of thing. He'd say, 'You're just wasting your bloody time, sit down you silly bugger, you don't influence me.' But there are other men who get very worried about this sort of tactic. (F1)

Teamwork

'One man leads the negotiations.'

It was clear that all our negotiators saw the value of a team approach to negotiations. But in each case stewards were there to support, give added detail and information. In the actual negotiations a united front is essential even if it has its difficulties. Clearly there may be a big problems *within* the negotiating team which may lead to friction. The examples that follow are a useful reminder that negotiations are for real and not just an academic exercise.

It's important that stewards are involved immediately in any case that's being negotiated. I have often insisted that all shop stewards should be there and the company couldn't refuse it; they would be seeing a delegation. It'll be at the discretion of the senior steward how he pursues the matter and how many stewards he has there. I always made it my business in these kinds of situations to have all stewards present. If the company is presented by all stewards he knows that there's a united front. The management find it more difficult to use their propaganda and cause a split between stewards and senior stewards. Stewards who are present can make up their own minds whether the senior stewards are correct or the management. If the senior misses detail in presenting his case the stewards will fill in on points of fact and details. (C1)

DISSENSION ON THE UNION SIDE

There are certain stewards you can't trust anyway, they may lean towards management and they may be doing the job only because of personal ambition, and these are the ones you have to watch and make sure they don't jump in and say something which is entirely different to the agreed presentation and weaken the case. You usually know that sort of person and then right from the start they're told, 'If you say something it's got to assist the case.' If they don't shut up then we would adjourn, take him outside and tell him exactly what the situation is. That sort of thing has happened, but it doesn't happen very often. If it does happen, adjourn, take the steward to one side and tell him he is damaging the case. (C1)

BACK-ROOM BOYS

Once I was involved in some very complicated negotiations and had a team of shop stewards working behind the scenes. We decided we should have a group of twelve stewards representing various sections of membership throughout the factory covering some seven thousand members. They would sit in permanent session in another room while we negotiated with management. They would do projects for us such as lay-off agreements, line reliefs and so on and they would think about the points they wanted us to raise with management. The management agreed with this and the team sat for about three weeks on full pay. I met them at the start of negotiations and said broadly what I was going after and then gave them projects to look at. (F1)

HOW NEGOTIATIONS CONSTANTLY CHANGE

I reported to the team but *not* on the details of the negotiations. I didn't keep them closely informed about that because – and many people don't realize this – negotiations are constantly changing. I didn't want the stewards to pick up a situation at a given moment which could have changed in a few days. So I didn't go back to report; only to find out what they had done, what their views were and to give new projects for them to work on. In that way we involved the stewards in all the details and it proved extremely useful. (F1)

WHO SPEAKS AND WHEN?

First of all, both for informal and formal conferences, if I am involved I make sure I make the major opening statement. So I will set the basis for the discussion. Now if it's an informal conference once I have made the major opening statement I welcome and encourage the senior shop steward to make comments and also any other shop stewards who happen to be present. If it is a formal conference within the formal procedure, because notes are being taken of everything said, I will make the formal presentation and the chairman of the conference, who is nine times out of ten the employer, knows that I will be content if he says to the rest of my colleagues, 'Is there anything else anybody wishes to add to what has been said?' My colleagues will not add anything unless I have actually said something which is incorrect and obviously needs to be corrected. Nine times out of ten they never make any comment. When the employer comes back with a formal reply I will formally reply to them and they will still say nothing. If they want me to raise a point they pass a note over to me and I will stop and read the note. If it's something I don't quite understand because the note's too brief or if it's a point that needs to be raised I will say, 'Will you come in on it?' So I try to control the discussion from my side. I do it this way because it's my experience that the employers operate that same system. One man leads the negotiations. (F1)

UNITY AT ALL COSTS

I have bad shop stewards who have not accepted my advice or are so enthusiastic that they have blurted something out and dropped themselves in the cart. Let me give you an example – it's bloody heartbreaking actually. I was negotiating with some employers over redundancy and the shop stewards were not very experienced. One of them had hardly seen any negotiations, and kept shooting his mouth off. I gave him a few stern looks and at one stage asked for an adjournment and said to him, 'Look, for Christ's sake keep your mouth shut, you're not helping things.' Well, we were negotiating redundancy pay and this laddie kept shouting his mouth off. He was one of those being made redundant. I got the employer to increase the amount over and above redundancy payments from the £98 entitlement to £120, then £150. When we got to £150 the employer said, 'That's as far as I can go.' This stupid clot says to the manager, 'Give me two hundred bloody pounds and I'll go.' I asked the manager if he'd made a note of it and he said he had. I said I'd got a note of what he'd said on my pad. I negotiated with the managing director two days later and finally he agreed that nobody should be made redundant except the one man who had demanded £200 and had got it. You see, there was a lot more bargaining to do. I never accept that I've got to the end until they just say, 'Look, no matter what you do to us there is absolutely nothing more to be had.' We were nowhere near that stage but this man through his lack of experience blurted out and he paid the penalty for it. (F1)

Adjournments

'The very important five or ten minutes.'

All the negotiators used adjournments to clarify details; communicate within the negotiating team; make decisions or even to discipline rogue members of the team. One of the negotiators pointed out that there are different kinds of adjournments.

When you're negotiating big deals it becomes very important you get everything absolutely right because it's going to set your conditions for a year or so. You've got to make sure that everything is right and correct and that your facts can't be challenged by management. We often have short adjournments, the very important five or ten minutes to make sure that things are right. But when it comes to annual reviews and things like that your adjournment may last for days, and sometimes even weeks or more. (C1)

Face-Saving

'Show them how you can agree.'

One issue on which the negotiators agree with the academics is the occasional need for 'face-savers'. In fact we collected much evidence of how the two negotiating parties collude in an attempt to meet the internal problems of either or both negotiating teams.

Sometimes management will want to agree to a settlement but they may be unable to because of higher instructions. A local manager may believe in what you're saying but can't do anything about it, he's being countermanded by higher levels. Sometimes local management will tell us this and we know the only way to put pressure on those higher up is by taking action. (C1)

WHEN THE LOCAL MANAGER CANNOT SETTLE

A manager in a multi-plant company once rang a district official I know and said, 'Look, I think what the lads are asking for is reasonable but I can't concede because the powers that be will cut my ears off. Can you get the lads out on strike for about four hours and I'll contact headquarters and tell them what's happened?' The district official said he didn't see why his members should lose four hours' pay because the manager hadn't got the authority to negotiate. But eventually he compromised and got them out for *two* hours. The lads came out and the manager rang up to say he'd been authorized to settle. The district official got the lads back to work and that was the end of it. (F1)

TOKEN CONCESSIONS AS FACE-SAVERS

Sometimes you must make token concessions and allow management to climb down gracefully and make sure they can make decisions without losing face. That's important in all negotiations. Always know your opponent and know how far they can go. If something must be agreed to give your opponent respect, show them how you can agree. I've done this many times. They have to provide us with a ladder sometimes too. In our situation, with hard-faced people on our side, it's necessary. That's what's known as compromise. (C1)

Flexibility

'You get to know these things.'

All the union negotiators emphasized one thing about facing an opponent across the table: that flexibility and intelligence were more important than the application of rigid rules.

You learn negotiating skills by experience and observation. You know how far they will go, they know how far you will go and there are certain steps which both sides can take to resolve the problem. But the two sides can misjudge each other. You can't be 100 per cent sure that you've judged your case rightly or you've judged their reactions rightly. You may hear certain statements and think, 'Ah, they've gone as far as they're going to go on this issue and there's no point in pressing them any further.' You agree and find you're wrong, and you could have got more if you'd pursued it. That teaches you you can't always be right in your judgements, though most of the time you are right if you have years of experience. (C1)

GETTING TO KNOW THE WAY MANAGEMENT REACTS

You can often sense from the way the management reply, the look on their faces, you know exactly whether they're telling the truth or not. The way they're speaking, the way they're reacting, the tone of voice – it's very important – someone may go red in the face or stop in his tracks and say nothing for a couple of minutes. You know if he gets to that certain point or that certain stage in the negotiations there's something suspicious. You get to know these things and you get to know individual differences the way they react, speak, the way their faces look. (C1)

BLUFF?

You do sometimes want to use a bit of psychology. You may feel that you've got a strong case but your members won't support the action and you have to bluff your way through because you know it's got to be done. Then you've got to display strength and bluff management. I'm sure they must do the same. Bluffing is sometimes necessary, I'm not saying it's an accepted practice but it is sometimes necessary, but you must never have your bluff called. You must gracefully save your face and give in. (C1)

ALL NEGOTIATIONS ARE DIFFERENT

Take negotiations in the restaurant trade. Here, the union members, mostly non-British, have different cultural assumptions about bargaining. Documents and agreements have to be translated – the terms cause a lot of difficulty – and interpreters have to be used. Words have different shades of meaning. For instance, the union sent out a circular about May Day 1975, recommending those free through shift work or on rest days to join the demonstration march. This was taken by the restaurant representatives to mean that they should all be there, and they went about closing all their work-places for the day. It's not just a question of language, but of customs and practices which are difficult to change and teach. There are often extremes of attitude, political and personal, which make conventional bargaining difficult. (F2)

EXPECTING IRRATIONAL ACTS

In bargaining irrational actions often upset everyone's calculations. In one engineering dispute after three weeks of strike and lock-out and patient successful negotiations for a return to work, the employer withdrew facilities enjoyed for years by a convenor in one of the firm's other factories. Out of spite? It took another day of bargaining to cool things down.

In a recent bookshop dispute the members wouldn't allow the officials in on the case at all.

In a factory which had run a check-off system and accepted the unions, a change of senior management altered the atmosphere and check-off facilities were withdrawn. (F2)

HORSES FOR COURSES

As a full-time official, faced by a variety of bargaining situations, an essential task is choosing horses for courses, the right people with a certain approach for the particular role, because of their bargaining style. And behind it all, keeping an eye all the time on the long-term objective in negotiations. (F2)

Rank-and-File Reactions

'They've the right to expect me to do my best.'

Trade unions exist to negotiate with management. But all our union negotiators stressed that they were often involved in 'negotiations' with their own members; either when members expected their negotiators to pursue an issue which the latter felt unreasonable or unpropitious; or, when the negotiators had reached a certain stage with management, they tried to convince unwilling members that they should endorse an agreement.

Sometimes you weigh up an issue and think it's not a very good one. Then, you can't convince the management because they know it's a bad one. It's the job of the senior steward then to tell the members the issue is no good and should be abandoned, that it could bring the union and senior steward into disrepute. Quite often the senior steward is in conflict with the membership because the members will want him to pursue something and he thinks it's indefensible. Yet minority groups and small sections still pursue it, and press it. Then it's the senior steward's job to call a meeting to convince the members that what they are pursuing is wrong and it should be dropped. It's the senior steward's job to convinced his shop stewards. It's absolutely essential that he sees that as his function. He's not just a mouth-piece. (C1)

Although our union negotiators clearly saw that they sometimes had to negotiate with their own members, they were prepared, in the last resort, to present poor cases if that was what the membership wanted.

Well, of course, there are many cases where I've had to go in and argue for the lads on the basis of a claim that in my heart of hearts I don't think is reasonable. Then I equate myself to a lawyer – I'm quite sure there's many a lawyer who is convinced that his client is as guilty as hell but he's being paid to put the best possible case he can to the judge. In those circumstances I'll put up the best possible argument I can. If I feel in my bones it's not right, that we haven't got a real basis for argument, I'll tell the members so. But in the final analysis they've the right to expect me to do my best. But by God I won't waste much time on it because if it's a poor argument and the man opposite you is any good he'll very quickly bloody shoot you down. (F1)

CONVINCING THE MEMBERS

Some branch meetings or meetings of shop stewards for reporting back are equally tough if not tougher than negotiating with the management. That's a task that some district officials won't take on. It's the easiest thing in the world to say to members, 'Yes, I think you're right, I'll go back and have another go.' But it's really being dishonest because you're misleading them; you're kidding them that there's more to be had. (F1)

CLOSING NEGOTIATIONS AND CONSULTING WITH MEMBERS

Atmosphere is all important when you have got to a stage with the employer where you're talking about recommending a deal. For instance, if the employer said to me 'There's nothing more to be had, will you please recommend this to your members?' and yet I felt there was more to be had but not that day because he was not prepared to talk any more, under those circumstances I would say 'Look, I will put this to my members,' those are the words I would use, and it will be for them to decide. But suppose we've got a situation where I feel in my bones that we've got all that we can get; where we've had good negotiations, I may even volunteer it myself. I would say, 'I am prepared to go back to the members now and fully recommend acceptance of this deal.' If I say that in that tone of voice I do not expect to go back to the management with a rejection, because that's when I get my jacket and my shirt off and argue with the membership. (F1)

PUSHING FOR A BIT EXTRA

We rarely bring in the full-time official: he may be invited in when we are near a settlement, to push for that little bit extra. For example, suppose we had been bargaining for £x basic increase: we might bring him in when we had got within £1 or 50p of what we'd hoped to get, to try to squeeze the balance out. If we plan to do this, we might receive the management's 'final offer', and take it to the membership with a recommendation of 'no acceptance'. With this decision agreed, the full-time official might come in and use the background of the 'no acceptance' and the possibility of industrial action to reopen negotiations which the stewards and management had suspended. (C2)

GETTING MEMBERS TO AGREE

I've recently had an example of this with some white-collar people. In my own mind the employer had gone to the maximum. I was satisfied – maybe my judgement was wrong – but I thought I had got the maximum possible. When I went back to the membership and reported I felt that the whole meeting was against me and that they were going to order me to go back. I didn't want to go back. By the end of the meeting I'd got sixty-eight people voting for my recommendation to accept and four voting against, whereas an hour before the figures were the reverse. (F1)

The Use of Sanctions

'Without sanctions . . . it won't convince the company one iota.'

The threat and use of industrial action is clearly always in the background of negotiating. Indeed, many would argue that potential sanctions are a prerequisite for genuine bargaining. As Allan Flanders once remarked, 'The threat of sanctions deprives both parties of the luxury of being irresponsible.' We noted above (p. 50) that the work force may be prepared before negotiations in order to show greater unity. Sanctions often start in these pre-negotiating manoeuvres.

Sanctions have to be there all the time because it is not an academic exercise. We're engaged in arguments which concern our livelihood and our future living conditions. The use of sanctions against the management is essential if you are faced with a completely uncompromising attitude. But when you are dealing with a serious attack by management even unofficial and unconstitutional action must be there if necessary to convince the company that you are powerful and the members are serious and are prepared to take action. Without sanctions you can have the best argument in the world. You can be the best intellectual but it won't convince the company one iota – you can just forget it. (C1)

QUICK ACTION ON VICTIMIZATION

If you failed in negotiations on an important issue, say a victimization case where a member or steward may be dismissed, you'd regard this as a vital principle. That's when you'd pull all the stops out to make sure the company doesn't get its way. If you don't stop the company in their tracks, if you use the procedure, the man is sacked anyway and by the time you've gone through procedure it's very unlikely that they'll reinstate him. Therefore it's essential that the action must be taken there and then. On victimization it's got to be quick, sharp and united. No time must be wasted to make the company aware immediately of how the members feel about it, not just in a verbal fashion but through action. (C1)

MANAGEMENT MANOEUVRES

Managements will create situations which will make it easier for them to get away with a low offer. They'll institute shut-outs, they'll do all kinds of things which will weaken people. They'll take a tough line on things that they would not normally do so and this creates strife inside the factory which may lead on to shut-outs. This weakens the labour force for the final negotiations. The management will do this practically every time and will continue to do so in the future. Obviously it's a question of wages and wages come out of profits. Their intention is to keep wages as low as possible. (C1)

The possibility of sanctions may be sufficient in itself to gain concessions; all that is needed is a *convincing* threat.

THE NEGOTIATOR'S THREAT

I've never taken it for granted that sanctions are there for the asking. But I've used an enormous amount of bluff about that power that I've got and I've got away with sheer bloody murder. On occasions, by quietly implying that there'll be the most massive reaction if I dare go back to the members with an offer, I've got more out of them. (F1)

THE MEMBERS' THREAT

But there are circumstances where the members have demonstrated their power before we ever get round the negotiating table. Then, it is very much in the mind of management. If the lads have come out on strike and I've persuaded them to go back to work on the basis of negotiations, that puts me in a very strong position. The membership may have made it clear they are going to withdraw their labour again if they don't get a satisfactory settlement.

Another way I've used the threat of sanctions is by advising the stewards to put it round the shop floor that we're only staying in work because we've been asked by the union, and that the minute the full-time official comes back and tells us it's not on – then we're outside the gates. That's a successful use of sanctions because it sometimes even helps local management who report to more senior managers. It's made it possible for him to say he's followed the company's line but that the pressures to concede were too great. (F1)

The threat of sanctions needs to be a realistic one, and to some extent this depends on the parties' impressions of how feeling is running on the shop floor. There is obviously much room for threatening bluff and counter-bluffing on both sides.

BLUFF AND INFORMATION

If it's a small factory of say 100–150 people the management may know how the members feel, but take an enormous plant where there's 9–10 000 people and maybe we're negotiating an issue that affects 5000 or 6000 of them. We've got our shop stewards in all the sections and we would know from them what the general reaction was likely to be. It wouldn't be completely accurate but it would be a fairly good assessment of the situation. The management would only have the information that came to them from the foremen and supervisors. If there's a volatile situation and the lads are waiting to take action – or maybe it's 80 per cent who are willing to take action and 20 per cent are not – under these circumstances traditionally the working man does not talk to the foreman or supervisor or give him any information which is likely to weaken his case. (F1)

IF WEAK, LOOK STRONG

We have educated the members and stewards now that even where they don't feel they've got a strong case they've got to let management think they have. The minute you let management know that you don't believe you've got a strong case, you'll get nothing. So therefore you must make them believe you are just dying to get out on strike or that you are dying to cause some inconvenience to them. In those circumstances our information on the situation is nine times out of ten much more accurate than the management's.

But I've noticed over the last two or three years, that the companies are becoming a bit more sophisticated in finding out what the views of the lads are. I have had one or two occasions where the management have said, 'Well, we know the membership isn't behind this,' and I've felt in my bones that they were right. Under those circumstances I go back to the membership and say, 'Well, who am I fighting for? What sort of an army have I got behind me because the bloody management are telling me that you're not going to fight, now are you management men or are you union men?' Normally that whips them back into line and I go back up there again and say 'Right, I think the situation has changed since you last met me,' and I invariably make sure that it has. (F1)

GAINING AND LOSING

A negotiator who uses the strike or other sanctions too readily is really a weak man at heart. He has to use brute strength to get what he can rather than his guile, ability and his arguments. The greatest joy I get out of my job is where I go in having spent a whole weekend working on a case thinking up all the possible arguments, all the possible moves that the other side are going to make, anticipating them, spending maybe hours and hours of arguing but at the end of it come out of there with something I can recommend to my members and they haven't lost a bloody penny during the whole process. That gives me much more satisfaction than getting the lads out. (F1)

The Media

'They are a menace to us in many respects.'

Some people argue that the media and public opinion are generally irrelevant to industrial negotiations. At least one of our negotiators thought otherwise, although his attitude towards the press was ambivalent. He felt that it was a major local disadvantage which the union suffered, but on the other hand he had learned to use the press for his own purposes on some occasions.

The media are a menace to us in many respects. Yet on the other hand I use the media. It's essential that the media do not know about an issue when we are locked in a battle where the outcome is uncertain. They will almost certainly take the employer's point of view. Almost on every occasion it will take the employer's point of view and you are not only fighting the employer but the media as well. So under those circumstances it is disastrous. (F1)

USING THE PRESS

But I'll give an example where it is helpful. Say I'm negotiating with one firm and I'm desperately trying to get a decent sick pay scheme in for the lads or lasses and I simply can't make any progress and there's no great enthusiasm amongst the lads for it. They may want a sick pay scheme but are not prepared to really fight for it. Then I go to another firm in the same locality and negotiate a good sick pay scheme. Under those circumstances I'd let the media know what has been achieved and they will publicize it generally. Invariably, when I go along to the branch where the lads were a bit lethargic they'll say, 'Hey, we see the buggers up the road have got a bloody sick pay scheme, why can't we have one?' The media may generate a desire for something. You could say, well why don't you tell them yourself? Well, I do, but either they don't believe me or they don't pay much attention to it. They seem to pay far more attention to it when they read it in the press. That sparks them off. (F1)

At the End of the Day

'I know what I've got.'

It is essential to be sure of exactly what has been agreed at the end of a round of negotiations. As a full-time official said:

I've learned from experience now. I often left the negotiating room saying 'I'm happy with what we've got, thanks very much indeed'; I've got nothing in writing except my notes and what I've got on my notes is *my* interpretation. Then to my horror I've gone to the lads at the report-back meeting, or written to the company, saying that I shall be reporting to our members that you have offered this, that and the other, and management have come back and challenged it. I now try to get in writing from the management what the agreed offer is; agree the interpretation of complicated clauses; and then once we've agreed in that way then I know what I've got. I think it is important to do that. (F1)

Why Get Involved?

'I enjoy every minute of it.'

A union negotiator's job is not an easy one. The work-load and generally pressing nature of the job may place considerable stress and inconvenience on the negotiator's shoulders. For the full-time official, pay is not high and hours are long. The convenor's pay is likely to be what he would get for doing his ordinary job in the factory, yet the position will entail much work in his own time.

THE CONSTANT STRESS

There's a great deal of stress if you're a senior steward. It's a job you're doing continuously. After working hours; branch meetings; branch committee

C

meetings; shop stewards' meetings; joint shop stewards' committee; confederation district committees; your own union committees; conferences of shop stewards; you're continuously on the go. It takes you away from home very often. You hardly ever see your own family. When you're at home you're thinking about problems and you've got to be ready for the next day and the stress is on you continuously. If you've a night shift, people will knock at your door twelve o'clock midnight, two o'clock in the morning – many times I've been called out in the middle of the night. It's very hard for your family to understand why you're doing the job under those conditions. (C1)

THE REWARD: JOB SATISFACTION

It's a very pompous thing to say but I have a deep and sincere belief in the work I'm doing. Much deeper than some people would appreciate. If anybody is getting more job satisfaction than I am bloody good luck to them because I enjoy every single moment. I'm not a clever guy, I haven't got great wisdom and all the rest of it, I get moderate successes and what I get I am immensely satisfied with. (F1)

AN EXAMPLE

I'll give you an example. I was in negotiations with a company and the employers came up with a massive offer for one group and a very poor offer for another group who are the lower paid. I was bloody livid with this because it was 47 per cent for the highest paid people in the industry and about 12 per cent for the others. It was simply because they wanted to favour one group. I went to the branch meeting with a recommendation that they should reject the offer and stand behind the low paid for a far bigger increase for them. The highly paid members sitting in the front of the meeting were going on like that to me – sticking their fingers up – and the others at the back were cheering me. It was an extraordinary experience because I almost felt remote from it as if I wasn't there, and yet I was there, in a fury. I talked for about a quarter of an hour and it was all pouring out. It was probably all disjointed but I poured out my venom against these people. They were not trade unionists, and all the rest of it. Then suddenly I was exhausted and there was a long pause and the next time I looked up they were all clapping their hands. The resolution was passed, they rejected the offer, and supported the lower paid. (F1)

What Makes a Good Negotiator?

'He's got to have principles.'

The question of what makes a good negotiator may be impossible to answer. Would we try to answer the question of what makes a good artist?

Dedication and experience clearly play a part. One of our convenors clearly feels that mechanical and rote skills are insufficient and that an educated (perhaps self-educated), committed 'whole man' makes the best negotiator. Is this one of the more important lessons we can learn from the union negotiators?

What makes a good negotiator? He's got to be intelligent for a start. He should have had some education or be self-educated. You get many stewards who believe in what they're doing but can't express themselves in words and even worse when it comes to writing it down. They've been deprived of education in their early childhood and they find it difficult to express themselves. I'm afraid they must learn the hard way. Start from scratch. I always see it as my job to see shop stewards before they are made up, explain everything to them and tell them if they are ever in any doubt to send for me immediately for guidance. (C1)

ON BEHALF OF THE MEMBERS

It's not just a game you're engaged in, because at the back of your mind you always know that the living standards of your members depend on the negotiations, the future depends on your negotiations and therefore you're not play-acting, you're not bluffing, you're using the best of your ability to secure a fair and just settlement on behalf of your members.

Secondly, he's got to have the vocation, he's got to believe in something; he's got to believe and have a consciousness of what he's doing. He's got to have principles otherwise he will never make a negotiator. It's no good just negotiating formally and academically, he's got to behave as a human being, he has to have ideas and to believe in what he's doing, that's the main thing. You want to represent people and you want to help people. The steward has to have principles, to have a reason for what he's doing, he's got to believe, he's got to have a faith in his members. (C1)

Notes

1. Chapters 6 and 7 by J. E. T. Eldrige and A. Fox in Charles, J. (ed.), *Man and Organisation* (Allen & Unwin, 1973) provide a useful sociological analysis of the different ideologies of manager–worker relations.

2. Warr, P., *Psychology and Collective Bargaining* (Hutchinson, 1973), pp. 21–2, is an example of this approach.

Industrial Reactions
by Ron Bean

It is interesting to move on from the oral comments in the last chapter
to see how they fit in firstly with the theoretical assumptions of Ron
Bean and Mike Pedler in the essays which follow, and secondly with
the contrasting ideas of other writers who see conflict as normal, but
capable of being resolved or mitigated by organizational, procedural
change, and by improved communications. A useful collation of
different approaches is set out by Tony Topham in his essay
'Approaches to Work-Place Organization in Industrial Studies' in
Industrial Studies 1: the key skills, pp. 75–99.

Ron Bean's essay bridges theory and practice: it describes what
actions and reactions can arise from the power relationship between
groups of opposed interests which he feels underlies collective bargaining.
The essay sets out the ways in which adjustment to industrial conflict
is expressed, the responses to grievances, and the sanctions and
bargaining counters which are deployed in the work-place. Some of
these are organized, like all the different forms of strike, working to
rule, overtime bans, and sit-ins. Some are unorganized, like
absenteeism, accidents, labour turnover, and forms of industrial
sabotage. The essay ends with comments on and an evaluation of inter-
relations between these reactions.

The essay relates to the continuing debate over the interaction of
'structured' influences on industrial conflict, that is, technological,
economic and political forces, and 'the action frame of reference'
described by Goldthorpe and others in *The Affluent Worker: Industrial
Attitudes and Behaviour* (Cambridge University Press, 1968, p. 184)
as one 'within which actors' own definitions of the situations in which
they are engaged are taken as an initial basis for the explanation of
their social behaviour and relationships'.

These are examined by Richard Hyman in *Strikes* (Fontana, 1972),
Chapter 3: he sees them as 'a complex two-way process in which

men's goals, ideas and beliefs influence and are influenced by the social structure'. Trade unionists will be able to judge how far these various theories match their own practical experience, and how far they are helped by them to understand and improve their own bargaining performance. (Eds.)

Owners and managers of industry and the wage workers whom they hire and direct can be expected to develop different orientations towards industry and different perceptions of their own interests. Despite heavy accent in recent years on common goals and on the virtues of industrial peace and harmony, the pursuit of opposed aims continues to cause strife.[1]

Inter-Group Conflict in Industry

It has been pointed out[2] that an employee selling his labour in the market is in an inherently unstable position at the mercy of economic and technical vicissitudes. This instability is reflected in the determination of his wages, conditions of employment and hours of work. An economic recession accompanying a sudden fall in demand for products and services may result in short-time working, loss of overtime, reduced earnings levels and, possibly, lay-offs and redundancy. Similarly, technological or organizational innovation may bring in its wake not only displacement of labour but also changes in production methods. These may intensify the work pressures upon employees through reducing manning levels or requiring employees to maintain improved standards of performance on newly installed equipment. It is out of this shifting complex of forces that many of the day-to-day issues of industrial relations are generated. Management demands for adaptability or the rationalization of production in a changing market and technological environment often contrasts with the needs of workers for job and income security. Thus real and fundamental conflicts of interest within the employment relationship are inevitable.

At a more fundamental level the alienating tendencies inherent in much of modern industrial work have been widely discussed since the days of Marx. For many employees, in an office as well as on the factory floor, the bulk of their time is spent in labour that is 'repetitive, routine, uncreative, unfulfilling, tedious, objectively and subjectively boring, deadening to the spirit and to the imagination'.[3] In car assembly plants employees try to blot out what is happening around them: 'When I'm here my mind's a blank. I *make* it go blank,'[4] is a typical remark. This dehumanization in the organization of work in our society can of itself generate conflict. The degree of alienation will vary from job to job and from industry to industry. Moreover, within a social structure based on class divisions and concerned with ownership, hierarchy and privilege, the inequalities are in power and status, as well as in economic position and monetary reward. Thus the 'deprivations' of employees will be qualitative as well as quantitative. As a result, differences of interest will centre not only upon the price of labour and how the products of industry are to be divided between employers and workers, but also upon the exercise and limits of managerial authority and control within the daily work situation.

The worker undertakes as part of his employment contract not only to supply his labour services but also to work, to a very large extent, on management's terms. That is to say, he agrees to subordinate himself to the existing pattern of work organization and to acknowledge the decision-making rights of management over work objectives, techniques, materials and other arrangements. Alan Fox has noted[5] that despite the lip-service which is paid to democracy in industry today, employers' behaviour still often shows their strong attachment to master–servant relationships within an ideology which originates far back in the historical fabric of class, status and power. A conflict rooted in divergent interests and values will be seen most clearly when management asserts its prerogatives, discretion and its rights to manage, prescribing the pace, methods and quality of work required of rank-and-file employees. Management may then be challenged by the workers' counter-assertions about their 'rights' to fairness, consistency and equity of treatment, together with more involvement and control over decisions which affect them on the shop floor.

Historically, collective bargaining has been used as a mechanism for redressing workers' grievances, regulating the work environment and improving the terms and conditions of employment. The basis of collective bargaining is the *joint* regulation by trade unions and employers of the rules which govern employment relationships.[6] These 'rules' require managements to observe agreed standards of pay, hours and working conditions, and to follow agreed procedures in such matters as job transfers, allocation of overtime and production standards. This prevents arbitrary decision-making and discrimination between employees. Since 1945 management has also been compelled to engage in collective bargaining with work-groups within the firm as well as with trade unions outside it. A long period of sustained full employment has greatly increased the bargaining power of work-groups on the factory floor and strengthened the authority of their representatives the shop stewards. This development has been particularly noticeable in issues arising out of working arrangements, the regulation of output, dismissals and the administration and enforcement of discipline.

Essentially, then, collective bargaining is also a power relationship between opposed interest groups. Pressure or sanctions will be brought to bear in order to force the other side to make concessions, restrict its areas of control or enforce and uphold the agreed work-place rules. Negotiating situations are therefore power situations. This essay, however, is concerned not so much with the sources and methods of adjustment of industrial conflict, but rather with its expression and various forms. The range of responses, which may be either collective or individual, to felt grievances on the part of the work force, will be examined. In particular, those sanctions and bargaining counters which are used in the conduct of negotiations and enforced, either by trade unions or independently by work-groups, in response to new needs and changing situations, will be analysed.

ORGANIZED AND UNORGANIZED REACTIONS

Although conflict within the industrial context is often regarded as being synonymous with a strike, a deeper insight requires consideration of its more latent, less spectacular dimensions. What needs to be considered is the entire 'range of behaviour and attitudes that express opposition and divergent orientations between industrial owners and managers on the one hand, and working people and their organisations on the other'.[7] Certainly, a strike is not the sole, nor necessarily the most important, expression of unrest among industrial workers; nor is it the only collective or mass technique through which pressure can be applied on an employer. Equally, workers may deploy on an individual basis a wide range of reactions and forms of resistance to the exercise of managerial authority, in order to gain some degree of control over their work situation.

We may distinguish firstly *organized* and overt patterns of conflict. These involve collective or group action and can include, in addition to strikes, go-slow and work-to-rule tactics, bans on overtime working, a concerted curtailment of output and (in recent years) sit-ins by means of occupation of factory premises. Then, at a more indirect and individually based level of expression, there are *unorganized* reactions and manifestations of unrest. These may comprise a high incidence of absenteeism and labour turnover, poor time-keeping and disregard of rules. Many forms of non-cooperation and withdrawal of goodwill may also be pursued, such as passive offhandedness, carelessness, or indifference to work. In addition, or as an alternative, the acts of defiance may be more formally articulated, like refusals to obey instructions, sabotage and even apparently unrelated social phenomena such as industrial accidents and pilfering. Indeed, 'as any manager knows there are a hundred small ways in which his workers can make his life a misery if they set their minds to it'.[8]

The more important of these collective and individual reactions will be examined below in greater detail, bearing in mind that the two forms may overlap. Absenteeism, for instance, may not only be an individual response to dissatisfaction but may also be organized, say on a rota basis, by a work-group.

Organized Reactions

STRIKES

Of all the forms of organized conflict strikes are the most apparent, glaring and palpable, and so command public attention and usually elicit adverse reaction. However, we should make it quite clear at the outset that the occurrence of a strike does not show conclusively that workers 'caused' it. The strike may well have been triggered off as a responsive or defensive reaction to adverse, unwanted and imposed change introduced into the work-place by the employer. Thus, many strikes are initiated not in support of a new demand on the employees' part but in immediate protest against an act of management. In the notorious Roberts–Arundel dispute in Stockport[9] the men struck when management began to employ women shortly after fifty men had been sacked as redundant. Although the press had presented this particular dispute as a strike against the employment of women, in fact action had been taken in response to the management's breaching of the engineering disputes procedure by replacing one class of labour by another without prior consultation with the unions. In a similar way, a dismissal may lead to a strike in order to obtain reinstatement of the employee, or a disciplinary suspension may lead to a demonstration stoppage to show opposition to that decision.

Why are grievances manifested in the form of a withdrawal of labour through strike action, rather than in the more diffuse expressions of discontent already mentioned? For discontent to be expressed as a strike there must be some social cohesion amongst the workers concerned, who have to be mobilized into an effective force. The strike is a collective act, so it is organized rather than unorganized workers who take strike action. It has been found[10] that plants with at least five hundred employees are more than twice as strike-prone as smaller ones. The explanation for this seems to relate not only to the stresses which can arise from the impersonality of the work situation and the resultant insignificance of the individual worker. A further important cause is that in these large plants, where considerable numbers of workers are employed on closely similar jobs, the formation of active work-groups which are more predisposed to take concerted, collective action in pursuit of grievances is encouraged.

However, strikes are complex phenomena and explanations of the circumstances in which they will be used which do not consider other interacting factors are likely to prove totally inadequate. For instance, among white-collar employees social and cultural attitudes have also been important. Traditionally many of them would have deprecated strike action as 'unprofessional', and would prefer to 'behave like gentlemen' and process their grievances through other, more socially acceptable channels. Nevertheless, this sort of inhibition about industrial action has been weakening in recent years, during which there have been, for example, strikes by airline pilots, bank staffs, teachers, hospital doctors and civil servants.

Financial considerations can also significantly affect strike decisions because during a prolonged stoppage there are bound to be severe financial losses. Thus, the unions' ability to provide strike benefits and the income and commitments of workers may also be relevant. As an illustration of the cost to those who take part, the strikers involved in the seven-week Pilkington strike at St Helens in 1970 forfeited up to £200 each in lost earnings. By the end, some of the younger unmarried men were absolutely penniless and were reduced to sleeping rough in disused brick kilns. Indeed, for everyone involved in that strike some hardship was entailed: 'standards of living had to be stripped to the bare essentials; many were obliged to go into arrears on rent and HP payments: savings were swallowed up; in some cases durable goods had to be sold; some strikers were forced to receive charity from relatives and friends.'[11]

Strikes are heterogeneous phenomena, as their scale, length and impact differ quantitatively and also qualitatively. There is clearly a wealth of difference between the national coal-mining strikes of 1972 and 1974 which took place in pursuit of an industry-wide wage claim after long drawn out negotiations had become deadlocked, and challenged the Government's pay policy, causing repercussions which were felt throughout the economy, and the small strikes or 'downers' which happen within a department of, say, a single car factory. This latter type of stoppage can be initiated and called off in minutes as the men do not leave the factory premises. The purpose of these 'downer' strikes is not to obtain general economic concessions but rather to get 'attention', to pressure management into giving certain shop-floor grievances priority so as to achieve an immediate resumption of work.[12] In much the same way most unofficial strikes (that is those not organized and sanctioned by the union) are concerned with localized plant grievances rather than with industry-wide issues and they are a means of demonstrating and deploying workshop power. They are often spontaneous rather than strategically planned and prepared for, they ignore union authority and they sidestep established disputes procedures. To counter management actions such as arbitrary curtailment of meal times, speeding up of production without warning, or employee victimization and 'unjust' dismissal, there may be no immediate forms of redress ready to hand through constitutional channels. In these circumstances prompt action is essential if the issue is not to be lost by default.

Whatever the type and magnitude of stoppage it remains true that strike action shows every sign of being a continuing feature of our society and that 'it has defied all prescribed solutions, both prophylactic and punitive'.[13] Moreover, the statistical trends of recent years would indicate that it is also a phenomenon which is spreading through most industries, even into those sectors of the economy which had been previously strike-free.

Strike Statistics and Their Interpretation

In contrast to other forms of organized and unorganized conflict where statistical information relating to incidence is limited and in some cases evidence is fragmentary,[14] strike statistics exist in great detail over a long period of time. There is a choice, depending on the purpose for which the information is required, of three basic units of measurement. The *number* of strikes shows the frequency of occurrence of separate outbreaks of collective work stoppages. However, this measure does not give any reliable information about their size or scale, nor of their severity in the sense of loss of working time. A one-day strike on a single coal face by ten men is counted as equal to an industry-wide stoppage lasting for six months. Measures are therefore needed of numbers involved, duration of stoppages and the amount of lost working time as a consequence. The *number of workers involved* is an indication of whether strikes are large or small, and the *number of working days lost* is a rough approximation of whether strikes are long or short. This latter measure is the product of the number of workers involved multiplied by the number of days' duration of the stoppage. Even this composite measure is not unambiguous: a total of one hundred working days lost may refer to a strike of one hundred men for one day, or to a strike of ten workers lasting for ten days.

Thus, the problem is not the lack of hard data but rather difficulties in interpreting the available information. The strike statistics published by the Department of Employment suffer, in fact, from limited definition, coverage and reporting. The method of compilation of the official statistics makes no differentiation between 'strikes' and 'lock-outs': both are included in the published monthly and yearly time series of work stoppages. Furthermore, the series relate to 'stoppages of work due to *industrial disputes*' so that 'sympathetic' strikes are included but not 'political' strikes. Unofficial stoppages are also not separately identified, although information about strikes *known* to be official has begun to be included during the past few years.

In practice, few complications arise from the inclusion of lock-outs within the strike series since these have been rare during the past few decades. The evidence on strikes compiled by the Ministry of Labour for the 1968 Royal Commission on Trade Unions (the Donovan Report) included a 'residual' category comprising lock-outs, strikes by non-unionists and unclassifiable disputes. This entire group accounted for less than 4 per cent of the number of working days lost by strikes each year. However, the exclusion of disputes not connected with the terms and conditions of employment (political strikes) is less satisfactory because although these stoppages may not have industrial causes they can still have serious industrial consequences. For example, twice as many workers were involved in three one-day strikes against the Conservatives' Industrial Relations Bill in 1971 as in the whole of that year's 'industrial' disputes. Similarly, in 1972, the statistics omit days lost by about 170 000 workers in various parts of the country for three days in July in protest against the decision to commit five London dockers to prison for contempt of the National Industrial Relations Court. In 1973 the strike figures omit absences from work on May Day by 1·6 million workers throughout the country who demonstrated against the Government's counter-inflation policy.

Further problems arise over the coverage of the official figures and the accuracy with which firms report their stoppages to the Department of Employment. Small stoppages involving fewer than ten workers and those lasting less than one full day are excluded from the statistics, except where the aggregate number of days lost exceeds one hundred. Thus the many local plant disputes which last for a matter of only a few hours will not find their way into the national figures, for instance the thirty or more strikes which occurred over a seven-month period in one particular car factory. The stoppages lasted only an hour or two but were 'sufficiently frequent to be regarded as a normal part of working life'.[15] Moreover in this plant the bigger disputes may have been under-reported because management kept no consolidated record of them.

Statistical interpretation is even more hazardous when comparing strike-proneness in various countries, since there are wide differences in the minimum required levels for recording disputes. In contrast to Britain, where the minimum duration for a stoppage to be recorded is one day, the minimum in Finland is two hours, in the USA it is one shift and in Belgium there is no minimum duration at all.[16] Therefore, other things being equal, the USA, Finland and Belgium would tend to show in ascending order more stoppages merely as a consequence of differences in definitional unit and scope of coverage. Finally, with reference to the secondary effects of strikes, in Britain the official statistics under-record the loss of working time experienced by workers *indirectly* involved in a dispute who, although not themselves a party to it, nevertheless lost time perhaps through shortage of materials or components. Only loss of time by workers laid off as a result of the strike at those establishments *actually experiencing* the stoppage is included, and not lost time at other non-struck establishments. Nevertheless, these secondary repercussions in an industry with a high degree of interdependence, such as motor vehicles, will be extensive. In this industry more than 300000 working days were lost in 1973 at establishments other than those at which disputes occurred and these went unrecorded in the statistics.

If these above qualifications are borne in mind, strike statistics can be employed as a useful tool in the analysis of industrial conflict. An examination of the salient features and trends in British strike statistics over the past few years follows.

Recent Strike Trends

The table opposite (Table 1) shows movements in the major strike indices in Britain during the years 1965–75.

There are a number of points to note about the use of aggregate strike statistics like those which appear in this table. The composition of the aggregates is very important. If the series of number of strikes were to be projected back to the late 1950s it would appear that between 1958 and 1968 the total number of stoppages in the country remained fairly static. However, this spurious stability was entirely the result of strike movements in one major component industry, coal-mining. In this industry the number of strikes fell by more than 80 per cent. This was mainly a consequence of the abolition of contentious piece-rate wage payment systems (which had led to fluctuating earnings) within an industry which was at the same time also experiencing a marked contraction in the size of its labour force. Such a rapid decline in strike frequency in one industry whose strikes used to contribute three-quarters of the overall recorded total of disputes in the country had the effect of offsetting strike movements elsewhere. It tended to mask the fact that in every other major industry strike incidence greatly increased over the same period. Likewise, the aggregate statistics in the fourth and fifth columns in the table are in any case dominated by the effects of big strikes, large-scale stoppages involving many workers and/or of long duration. In 1971 the 13½ million working

Table 1: Industrial Stoppages, 1965–75

Year	Number of stoppages beginning in year	(Of which known to have been official)	Number of workers involved[1] in stoppages in progress[2] in year '000	Aggregate number of working days lost[3] in stoppages in progress in year '000
1965	2354	(97)	876	2925
1966	1937	(60)	544	2398
1967	2116	(108)	734	2787
1968	2378	(91)	2258	4690
1969	3116	(98)	1665	6846
1970	3906	(162)	1801	10980
1971	2228	(161)	1178	13551
1972	2497	(160)	1734	23909
1973	2873	(132)	1528	7197
1974	2922	(125)	1626	14750
1975	2263	n.a.	805·6	5957

Notes

[1] The figures include workers both directly and indirectly involved, the latter being those workers thrown out of work *at the establishments where the disputes occurred*, although not themselves parties to the disputes.

[2] Stoppages 'in progress' include stoppages continuing from the previous year.

[3] Excluding loss of time caused *at other establishments* by the stoppages.

Source: Department of Employment *Gazette*

days lost included more than 6¼ million days lost through the national stoppage by Post Office workers and a further 2 million as a result of a ten-week stoppage by car workers. Similarly, in 1972 45 per cent of the days lost were attributable to the national coal-mining strike in the early part of that year.

It is also apparent from the table that only a small proportion of the annual number of stoppages takes the form of official strikes. The real incidence of unofficial strikes will be even higher than the statistics indicate as many small strikes are never recorded. Nevertheless, the fact is that the few massive, official 'confrontations' are responsible for the bulk of days lost and workers involved. In 1973, for instance, a mere 1 per cent of the total number of stoppages accounted for 15 per cent of all workers involved in strikes that year and for 20 per cent of the days lost.

From 1968 to 1974 the number of stoppages, the number of workers involved in strikes and the number of working days lost entered a new dimension of magnitude, especially as a result of the resurgence of the national, official type of stoppage. In 1970 there was the largest number of stoppages ever recorded and in 1972 working days lost were the highest in any single year since 1926, the year of the General Strike. It is clear from the table that in 1971 both the number of strikes and number of workers involved declined, so that the increase in the number of working days lost was the consequence of the fact that the *duration* of strikes (days lost per striker) doubled. Once again it is true that strike-proneness is exceptionally unevenly distributed throughout the various industries in the economy: strikes in engineering, motor vehicles, mining, shipbuilding, docks and transport have been predominant since the Second World War. However, it has been shown[17] that in recent years strike trends among different industries have been relatively uniform, that although levels of strike activity differ between industries, increases in strike activity have been spread evenly over almost the entire economy. Nevertheless, to preserve an overall perspective, it is worth noting that in 1969 there was a strike loss of only 0·13 per cent in man days as a percentage of total work-time available.

What the statistics in the table do not reveal is that there has been a noticeable change in the character and precipitating causes of strikes during these years. The biggest proportion of the increase in strike frequency since the early 1960s has been due to disputes over wage claims, that is, strikes are about money rather than management control. This was something of a reversal of the dominant trends which had appeared in the 1950s. It is possible to attempt to account for this recent acceleration in strike activity by using statistical analysis in the form of econometric techniques. This avoids an oversimplified, single factor explanatory approach by taking into account other possible causal influences and separating out the interacting variables involved. Preliminary work in this area[18] provides support for the hypothesis that the heightened level of strike activity may be connected with the recent unaccustomed and unexpected acceleration in the pace of inflation. This has led to problems caused by different speeds of adjustment in the relative earnings (differentials) of particular groups of workers. Whether or not these trends in strikes will continue must, however, remain a matter for speculation as these movements are not easily predictable.

It is also worth remembering that most employees do not seem to favour using the power tactic of the strike in any situation in order to gain what they want. A recent Government-sponsored survey of shop-floor opinions[19] found that only a quarter of the sample of workers interviewed across a wide range of industries said they would support strike action under any circumstances to remedy grievances. However, about two-thirds of the total of employees were in favour of taking strike action in three specific sets of circumstances: where management broke an agreement, delayed dealing with grievances, or discharged workmates unfairly. Nevertheless, a large majority of both employees and shop stewards preferred wherever possible 'going through procedure' for settling disputes, to strikes and other forms of pressure.

NON-STRIKE REACTIONS

Some of the other important collective expressions of organized conflict in industry usually have a less dramatic impact than strikes on public opinion, and they also result in a smaller loss of earnings for their participants. Like strikes these actions do not have to be pursued by unions; they can be directed by organized work-groups who can impose their own sanctions in order to regulate work-place relations. The evidence on the extent to which these other reactions and forms of pressure are utilized comes from the 1972 *Workplace Industrial Relations* survey previously quoted (see note 19). The informants were asked whether forms of pressure other than strikes had been used against management in the previous two years. It was found that overtime bans (particularly in engineering), threats to strike, and working to rule were the most frequent other types of pressure employed.[20] The only groups of industries which were relatively free from these were the distributive trades and offices, both of which are largely non-unionized. The percentage of shop stewards who replied that various sanctions other than striking had been used at their place of work during a two year period is shown below (Table 2):

Table 2: Non-Strike Forms of Pressure Used Against Management
(All Industries)

	%
Overtime bans	38
Threats to strike	24
Working to rule	30
Go-slows	7
Blacking	3
Other forms of pressure	4
At least one form of pressure	60
None	40
Total	100

Source: extracted from Table 12.7, *Workplace Industrial Relations*, 1972
Note: the table adds up to more than 100 per cent because some shop stewards had used more than one form of pressure.

In a similar, earlier survey[21] a substantial majority of works managers, personnel officers and foremen felt that these other forms of pressure were, in fact, more effective than strikes in securing results, although the majority of shop stewards questioned thought that strikes were the more effective.

Some of the more common types of collective sanctions will be considered below, recognizing that the range of irregular action which stops short of strikes is much wider than the table indicates. In shipbuilding, for example, such action has included bans on night-shift working, restrictions on the use of tools and refusals to operate the flexibility provisions of productivity agreements.

Work-to-Rule and Overtime Bans

The phrases 'work-to-rule' and 'go-slow' are often used interchangeably. Sometimes other terminology is employed such as the old 'ca' canny' practices of dock workers and the euphemistic 'working without enthusiasm' of certain groups of white-collar workers. They represent a type of passive reaction resorted to by organized (and sometimes unorganized) workers so that although it is not a strike in the sense of a temporary and concerted *cessation* of work, so little work may in fact be performed that it becomes a 'strike on the job'. Working to rule is especially effective in jobs which are governed by closely detailed rules. A good illustration relates to the railways where during the official work-to-rule in 1972,

there was much scope for the imaginative worker-to-rule. During a normal rush-hour passengers would not thank railway staff for attending too conscientiously to their safety. Before a train starts a guard must examine notices to see if anything needs his special attention. He must see that the train is correctly labelled and has the necessary lamps. It is also his task to see that all couplings are properly connected and that the doors of the carriages are properly closed. He could, if he so chose, spend a considerable amount of time ensuring that his watch was exactly synchronised with other clocks in the station and that the train's first aid and emergency equipment was intact. . . . What emerges is that if the rules were seriously or conscientiously obeyed no train would ever leave the station.[22]

Another bargaining weapon widely used is the overtime ban. It appears to be as frequent as an actual strike, considering the large amounts of overtime regularly worked in Britain since 1945. It is a particularly potent force in certain industries such as ship repair. Here penalty clauses, sailing schedules and the economics of ship chartering all restrict the time allotted to complete work down to fine limits.[23] The uncertain nature of the work flow into the yard makes the employer rely on overtime to meet the demands of the shipowner; thus an overtime ban can be extremely damaging.

In these circumstances it is seldom necessary for workers to come out on strike in order to make their point to the employer. In the allied ship-building industry bans on overtime have been very common shortly before a launch or delivery date to put pressure on an employer when he is at his most vulnerable.

In the coal industry a national overtime ban escalated three months later into the strike of 1974. This was accompanied by a three-day working week in other major industries imposed by the Government in order to conserve fuel stocks. In electricity supply a combined work-to-rule and overtime ban in 1970 in support of a pay claim resulted in widespread power cuts and black-outs.

Sit-Ins

'Sit-ins' may be defined as the occupation of a work-place by employees against their employers' wishes, in which control (or partial control) is exercised over the access to and the use of the work-place.[24] The duration of occupation will need to exceed a minimum of a half-day in order to constitute more than a token protest. The emphasis of definition here is on the intent to occupy, in order to distinguish sit-ins from 'sit-down strikes' in which there is no intention to occupy and control the work-place. Occupation has not been a part of traditional industrial action in Britain, although it was popular in France and the USA in the 1930s, and it has only become more widespread in this country since the end of the 1960s. It has generally originated in local action often by shop stew-ards, rather than in national union action. Work-place occupation has been used mainly to combat threatened closures and accompanying redundancies by taking physical control of the factory premises so as to frustrate management's closure procedure. It has also achieved some success by causing management to reverse, or modify substantially, their closure and redundancy policies, as for example at Upper Clyde Ship-builders, Fisher-Bendix (IPD) and Plessey. When work continues during the occupation the sit-in becomes a 'work-in'. For this to be possible a large amount of work has to be already in progress, or else customers and suppliers have to be confident enough to continue to carry on normal business relationships, or else support from the Government in the form of loans and grants needs to be forthcoming.

Certainly, the sit-in as a form of action may both reduce the possibility of conflict and clashes with the police in picketing outside the gates and at the same time may help maintain the morale of workers by keeping them all together within the work-place. In some circumstances it may therefore prove superior to the strike. It is a type of offensive industrial reaction which, when it becomes a work-in, reflects not merely a further, gradual shop-floor encroachment on management authority but a bold stepping over on to the management power base itself. In the workers' takeover at IPD (afterwards a workers' cooperative) managers, not employees, found themselves out in the street. In the words of the factory convenor to the Works Director,

In 1963 there were 2,500 people who worked here, and every time a product was sold off (to another company) and you made money – you made redundancies. Now we have a work force of 700, well we've had enough, we're giving you formal notice now, in our own little way – we've got no papers – but as from today *you're redundant.*[25]

Unorganized Reactions

In the major forms, considered above, of organized industrial reactions, the employees have group cohesiveness, effective leadership and a willingness to take concerted action. There follows a discussion of the unorganized, more individual and latent expressions of employee dissatisfaction. It is important to notice, however, that unlike the industrial actions described above, these unorganized expressions often have less definite aims, although they arise from the nature of the work situation. Indeed, they are not usually employed in the same way as part of the bargaining strategy in an attempt actually to *alter* the work situation by resolving specific demands and grievances.

ABSENTEEISM, ACCIDENTS AND LABOUR TURNOVER

Negative reactions to a work situation which causes discontent, unrest and deprivation can be demonstrated by employees as a high incidence of voluntary absenteeism or of labour turnover. Absences, that is being away from work whilst still remaining an employee, may be contrasted with labour turnover which is leaving one job for another. Essentially then, absence can be regarded as a 'stayer' phenomenon in that one of its uses is to provide a means of temporary withdrawal from the stress of continuing in, as distinct from breaking (by permanently leaving), a specific work situation.

It is true that sickness absence is the main component of overall industrial absenteeism. But most of the factors which have been found to be significantly associated with sickness absence can also be considered to be behavioural, rather than medical, environmental or economic. In a recent study of male workers in an oil refinery[26] it was shown that sickness absences are by no means all random phenomena related solely to medical factors. Job dissatisfaction was found to be an important influence on 'sickness' absence, in that people who took frequent spells of absence from sickness very often disliked their jobs. Thus job involvement and satisfaction would appear to be crucial factors in improving attendance records. Furthermore, it has been suggested that sickness absence and other absences are to some extent interchangeable, depending on whether in any particular plant absence without sickness is tolerated as a mode of behaviour by both employers and workers. It also is probable that even in those cases where medical reasons are applicable, at least part of the marked increase in industrial absence rates in recent years has arisen from the fact that less serious illnesses are assumed to justify absence from work.[27]

Another form of temporary withdrawal in which the employee takes up the role of absentee in a way acceptable to both himself and his employer, is the industrial accident. These accidents can be analysed from the standpoint of the quality of the relationship between the employee and his employing institution, that is although accidents happen to individuals they are social events. Accidents cause not only injury but also absence from work and, although an infrequent form of absence, they are nevertheless readily sanctioned as such. In a case study at an iron and steel works[28] it was found the prevailing pattern of accidents was one of common mishaps (sprains, cuts, burns, etc.) resulting in superficial injuries which led to relatively short absences. It was concluded that an accident is a form of motivated absence, however unconscious the motivation on the part of the individual concerned.

Some studies[29] have shown that industrial unrest is also often expressed in the form of a high rate of labour turnover, especially among unskilled workers. If employees are dissatisfied with their existing work situation they may not take industrial action. Instead, they can 'vote with their feet' and simply leave. However, the validity of labour turnover as evidence of dissatisfaction is considerably reduced by the effect of general economic conditions on turnover. Its validity depends on the ability of workers to express their unrest by leaving their jobs and going to work elsewhere. Its magnitude will therefore be affected by the job opportunities available in the labour market at any one time. Similarly, the statistical evidence is not easy to evaluate because 'quit' rates (voluntary withdrawals) are often not available and the more commonly used 'discharge' rates include the involuntary aspects of turnover as well as voluntary terminations of employment.

INDUSTRIAL SABOTAGE

Industrial sabotage is the destruction or deliberate breaking down and impeding of factory plant and equipment and sometimes the mutilation of its products. There are many ways of disconcerting management with this technique:

Materials are hidden in factories, conveyor belts jammed with sticks, cogs stopped with wire and ropes, lorries 'accidentally' backed into ditches. Electricians labour to put in weak fuses, textile workers knife through carpets and farm workers cooperate to choke agricultural machinery with tree branches.[30]

Sabotage is included here among the unorganized expressions of conflict because it is more covert than strikes or overtime bans and, like sickness and accidents, it is more ambiguous of interpretation. Sometimes it involves informal and individual actions as a means of relieving frustration. In car plants when lay-offs are impending, employees may work out their anger and frustration by going down the line with pennies or knives scraping the paint off car bodies. These actions could however also be more purposive, representing the operatives' search for greater job control over work speeds. In the early days at Ford's Halewood assembly plant there were no agreements about the speed of the line and the pace of work demanded. This is the sort of thing that happened: 'Individual acts of sabotage were common. . . . Men pulled the safety wire and stopped the line. These acts were part of a general movement toward job control.'[31] Or 'Bostic bombs were manufactured and hurled into the steel dumper rubbish containers. Explosions . . . flames twenty feet high.'[31]

However, such uncoordinated and individual acts of sabotage were a feature of this plant in the early stages of shop-floor organization before stewards had control of the membership. Once a plant becomes well-organized, individual sabotage may then threaten the unity and organization achieved through collective action. Thus in most instances sabotage involves the active or passive cooperation of many employees and can be a concerted, cohesive and group act towards a definite aim. It then becomes an organized reaction used as a bargaining weapon to wear down management so that it makes concessions. For example, a group of bakery workers did not welcome being put on to night-shift work. They therefore deliberately engineered a regular series of breakdowns in the ovens so that they would be sent home early and ultimately put on to different hours.[32]

The Interrelation of Reactions

It remains to examine the relationship between the main organized and unorganized varieties of conflict response by work forces in terms of the kinds of response and reactions which will emerge in different situations. To what extent are they interchangeable and therefore *alternative* forms of unrest or, conversely, might they be *additive* forms of expression whereby both organized and unorganized responses move together, either upward or downward, in unison? It is hardly surprising that the available evidence is conflicting, because industrial unrest is in itself a complex phenomenon.

In the coal industry it was concluded that strikes and the various types of unorganized conflict function as alternative manifestations of discontent. Whereas absenteeism increased after 1957, the frequency of strikes, even after allowing for the subsequent decline in the size of the industry's labour force, decreased substantially, as has already been noted. Likewise, accidents per 100000 man-shifts and voluntary turnover all increased over the same period.[33] In contrast, other studies have shown that in pits where discontent is very prevalent the accident rate rises before the pit is due to go on strike.[34] In the case of the Yorkshire coalfield[35] absenteeism and strike propensity appear to be positively related, so that unrest manifests itself in both forms where conflict is acute. A recent statistical analysis across a number of manufacturing industries[36] supports a direct rather than inverse connection, in that the same forces which operate on sickness absence, voluntary absence and lateness may also affect the propensity to take strike action. Another study, in Irish industry, has found that some thirteen days per worker per year are typically lost through absences of one kind or another but that strike-prone firms have significantly higher absence rates than the norm.[37] This would again suggest that at least some of the underlying causes are the same for both phenomena.

There is clearly evidence, however, of a relationship between the skill, status and rewards of an occupation and the willingness of employees to take organized action in support of grievances: the higher the occupational status the greater the willingness to support organized action. In coal-mining it has been found that the face-workers, rippers, cutters and fillers, took concerted group action through strikes and the grievance procedure, whereas the less well-organized packers expressed their discontent through absenteeism or quitting the job, and the low status and less skilled conveyor movers by 'grumbling without action'.[38] This close association between occupational status and organized conflict was said to be a consequence of three main factors:

1. Higher status groups have a more secure market position and are less easily dispensable or replaceable.
2. These groups usually display greater solidarity and more group cohesion than lower status groups.

3. The groups are composed of more experienced and older workers, as promotion within the manual category depends to a large degree upon seniority.

It has also been more firmly established that if the collective expressions of discontent are suppressed or inhibited then they are likely to find an outlet in a more dispersed and individual fashion. A car firm which began dismissing unofficial strike leaders sustained fewer strikes but its labour turnover doubled, the accident frequency rate rose by more than 40 per cent and absenteeism increased significantly as well.[39]

Evaluation

In this essay we have defined industrial relationships within the bargaining context in terms of divergent interests, values and orientations. These separate employers and managers to one side of the employment situation and workers and trade unions to the other. We have examined the methods used in national, 'set-piece' confrontations and the numerous types of work-place sanctions involving skirmishes on the shop floor, by which means bargaining is continued through the use of pressure tactics. It is true that powerful trade unions may be able to put employers under severe pressure as a result of taking industrial action. But although they may adopt postures which look aggressive, their underlying psychology is basically defensive. Unions react to events. Indeed their resources are always, in the last resort, inferior to the resources which employers could mobilize if they were to decide on a fight to the finish. Plants may be closed and investments written off whilst fortunes still remain intact; but men are risking their very livelihoods in a sustained strike.[40] The power of employers can be very real despite the fact that it is less overt and that its full weight is kept in reserve rather than being continuously deployed. For example, a demand backed by strike action that wage earners receive equal rewards with top management would soon demonstrate which side was the stronger and which could last out the longer.[41]

Furthermore, workers and their organizations have no monopoly of sanctions in industrial relations matters. Employers, either singly or collectively, may also take industrial action against unions or unorganized individual workers in the form of black-lists, intimidation, or lock-outs. These may be applied either as an offensive measure in their own right, or as retaliation against measures initiated against themselves. Managements also can invoke a variety of sanctions. They can suddenly become less cooperative, tighten up on (or withdraw) concessions previously made to their work forces and be unwilling to concede even the most insignificant matters in negotiations. They too can apply pressure and clamp down. Conversely, on some occasions, management can pursue its own interests by doing nothing in relation to its labour force: by, for instance, allowing during inflationary conditions increased values of output to be reflected in higher profitability rather than in adjusted wage levels.

In work-place bargaining then, the parties directly involved have come to accept that at least some of the sanctions, pressures and techniques of industrial action considered here will be used by both sides. In many industries they are part of the normal background against which negotiations are conducted on the shop floor on a day-to-day basis.

Notes

1. Kornhauser, A., Durbin, R., and Ross, A. M., *Industrial Conflict* (New York: McGraw-Hill, 1954), p. 3.
2. Allen, V. L., *Militant Trade Unionism* (Merlin Press, 1966), p. 12.
3. Blumberg, P., *Industrial Democracy: the Sociology of Participation* (Constable, 1968), p. 48.
4. Beynon, H., *Working for Ford* (Penguin, 1973), p. 109.
5. Fox, A., *Beyond Contract: Work, Power and Trust Relations* (Faber, 1974), p. 250.
6. Flanders, A., *Management and Unions* (Faber, 1970), p. 220.
7. Kornhauser, A., *et al., op. cit.*, p. 13.
8. Fox, A., 'Labour Utilisation and Industrial Relations', in Pym, D. (ed.), *Industrial Society* (Penguin, 1968), p. 55.
9. See Arnison, J., *The Million Pound Strike* (Lawrence & Wishart, 1970).
10. Government Social Survey, *Workplace Industrial Relations* (HMSO, 1968). See also Shorey, J., 'The Size of the Work Unit and Strike Incidence', *Journal of Industrial Economics*, Vol. 23 (1975), pp. 175–88.
11. Lane, A., and Roberts, K., *Strike at Pilkingtons* (Fontana, 1971), p. 107.
12. See Clack, G., *Industrial Relations in a British Car Factory* (Cambridge University Press, 1967), p. 61.
13. Allen, V. L., *op. cit.*, p. 112.
14. It is usually based on sample data for a limited number of workers or establishments, or else relates only to a single industry.
15. Clack, G., *op. cit.*, p. 88.
16. Fisher, M., *Measurement of Labour Disputes and Their Economic Effect* (Paris: OECD, 1973), pp. 88–9.
17. Silver, M., 'Recent British Strike Trends: A Factual Analysis', *British Journal of Industrial Relations*, Vol. 11 (1973), p. 77.
18. See for example Bean, R., and Peel, D. A., 'A Quantitative Analysis of Wage Strikes in Four U.K. Industries, 1962–1970', *Journal of Economic Studies*, N.S., Vol. 1, No. 2 (1974), pp. 88–97.
19. Parker, S., *Workplace Industrial Relations 1972* (HMSO, 1974), p. 69.
20. *Ibid.*, p. 67.
21. McCarthy, W. E. J., and Parker, S. R., *Shop Stewards and Workshop Relations*, Royal Commission Research Paper No. 10 (HMSO, 1968), p. 91.
22. *Sunday Times*, 2 April 1972.
23. Commission on Industrial Relations, *Shipbuilding and Shiprepairing*, Report No. 22, Cmnd. 4756 (HMSO, 1971), p. 92.

24. See Beever, C., 'Sitting It Out', *Industrial Society*, Vol. 55 (May 1973), p. 13.

25. Quoted in Clarke, T., *Sit-In at Fisher-Bendix* (Institute for Workers' Control, Pamphlet No. 42, 1975), p. 5.

26. Taylor, P. J., 'Personal Factors Associated with Sickness Absence', *British Journal of Industrial Medicine*, Vol. 25 (1968), pp. 109–13.

27. See Office of Health Economics, *Off Sick* (HMSO, 1971), p. 6.

28. Hill, J. M. M., and Trist, E. L., *Industrial Accidents, Sickness and Other Absences*, Tavistock Pamphlet No. 4 (1962), p. 3.

29. See for instance Scott, W. H., *et. al.*, *Coal and Conflict* (Liverpool University Press, 1963), pp. 174–5.

30. Taylor, L., and Walton, P., 'Industrial Sabotage: Motives and Meanings', in Cohen, S. (ed.), *Images of Deviance* (Penguin, 1971), p. 219.

31. Beynon, H., *op. cit.*, p. 139.

32. Taylor, L., and Walton, P., *op. cit.*, p. 238.

33. Handy, L. J., 'Absenteeism and Attendance in the British Coal-Mining Industry', *British Journal of Industrial Relations*, Vol. 6 (1968), pp. 45–50.

34. Revans, R. W., 'Industrial Morale and Size of Unit', in Galenson, W., and Lipset, S. M., *Labour and Trade Unionism: An Inter-disciplinary Reader* (New York: Wiley, 1960), p. 298.

35. McCormick, B. J., 'Strikes in the Yorkshire Coalfield, 1947–1963', *Journal of Economic Studies*, Vol. 14 (1969), p. 193.

36. Bean, R., 'The Relationship Between Strikes and Unorganised Conflict in Manufacturing Industries', *British Journal of Industrial Relations*, Vol. 13 (1975), pp. 98–101.

37. O'Muircheartaigh, C., *Absenteeism in Irish Industry* (Irish Productivity Centre, 1975).

38. Scott, W. H., *et. al.*, *op. cit.*, pp. 174–5. It can also be argued that strike-proneness in this industry has now been reduced because of the changeover from piecework to day work *payment* systems, under the national power loading agreement which applies to all mechanized coal-faces.

39. Turner, H. A., Clack, G., and Roberts, G., *Labour Relations in the Motor Industry* (Allen & Unwin, 1967), p. 190.

40. Flanders, A., 'The Tradition of Voluntarism', *British Journal of Industrial Relations*, Vol. 12 (1974), p. 355.

41. Fox, A., *Beyond Contract*, p. 284.

Learning to Negotiate
by Mike Pedler

The following essay, in two parts which are complementary, assumes
a theory of conflict. The first analyses conflict from a behaviourist
point of view, and the second sets out ways in which negotiating
can be taught against this background of analysis, ending with a
selection of eleven training exercises and some notes on closed-circuit
television.

They offer useful comparisons and contrasts with the practical
experience of the trade union negotiators (pp. 43–67) and with the
industrial reactions described by Ron Bean.

Trade unionists and tutors may choose to set the behaviourist
approach in the kind of context given by Hyman (pp. 68–9 above), and
introduce economic, political, legal, historical, social and institutional
elements which add to the richness of both theory and practice.

The question of 'teaching' bargaining and negotiating in any case
raises a number of issues. There is little agreement on what constitutes
the 'best' kind of training for negotiators. Many industrial tutors use
well-tried teaching methods, usually based on case studies and role-
playing exercises. Yet many trade unionists still insist that practical
experience is the key to becoming a good negotiator. There has been
little or no research to tell tutors whether their methods are the right
ones. Then again, some writers think that negotiating skills are diverse
and that only a negotiating *team* can satisfy the requirements of good
negotiating. (See for example B. H. Kniveton, 'Industrial Negotiating:
Some Training Implications', *Industrial Relations Journal*, autumn 1974.)

These ideas should not be lightly discarded if only because we as
tutors know so little about the effectiveness of our training methods. In
any case, the union negotiators we interviewed (pp. 43–67) told us how
experienced negotiators selected promising stewards and 'brought them
on' by encouragement, advice and gradual planned exposure to the
real thing. And all this was done without removing them from the

work-place and running the risk of isolating them from their members. Many stewards learn to be effective negotiators without seeing a classroom at all, and we would be wrong to assume that this is some accident of nature.

'Training' on the shop floor may be more effective than we realize and more systematic too, possibly because it arises out of the participative and democratic nature of union activity of which it is itself a part. The union negotiators described (pp. 49–56) how different forms of 'team approach' were used, all of which drew on the varied skills and abilities of the shop stewards' committee within the factory.

If we look closely enough at what the practitioners do, we may learn more about the phenomenon as an art, a skill or a process, and the best ways to teach it.

Against this background, Mike Pedler's approach to the question offers a different dimension to tutors and students teaching and learning about negotiating. What other possibilities may develop with the application of research and sophisticated technical equipment in the future? (Eds.)

Foreword

This essay is in two parts. The first part describes the nature of conflict, conflict resolution, negotiation and communication, using recent research to build up a model of the negotiating process primarily from the point of view of behavioural science. The major disciplines from which the theory is drawn are social psychology and sociology, and the emphasis is upon negotiation as an interpersonal and inter-group process. Negotiation is seen as a basic human activity, practised in many situations, and not as something limited to union–management relationships. For this reason some of the important aspects of union and management collective bargaining are deliberately neglected and referred to only in passing. Examples are the collection and selection of information for negotiation, case preparation and strategy develop-ment (to which references are given where appropriate).

The second part contains exercises for the development of negotiating and conflict resolving skills, together with a brief discussion of teaching and learning theory. In broad terms the exercises follow the theory outlined in Part 1. A note on the use of closed-circuit television (CCTV) is also included, as it is becoming more and more available and is a valuable tool for studying negotiating behaviour.

Part 1

A Behavioural Approach to Negotiating Skills

Introduction

In recent years, a number of developments have combined to make industrial relations a high priority for management and Government. Trade unions have always given industrial relations a high priority, yet the effects upon them are also obvious in the increasing number of unionists actively involved. This activity can be seen as a response to the need for the management of organizations to cope with change and to become more collaborative and consultative. 'Full employment', inflation, the development of post-industrial society, increasing white-collar and managerial unionism and the higher expectations of an ever more skilled, educated and flexible population are some of the pressures underlying this movement.

At a wider, societal level, the acceleration of change is putting new demands upon human relationships and personal skills. Frankenberg[1] has pointed out that the move from rural to urban society involves replacing few, relatively permanent role relationships with many, more transient ones.

The increasing pace of life creates a high 'turnover' of relationships with people, things, places, ideas and organizations. Not only do we change jobs more often, but we change homes, interests and even mates more frequently too.[2] This in turn creates a need for being able to develop relationships quickly to resolve conflicts and establish trust and communication on a fairly deep level, in order to operate effectively either at home or at work.

A consequence of these pressures is the greater likelihood and frequency of conflicts and the need to resolve them. Negotiation is perhaps the most widely applicable tool for resolving conflicts, and as there are more conflicts, so will there be more negotiating. At work for example, both managers and other employees are more involved in negotiating as the level of decision making comes down and the range of negotiable issues widens.

Unfortunately much of the existing training for negotiation is inappropriate. As Rackham has pointed out, many programmes do not allow for the development of skills, and concentrate overmuch on knowledge.[3] Those that do include skills practice almost always try to do this by means of role play. In such exercises role players adopt the stereotyped behaviours they think are appropriate. 'Managers' nearly always behave authoritatively or at best 'firmly but fairly', whilst 'shop stewards' are consistently obstructive, belligerent and 'chip-on-the-shoulderish'. Consequently all the participants end up learning are the bad old ways, and the lessons teach competition, blocking, resistance, points scoring and over-exaggeration. It has sometimes seemed to me that industrial relations practitioners value deviousness and toughness above all else. In training newcomers these tend to be the values passed on and they underlie the skills developed.

There is a time for toughness and perhaps even a time for deviousness too, but very often a yielding or straight approach might be valuable. What is needed is the development of skill in a number of styles and the judgement necessary to select appropriately. We all sometimes seem to operate on self-fulfilling prophecies: we go in hard, withholding information and manoeuvring skilfully, and meet the counter-attack which we expect (and create!).

The Nature of Conflict

Conflict can be defined as a situation in which the specific demands of one party are frustrated by one or other of the parties to a relationship or contract. In fact the word 'conflict' is used to describe more than a situation. Descriptions of conditions, such as scarcity of resources, differences in objectives; attitudes, such as stress, anxiety, tension; behaviours, such as resisting, aggression, all appear in the literature. Indeed conflicts may be described as episodes, during which all the various definitions can be related.

Before moving on it is worth making the point that this definition and description of conflicts applies to the frustrations of any contractual relationship. The ideas are every bit as relevant to husband–wife and neighbour–neighbour relationships as they are to those between union and management. Within organizations there are numerous opportunities for conflicting. There are, perhaps, four major categories, as can be seen on p. 93.

POTENTIAL CONFLICT FOCI IN AN ORGANIZATION[4]

1. *Interest groups*, such as union and management or craft unions and manual unions, may compete for scarce resources.

2. *Control*. The parties to an authority relationship may come into conflict when one tries to exercise control over some activity that the other regards as his sphere. These conflicts take place in the vertical dimension of an organization between a superior and a subordinate. Conflict arises here when either tries to extend his control and influence. This type of conflict is increasing as individuals seek more autonomy, that is control over the conditions of one's existence, because of the large size of many modern organizations where leaders are distant and impersonal; sub-unit goals are different from and hard to relate to the goals of the organization's leaders; procedures are formalized and rank-and-file are treated impersonally, instrumentally or as factors of production.

3. *Coordination*. Sub-units or departments which should be cooperating on some joint activity may be unable to act concertedly and so compete with each other. This is a problem of coordination and takes place on the lateral dimension of an organization. The departments (or they may be individuals, or teams within a department – hence the term 'sub-unit') will have different sub-goals but are often interdependent through the common usage of services or facilities; the work flow sequence; rules about joint activity. Well-known examples in this category are sales and production; staff and line; maintenance and production; merchandising and marketing.

4. *Role sets*. Role sets are composed of individuals in an organization and all the other individuals in his social network who have role expectations of him. The supervisor, for example, has a role set which may consist of certain members (see Figure 2 on p. 94).

Each of the members of the role set is a 'sender' of expectations. Obviously these expectations can never completely match up. Role conflicts arise from differences between the demands of different senders and differences between these demands and the job holder's wishes and expectations.

If we regard the organization as composed of different but overlapping role sets, then the opportunities for this type of conflict are numerous.

At any one time of course, more than one form of conflict may be present.

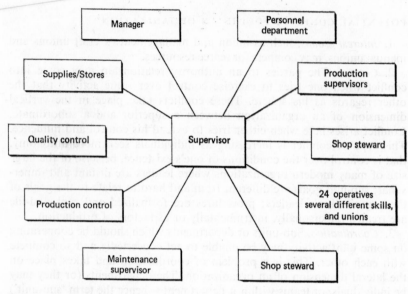

Figure 2

The relevance for bargainers of these different sources of conflict is that the normal negotiating process is best equipped for dealing with interest group conflict (no. 1, p. 93). A danger here is that, say, a role conflict may be expressed in terms of an interest group conflict because this is where the available procedures for resolution are.

A recent example concerns a large wholesaling organization in which a group of girl clerical workers got angry because they felt that the quality standards applied had suddenly been stepped up. In addition they had a long-standing sense of grievance about the quality standards as they claimed that a certain margin of error was beyond their control. The supervisor felt he should make management instructions 'stick', yet he sympathized to some extent with his girls. He did not in fact tell his boss about his difficulties as he felt that this would unfavourably reflect upon his abilities. He soldiered on, trying to patch up the errors and protect his work-group, whilst at the same time meeting perceived quality demands. This man eventually gave up his job and left the company, no doubt partly because of the pressures upon him. His successor tried to enforce the quality standards and met a great deal of opposition. A management–union dispute was officially filed by the union full-time official. Upon examination of their case, management discovered a fairly simple error in the way quality standards were being applied in this section, one which would quickly have come to light if either supervisor had queried his instructions.

This case is a good example of how organizations have procedures and methods of resolving interest group conflicts, but very few for resolving conflicts such as nos. 2, 3 and 4 (p. 93). In this case a role conflict for the supervisor (no. 4, p. 93) had to become an interest group conflict (no. 1) before it could be sorted out. This resulted in frustration and loss of morale for a work-group and personal stress for the supervisor.

Similarly, conflicts between two managers or heads of department over resources are commonplace within organizations. In my own organization, a Polytechnic, this type of conflict (no. 3) is far more common than interest group conflict (no. 1). Whilst there exists in most organizations some sort of procedure for individual grievances (often no. 2), these procedures make grievances unduly formal and can endanger ongoing relationships. For this reason they are often not used even where genuine conflicts exist.

Negotiators should examine their cases and look for the different conflict components. This will aid the sifting of those which are genuine interest group conflicts from those which have been caused by other types of pressure. These other conflicts may have been pushed into the interest group category because of the inadequacy of procedures elsewhere; if this is so they may require different negotiating treatment.

CONFLICT AND CHANGE

The Introduction referred to the changes taking place with accelerating rapidity, not only within organizations, but outside as well. The relationship between conflict and change is a close one. Theories of human and organizational behaviour often dispute whether equilibrium or disequilibrium is the normal, desired state. Theories which stress the value of stability or homeostasis see change as creating conflict and vice-versa. Change is often therefore something to be resisted and is negatively valued. Other theories hold that men and organizations actively seek a measure of uncertainty and change; this forms the basis of some learning theories. In industrial relations, holders of a unitary concept of organization will perhaps tend to regard conflict in negative terms, and as illegitimate. Those who accept a pluralistic point of view will tend more to emphasize the creative aspects of conflict.

Conflict and change are certainly interdependent. Change is something which may arise from the expression and resolution of conflicts, as the early sociologists believed.[5] On the other hand, change can come from outside and create conflict.

Conflict can be regarded as functional (good!) or dysfunctional (bad!) and in the end this rests on the values and beliefs of the regarder. Few people nowadays regard all conflict as undesirable and writers now tend to stress the desirable aspects.

Some of these are as follows:

1. 'Conflict is essential for the continued development of mature and competent human beings.'[6]

2. An optimum level of conflict is seen as necessary for progress and productivity.

3. Conflict with an out-group establishes or re-establishes internal unity and solidarity.[7]

4. Conflict frequently revitalizes and establishes new norms.[7]

5. Inflexible systems conflicts produce bonds and coalitions which allow for the expression of alternative ideas.[7]

6. 'It prevents stagnation, it stimulates interest and curiosity, it is the medium through which problems can be aired and solutions arrived at . . . part of the process of testing and assessing oneself and, as such, may be highly enjoyable as one experiences the pleasure of the full and active use of one's capacities.'[8]

Alternatively there are those who regard conflict as largely undesirable:

1. 'Common reactions to conflict and its associated tensions are often dysfunctional for the organization as an on-going social system and self-defeating for the person in the long run.'[9]

2. Conflict is 'a breakdown in the standard mechanisms of decision making'.[10]

3. Although stress and tension are necessary in individuals or organizations for maximum effort, progress, learning and productivity, conflict is primarily a social and personal cost by threatening the emotional well-being of the person or organization and by absorbing enormous amounts of energy.

4. Conflict is a cost, sometimes deliberately fostered, which induces negative and unproductive behaviour such as blocking, defensive resistance, destructive aggression, points scoring, 'knocking' and withdrawal from the relationship.

In fact, as mentioned above, which side you take depends very much upon your value system. One approach might be to accept that conflict *is*, that the potential for it is increasing, and that the important question is how to harness it for creative rather than destructive purposes.

One key question here is whether conflict and change can be managed in any sense of the word. Later parts of this essay discuss the use of power and different strategies for resolving conflict, omitting the question of whether change can be managed. It has been extensively written about in recent years and a growing emphasis is being put upon the manager as a 'change agent', that is, as someone who actively tries to promote desired changes rather than simply cope with those forced on him.[11] This emphasis goes hand in hand with a philosophy of optimism regarding the possible uses of conflict. It does not ignore the other obvious point that whilst we are learning to manage change, we are all past masters of resisting it.[12] Those who seek to use conflict to achieve changes or to innovate in any other way would do well to heed the words of Machiavelli:

And it ought to be remembered that there is nothing more difficult to take in hand, more perilous to conduct, or more uncertain in its success than to take the lead in the introduction of a new order of things. Because the innovator has for enemies all those who have done well under the old conditions, and only lukewarm defenders in those who may do well under the new.[13]

Methods of Conflict Resolution

In dealing with any conflict, major or minor, interpersonal or inter-party, there is a range of strategies that can be adopted. Figure 3 suggests a model of these strategies.

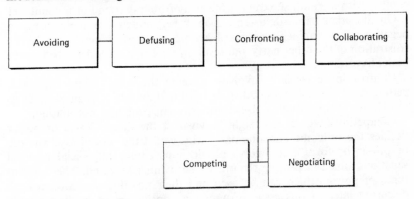

Figure 3: Conflict Resolution Strategies

Avoiding can really hardly be classed as a resolution strategy, but it is a response to conflict and probably a very popular one. We all of us avoid some situations because we cannot summon up the emotional energy, the courage or the necessary skills to negotiate or solve the problem.

D

Avoiding behaviour leaves the conflict unsettled and requires the avoider to change himself or adapt in order to 'manage the dissonance' caused by the conflict.[14] Usually the individual or party is unsatisfied and this leads to a number of states variously described as 'withdrawal', 'alienation', 'powerlessness', etc. Within the organization these states can result in a number of responses such as apathy, avoidance of responsibility, rigidity of behaviour, daydreaming, absenteeism, leaving, psychosomatic illness, etc. The same can of course happen in a marriage or within any close community. The costs to the marriage or the company are as great as to the individual. Avoidance of conflict can increase rigidity, a pathological clinging to the status quo and resistance to change, and an absence of creativity and development, if it is followed habitually.

Defusion is essentially a delaying tactic, either to cool a situation or to keep it going. Defusion often takes the form of resolving minor conflicts or giving minor concessions whilst the real, major issues remain. There can be good reasons for adopting a defusing strategy, for example in order to arrive at a confrontation at a more propitious time. A union leader may try to time the emotions and perceptions of his membership to peak at a particular time, perhaps the end of a wage freeze or the beginning of a 'season'. Defusion allows the conflict to simmer for longer than it would naturally and thereby increases eventual chances of success by confronting in a position of improved power. Similarly, my wife may avoid or defuse a conflict with me until she can get me away from my friend or my mother!

On the other hand, defusion can look very much like avoidance or a negative, if determined, rearguard action. As such it may increase the frustration of the other party and result in the behaviours described above under 'Avoiding'.

Confronting essentially involves bringing the conflict into the open, getting it recognized by the other party so that an attempt can be made to resolve it. There are two sub-categories, competing and negotiating.

Competing involves a straight survival of the fittest. Force or power decides the outcome and one party wins whilst the other loses. The use of power or force can involve physical, psychological, social or legal sanctions aimed at beating the other side: winner takes all. The different types of power which can be used and their possible consequences are discussed later in this essay. Competing approaches to conflict usually result in one party 'winning' and the other 'losing', and are hardly conducive to effective long-term relationships. If there is a reasonable power parity such methods result in battles of attrition, long-term struggles which eventually result in both parties exhausting each other. Such struggles are easily recognized in diverse circumstances like in Albee's *Who's afraid of Virginia Woolf?* or the First World War. Examples from industrial relations are perhaps less dramatic. However, the Roberts–Arundel and Fine Tubes disputes have displayed the deadlock which such conflicts can result in. If there is no parity of power then a 'master-slave' situation may develop with subsequent brutalization on both sides. Power struggles, exhausting and negative though they may be, nevertheless are sometimes unavoidable. They have been initiated by both sides to establish or maintain a principle. In Roberts–Arundel, for example, the unions held that the case served as a warning to any non-union employers thinking of coming in. Race relations show that often the (white) 'masters' do not begin to take the (black) 'slaves' seriously until the latter adopt outright power tactics or direct action. This has often paved the way for later and peaceful negotiations.

Negotiation, which is treated more fully later, is a strategy which aims to resolve a conflict to the mutual satisfaction of both sides. It is an appropriate strategy for long-term relationships where there are genuine differences in objectives but approximately equal power. At one pole it can lean towards the win or lose strategy outlined under 'Competing' above. At the other, it approaches the creative, problem solving, collaborative mode described below. In mid-ground, it is a compromising position, one of exchange, where I promise to give up X if you give up Y. The success of negotiation depends upon both parties feeling that the outcome is 'fair' or 'just', and the process involves a mutual exploration of what is acceptable. This essay is addressed to the developing of skills in this area, but in the slightly wider sense of negotiation including aspects of avoiding, defusion, competing and collaborating. An assumption is made that negotiation as a distinct approach to conflict resolution is more common than the other methods.

Collaborating is perhaps an ideal state requiring significantly greater skills, levels of trust, power equality and creativity than the other approaches. The management of differences is seen here as joint problem solving rather than negotiation. Perhaps this was the Webbs' vision of joint consultation! The conflict is treated as something to be overcome together, rather than as a frustration of one's objectives by the other. The emphasis is upon developing what might be called 'win-win' solutions where the result benefits both parties more than a negotiated or compromised outcome. The concept is closely allied to that of 'synergy', that the ultimate product is greater than the sum of the two parts.

An alternative scheme of conflict resolution behaviour has been developed which improves upon the one-dimensional continuum described in Figure 4 (p. 100). Figure 4 is taken from Jamieson and Thomas' work,[15] though originally developed by Blake and Mouton.

Two dimensions of behaviour, unassertive↔assertive, and uncooperative↔cooperative, are seen as fundamental. One measure sthe extent to which a party attempts to satisfy his own objectives, and the other measures the extent to which a party attempts to satisfy the other's objectives. The grid then gives five conflict-handling modes, as follows.

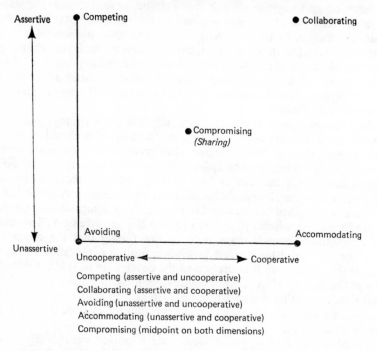

Competing (assertive and uncooperative)
Collaborating (assertive and cooperative)
Avoiding (unassertive and uncooperative)
Accommodating (unassertive and cooperative)
Compromising (midpoint on both dimensions)

Figure 4: Five Conflict Handling Modes

The positions in the figure above are similar to the range of conflict-resolving strategies (see p. 97). 'Accommodating' has been added, which is behaviour which attempts to satisfy the other party at all costs, and is characterized by a low concern for one's own objectives.

Other dimensions could be used. Bartos has developed a theory about 'toughness', and he measures the effectiveness of the soft↔tough continuum against time and pay-off.[17] A group of industrial relations officers developed two dimensions, soft↔hard and straight↔bent, to analyse their behaviour. The soft↔hard continuum was obviously similar in concept to tough↔soft and assertive↔unassertive, but the straight↔bent continuum was a measure of trustworthiness.

These different modes of handling conflict offer something of a repertoire of styles to the negotiator. He or she may not always be able to freely choose a given style because of the situation or the stance of the other party, but at least the possibilities for varying behaviour need to be recognized. Behaviour, and its effect upon others, is often something of which we are at least partially unaware. These categories can be used as a checklist for looking at one's own bargaining behaviour and comparing outcomes and effects with initial strategy. It may well be that different styles are appropriate to different personalities: individuals, unions and managements differ widely in character. Meeting a competing opponent with an accommodating stance is clearly to back a loser.

Certainly styles vary over time in a negotiation. A veteran chief negotiator in the USA (where contract negotiations are 'stagey' by our standards) has retailed how the normal pattern was non-committal, then fiercely competitive, and finally compromising. In public exchanges were nearly always competitive, with some avoiding and compromising, but in private there were frequent examples of collaborating especially as the contract deadline approached.[18]

Training in the various styles or modes of handling conflict is now becoming recognized as useful. The prime needs are the ability to diagnose what styles your opponent is using, and to decide upon and use the appropriate responses.

Power

No discussion of negotiating would be complete without some reference to power and its effects. Power can be defined as the potential influence of one party over another, where influence is defined as a change in the behaviour of one party which can be attributed to the other.[19] In other words, I have power in so far as I can get you to do something.

Here is an outline of six types or bases of power.[20]

1. Informational: this refers to the content of communication and not an attribute of the person influencing.
2. Coercive: this is based on the ability of the influencer to punish, force or compel.
3. Reward: this is based on the ability of the person influencing to get rewards, eg pay rises.
4. Referent: this stems from the liking or identification of the person influenced for the person influencing, and the wish to maintain this.
5. Expert: this stems from the attribution of superior knowledge or ability to the person influencing by the person influenced.

6. Legitimate: this is based on general norms about what is appropriate behaviour.

Power and conflict style are to some extent related. Jamieson and Thomas reported that the use of coercive power is likely to make students more competitive and less accommodating, whilst referent power produces more cooperating responses, both accommodating and collaborating.[21] Coercive, legitimate and reward power are mainly found to be used by superiors, whilst referent, expert and informational power is associated more with peers.

Another important point is that influence, and the type of power used to achieve it, varies in its potential permanence or likelihood of being maintained in private. Collins and Raven see reward and coercive power depending on *public* compliance, whereas referent, expert and legitimate power will be maintained in *private* without surveillance. Kelman has distinguished three processes of social influence:[22]

Compliance, where a person accepts influence because he sees it as a way to get the other to do what he wants. He does not change behaviour because he believes in it, but purely for instrumental reasons. The behaviour will only be maintained in special, public situations and the personal private beliefs may be quite different.

Identification, where a person identifies with another and attempts to be like or actually to be the other person. A man may imitate his boss, for example. Identification involves a belief in what is said or done and the behaviour is maintained privately, but only in the appropriate role, for example as shop steward or boss. Therefore behaviours acquired through a process of identification remain dependent on the external source of social support. They do not become part of the person's integrated value system.

Internalization, where influence is accepted because the behaviour is congruent with the person's value system. The content of the behaviour is intrinsically rewarding, the characteristics of the influence are less important. The behaviour becomes part of a personal system and is exhibited independently of any external source.

If these can be related to bases of power, it appears that reward and coercive power are more likely to produce compliance. Referent power would seem to relate particularly to identification, whilst legitimate, informational and expert power might be expected to result more in internalization. The strength and relative permanence of influence may therefore be related to the type of power used and perhaps to the style of conflict handling used.

If this were to be assumed, it would suggest, for example, that in the union–management situation competitive, win or lose strategies characterized by the use of force and threats should result in compliant behaviour. This might be said to be a shallow level of commitment to organizational objectives and result in relatively low productivity. Jamieson and Thomas have shown that the use of coercive power by teachers reduces student satisfaction and learning, and increases the likelihood of compliance rather than internalization.[23] Learning is particularly important for both organizations and individuals as a means of coping with change and conflict. When defined as 'a more or less permanent change in behaviour', learning is obviously related to internalization as an influence process and almost certainly also to the more 'democratic' forms of power, expert, informational and referent.

It would not do to make too much of this speculation. Some of the available laboratory evidence suggests that some types of power, the ones here termed 'democratic', produce more cooperative responses as well as responses which are likely to be internalized. A complementary suggestion is that coercive and reward powers tend to induce competitive behaviours and compliance rather than internalization of influence, especially where power is unequal.

There are, however, fundamental inequalities in societies and relationships which prevent 'ideal' choices from being made. It is at least questionable whether a cooperative response to a particular issue is appropriate in a situation where the whole basis of a relationship is unjust. Whether a relationship is unjust or not depends as much upon values and consciousness as upon 'facts'. Whilst the master–servant relationship was accepted as fixed and proper in Britain, this was the frame against which responses were made. After Rousseau and Marx, this framework became unacceptable to many people and along with it most of the hitherto accepted ideas about resolving industrial conflicts.

Similarly it could be held that women's liberation is changing the basis upon which conflicts are resolved in the home, through changes in consciousness and an increasing equalization of power.

THE EQUALIZATION OF POWER

It is fairly clear that negotiation or collaboration is more likely where power is balanced.[24] Refusals to negotiate, accommodations or one-sided competitions result from situations of unequal power or perceived unequal power. In such circumstances, Deutsch suggests low-power parties should be built up in order to make cooperation more possible.[25] Possibilities are:

Building up internal resources.

Forming coalitions.

Attempting to change high-power party attitude through education and moral persuasion.

Looking for new bases of power.

Using legal procedures.

Using harassment techniques.

Most of these tactics can be seen, for example, in the activities of trade unions trying to gain recognition to negotiate in a company. Negotiation is not on until some sort of power parity is brought about.

All of these manoeuvres help the low-power party to get the high-power party to 'listen'. Deutsch points out that high-power parties have many defence mechanisms which prevent them 'hearing' the claims of low-power parties.[26] These are:

Denial, that is blindness and insensitivity to dissatisfactions.

Repression, in which dissatisfactions are pushed underground, often to guerrilla action.

Aggression, which may lead to counter-escalation.

Displacement, which diverts dissatisfactions to other targets, eg government.

Sublimation, substituting solutions, for instance appointing a worker director instead of widening the range of negotiable issues.

Students of British industrial relations will recognize most of these!

Denial and aggression can often be seen together, as where 'agitators' and 'outside' influences are blamed for raising issues which are not supposed to exist. Real issues are denied and, just to add force to the argument, an attack is made at the same time. Denial is a much-loved response of employers who hold a 'unitary' frame of reference on industrial relations,[27] and if it is maintained over a period of time, it effectively becomes repression.

Repression seems often to be a perfectly normal response of industrial relations managers, who see their role as containing and minimizing conflict. In one sense the 'Red Clydesiders' and the shop steward movement during the First World War were responses to the repression of shop-floor activity by both management and unions.

The implication for negotiators here is that conflict can only be avoided or repressed for so long, and only then with a danger of eruption. At some stage, if there is a genuine conflict of interests, conflict has to be confronted, and it would often cause less harm if it were done sooner rather than later.

Displacement is a defence mechanism for us all when we need a scapegoat, but for political reasons, cannot blame the other side. Hence the Government frequently and conveniently offers itself to both management and unions during periods of wage or price restraint. Scapegoating does little to resolve the immediate problem, but it may make you feel a bit better.

We have plenty of examples of sublimation, which is akin to defusion and avoidance discussed earlier. Here the real problem is ignored and a substitute is offered. So, for example, if I wish to avoid relinquishing my right to bargain over overtime, I might convince myself that management is really asking for, say, more flexibility, and offer a solution in this area. In attempting to grapple with the current concern of 'participation', a whole range of panaceas is being offered all of which obscure the real nature of the problem.

Communication and the Development of Trust[28]

Power equalization makes negotiation and problem-solving modes of conflict resolution possible, but does not alone make them happen. The development of full communication and the establishment of trust are important preconditions.

By full communication I mean not just the articulation of a messsage but the 'hearing', understanding and acceptance of it. (See Figure 5.) In this sense communication and influence are very similar processes: if you accept my message, I have influenced you.[29] This connection is not always recognized, and it is perhaps the major reason why people consistently underestimate the difficulty of communication. Talking to stewards or managers in industry about industrial relations one becomes very aware of this dustbin category of 'bad communications' which is used to explain almost anything from lapses in safety to strikes. If communication equals influence, that is, 'If I listen to what you say, I will be influenced,' then it is easier to see why so much is not 'heard'. When we use the excuse 'bad communications' as a modern-day equivalent of witchcraft to explain things we do not understand, we are forgetting this point. Behind the information transmission aspect of communication lurk the other types of potential power – and knowledge is power in itself. Talking about improving communications therefore involves losing our fear and sus-picion about the use of power: learning to handle power and use it to achieve desirable rather than undesirable ends. Full communication requires an equalization of power.

For example, a major barrier to communication in organizations and in classrooms (and perhaps in male or female dominated marriages) is that information comes *down* from superior to subordinate or from high status to low. Behind each message is the threat of coercive, reward or legitimate power which (as discussed) can lead to avoidance, compliance, and repression of dissatisfactions. This is an inherent possibility in relationships of unequal power.

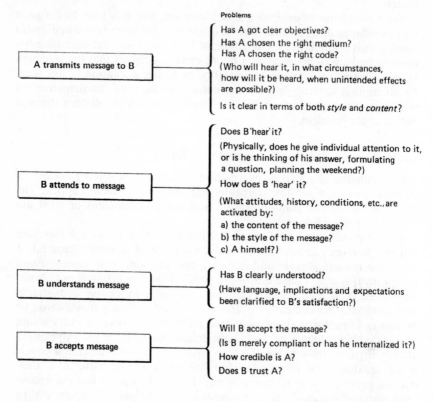

Problems

A transmits message to B
- Has A got clear objectives?
- Has A chosen the right medium?
- Has A chosen the right code?
- (Who will hear it, in what circumstances, how will it be heard, when unintended effects are possible?)
- Is it clear in terms of both *style* and *content*?

B attends to message
- Does B 'hear' it?
- (Physically, does he give individual attention to it, or is he thinking of his answer, formulating a question, planning the weekend?)
- How does B 'hear' it?
- (What attitudes, history, conditions, etc., are activated by:
  - a) the content of the message?
  - b) the style of the message?
  - c) A himself?)

B understands message
- Has B clearly understood?
- (Have language, implications and expectations been clarified to B's satisfaction?)

B accepts message
- Will B accept the message?
- (Is B merely compliant or has he internalized it?)
- How credible is A?
- Does B trust A?

Figure 5: The Process of Communication and Influence, and Some Problems

The difficulty of understanding and accepting messages in negotiating situations given the threats, distortion and stresses that surround them helps to explain the use of ritual. Ritual is procedure which both sides carry out for 'show'.[30] It is, however, functional. As Kniveton points out, it eases anxiety and tension through establishing predictable patterns.[31] When management expresses surprise or the union walks out, both are fulfilling important expectations whose absence would really rattle the other side. Similarly husband and wife may have certain rituals through which they proceed when approaching a conflict and each is acutely aware of the stage or level of behaviour reached. A sudden departure from this ritual such as either giving in or leaving home after the first exchange would be disastrous. This is not to say that ritual is not time-wasting, but that it does fulfil an important role in reducing uncertainty and attendant stress. Secondly ritual performs an important role in testing understanding, acceptability and trust, which are difficult problems in understanding and accepting communication. Thirdly, ritual moves may be necessary to show the potential power of a party and the willingness to use it.

Ritual and game playing can take over entirely, however, and communication becomes unreal and unproductive. The word 'game', incidentally, is not just used to describe 'fun' things, but also very serious behaviour, including negotiating, suicide and schizophrenia.[32] Berne suggests that a major problem of relationships concerns the structuring of time, and that there are five options for doing this: ritual, pastimes, games, intimacy and activity, in order of complexity.[33] He sees pastimes and games as substitutes for 'real living', which consists of intimacy and activity. The danger of ritual is its domination of the relationship to the exclusion of 'real' intimacy and activity. Berne's theory of transactional analysis, which seeks to develop authentic relationships between people, has become quite popular.[34]

Rackham has applied the idea of analysing transactions to the negotiating process and has developed lists of behavioural categories with which to examine communications.[35] Here are some of the categories from Rackham's article:

Proposing   Open
Building   Testing understanding
Supporting   Summarizing
Disagreeing   Seeking information
Defending, attacking   Giving information
Blocking

Whilst these categories help to analyse communications and expose the misperceptions and distortions which take place, they do not of themselves create full communication. This process is closely bound up with the development of trust which is essential to full communication whether it be in a negotiation, an interview, or a conversation between mother and child.

Trust can be defined as a confident expectation that another will do a given thing. Trust is essential to the influencing and negotiating process; without it no agreement is possible, as agreement implies a commitment on future behaviour. The ability to trust is also fundamental to our own sense of identity and the stability of the world; complete loss of it would be personally shattering.[36]

Figure 6 shows the Johari Window[37] which depicts four parts of a person. The open self is the part a person is aware of and is willing to reveal to another in open communication.

The hidden self is the more private part of us: the religious, political or other controversial beliefs, bad memories, feelings, impulses and behaviours which we think are antisocial or unacceptable and might hurt us or others if revealed.

The blind self is an area of deeply repressed feelings, unconscious impulses or hidden talents. It affects our behaviour and is often clearly seen by other people, for example, my habit of waving my hands about when I talk or showing anger on my face at the same time as I am saying 'I'm not angry'!

The unknown self is unseen by ourselves and by others. It is somewhat similar conceptually to the 'unconscious'; it influences our behaviour and 'leaks out' from time to time. This is an important area but difficult to talk about meaningfully because we cannot see it.

At the beginning of a relationship or encounter this 'open' part is small. It increases with time and the responsiveness of the other person or party. Initially, the blind, hidden and unknown areas are large, but given the development of trust in the other, the blind and hidden selves will be brought more into the open area.

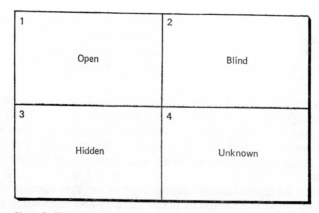

Figure 6: The Johari Window

For example, when I meet someone for the first time we invariably talk about 'safe' and public things such as my name, job and family. If we wish to continue our relationship then we need to know each other better, which involves risk in revealing more private information about politics, religion, fundamental beliefs, and so on.

The 'open' self can be enlarged by two basic processes. These are:

1. Self-disclosure, deliberately revealing information which is normally kept hidden. This decreases the hidden area. We do talk, in fact, of someone 'opening up'.

2. Receptivity to feedback. Feedback from others is the main way in which we can become aware of our blind selves.

Many errors of communication occur simply because all four parts of the self influence the transmission and reception of messages, but only the open self is acknowledged.

In the establishment of trust we are particularly concerned with increasing the 'open' self and decreasing the 'hidden' and 'blind' parts of ourselves. This process will probably include the following:

1. Personal risk-taking and innovation in revealing self or information; and in feeding back information about the other.

2. Establishing a degree of power relativity through some of the methods described earlier.

3. Allowing self to be increasingly influenced by the other party.

4. Getting and feeling 'closer' to the other party.

5. Developing mutual rules and regulations for maintaining the relationship. These might be written or unwritten, but need to ensure that:
Both parties know them and they are unambiguous and consistent.
Both parties adhere to them.
Social approval exists for adherence and disapproval for violation.
Violations are quickly known and public.
Adherence results in benefits for both sides and both parties wish to use them again in future conflicts.[38]

Present lack of trust is apparent in the panic shown about the legislation concerning disclosure of information. It is the fear within the management–union relationship which prevents the building of trust and full communication. There are those who persist in thinking that 'communications' are something that can be treated and dealt with like an aberrant tropical disease, but this is a naive view. The development of openness and the establishment of mutuality in rule- and decision-making is a long and difficult process requiring exceptional maturity and goodwill on both sides. Negotiators need to be aware that trust-building and the establishment of open communication affects, and is in turn affected by, the complete management–union relationship.

It should be pointed out that 'trust' can characterize either a long-lived or a very short-lived relationship. We may often think of it as something that endures, for instance between husband and wife or union and management, for many years. It can be seen on the other hand as a very specific short-term commitment. Given the multiplicity of demands and contradictory pulls on us all it may be naive to enter into long-term trust arrangements, making promises that cannot be kept. It is the violation of expectations that causes the damage, not lack of help from someone whom you do not expect to help. For example, if management announces redundancies having made a promise only two years ago that there will be none, then trust is deeply and perhaps irreparably damaged. If, on the other hand, no promises are made about the future, the lack of information and certainty may lead to just as much anxiety and mistrust. The only answer would seem to be an openness about intentions, constraints and possibilities.

The ability to regard 'trust' as a relatively specific and short-term commitment to be entered into quickly is essential to the building of relationships, the resolving of conflicts and quick recuperation for the next episode. This is not to say that there is no room for more permanent and general trust, such as mine that tomorrow the world will look very much the same as it did yesterday. It is a question of appropriateness, and here there is a need to assess and continually reassess.[39]

The Negotiating Process

Any negotiation can be seen as a process which passes through stages like a conflict episode. These stages are notional in that they are an abstraction of the real thing; in practice negotiations do not conform to tidy patterns. A negotiator may be replanning in the middle of a session; the negotiations may go through the stages more than once; and so on.

Table 3 shows the possible stages of a negotiation and some of the attendant skills and knowledge required at each stage. (It was developed from an idea by David Megginson to demonstrate the requirements at successive stages of a negotiation.)

Table 3: Negotiation: Stages, Skills and Knowledge

Stage	Skills required	Knowledge, information required
1. Setting objectives	Identifying problems Diagnosing the nature of the conflict, eg tangible or ideological or both? Identifying which objectives are integrative (ie cooperative) and which are distributive (ie competitive) with other party[40]	National/legal policies Company policies, eg: 　pay levels 　profit margins 　redundancy policy Local conditions Data collection methods Own authority Types of conflict resolution modes Issues involved
2. Planning negotiation	Choosing strategies, eg emphasizing differences between parties (competitive) or emphasizing common ground (cooperative) Planning in units rather than sequences (ie not having one point determine the outcome of the next) Planning to retain flexibility and enough ambiguity to respond yet maintain direction Ability to identify all resources in a situation	Sequence of negotiation stages Significance of ritual Information relating to issues
3. Negotiating	Awareness of own style and behaviour Understanding of other's style and behaviour Communication/influencing skills, eg 　expression 　listening 　questioning 　persuading 　resisting 　establishing trust 　summarizing, etc.	Constraints on self and other Information relating to issues Effects of stress, conflict and ambiguity on self and other

Stage	Skills required	Knowledge, information required
3. Negotiating (cont.)	Maintaining consensus in own party and between negotiators and those they represent[41]	
	Compromising between the demands for rigidity by own group and demands for flexibility by other party[42]	
	Ability to initiate confrontation and other styles of conflict handling including problem solving	Effects of different styles
	Uses of adjournments and recesses	Functions of adjournment
	'Flags' behaviour	
	Interpretation and judgement, ie 'assessing a complex interaction of factors and coming to a conclusion, based on an estimate of what is acceptable to the values of all the persons affected by any decision that is reached'[43]	Distortions possible in perception and difficulties of 'objective' judgement
	Ability to learn from experience	
	Ability to accept reversals and recover	
4. Concluding negotiation	Testing for: understanding acceptance agreement	What will be 'acceptable' to own and other party Procedures and precedent
	Writing of agreements and mutually acceptable rules	
	Establishing follow-up, review and evaluation procedure	Possible effects of conflict aftermath on long-term relationship

Table 3 does not purport to be an exhaustive classification,[44] but a way of showing some of the important skills and knowledge involved in the various stages of a negotiation. I have severe doubts, for example, about being able to pigeonhole 'judgement', for example, as skill or knowledge.

It is difficult to define, as it is a complex of sub-skills, attitudes, knowledge, and so on.

Table 3 is an attempt to provide a framework from which to develop teaching and learning programmes and strategies. My belief is that the skills mainly required are those variously called interactive, social or interpersonal skills and also those called interpretative, analytical or judgemental. The acquisition of information for negotiating, whilst undeniably important, seems to me decidedly secondary. Information is dependent upon the aims and attitudes of the person who is seeking for or using it. It is theoretically value-free, whereas negotiating seems to involve personal values and beliefs to a very high degree. Information is usually carefully selected and presented to justify one's own case or destroy another's. It is frequently used for bamboozling the opposition and clouding the vital issues. For example, the implications of productivity bargaining were scarcely realized by the early participants, and what characterized the process was usually a massive presentation of data.

Information is important: more access to information is to be warmly welcomed as a help in improving communication, trust, influence and problem solving. These processes, however, do not take place through the provision of information but through the exercise of will and skill. Unfortunately much of our present provision for negotiation training concentrates on the information aspect and indeed this is perhaps the most straightforward to teach, yet it misses the more difficult and vital issues.

The Problem of Creativity

This discussion of negotiating and the related issues of conflict, change, power and communication, has rested on a number of assumptions. A major assumption is that much of present-day negotiation is of the win or lose or exchange variety; some of it is even lose/lose. A further assumption is that change of various kinds is creating more potential conflicts and over a wider range of relationships than the various mechanisms for resolving it can cope with. Argyris, for example, has stated that one of the requirements of effective organization for tomorrow is that: 'Conflict is identified and managed in such a way that the destructive win/lose stances with their accompanying polarisation of views are minimised and effective problem-solving is maximised.'[45]

The aim of this essay has therefore been to open up new perspectives on negotiating skills and lay down a framework for their development. In no way do I want to pretend that the need for traditional power-bargaining has disappeared. It seems to me that coercive power will always be used to resolve genuine conflicts of interest, and that trainers and teachers can help people to explore the nature of power and its effects. For this reason the tactics surrounding bargaining will also continue: examples are over-statement of objectives, threats, red herrings, deliberate attempts to confuse, withholding of information, and every kind of devious behaviour known to man. Power strategies can be employed quite deliberately in order to create attitude changes. For example, in race relations, militancy in a minority group, whilst initially offending the majority, may eventually overcome the 'hearing' blocks and create some power parity and respect with the majority. Taking a long-term view, both integrative and distributive bargaining are likely, and nowhere more feasibly than in industrial relations. Power tactics can be used to build up identity and solidarity on one side, prior to more collaborative negotiation. One could argue that problem solving is likely to be enhanced by the mutual respect gained during power struggles. If trust is defined as a relatively specific, short-term characteristic of a relationship, then there is more credibility in operating both types of strategy over a certain length of time.

There is another contention and that is that there are more opportunities for integrative or cooperative bargaining as opposed to distributive or competitive bargaining than are sometimes realized. There is a danger of becoming locked into one style or approach to negotiating with no appreciation or ability to use other approaches. The emphasis therefore is on flexibility and multi-skilling in conflict resolving.

Traditional win or lose negotiating is, for example, often anti-creative and conservative. The status quo is emphasized, old positions are taken up and change of any kind is firmly resisted. Threats induce defensiveness and rigidity rather than the openness to new ideas and risk-taking which characterize a creative, problem-solving approach.

The process of problem solving may be described as a series of phases characterized by particular sorts of activity:

1. Defining the problem: establishing the basic issue as each or every party sees it.

2. Clarifying or re-defining the problem: experiencing the various positions taken and the dimensions of the problem. This is followed by staying away from solutions long enough to let optimum tension or motivation be aroused. Then comes defining the problem. This is a vital stage. If it is a 'problem' then past 'solutions' are useless. It may be necessary to allow the routine and habitual processes to be applied and fail before problem reformulation can take place.

3. Generating solutions (this stage may also lead to problem reformulation): can be done by 'brainstorming'. This process involves a free-wheeling and non-evaluative generation of all possible ideas, however bizarre or unlikely. A willingness to fool about and take risks, suggesting 'way-out' ideas, is valued.

4. Evaluating and choosing a solution: this is best done by some sort of consensus of all parties. Willingness to give up positions and be flexible are valued.

5. Planning, implementing and evaluating solutions: careful introduction, communication and monitoring of solutions. Most have a limited lifetime and eventually the problem-solving process may begin again.

Problem solving is not a simple matter of following a procedure. Successful collaboration involves free access; open communications; trusting and helping rather than defending and resisting, and a willingness to contribute to an integrated solution rather than needing individual reward. These characteristics are not easy to develop and many aspects of organizational life relating to industrial relations militate against them. However, change, as we have seen, can come from within an organization or relationship as well as from without.

Part 2

Learning Negotiation from Experience

This second part of the essay offers some ideas and exercises for learning negotiating and allied skills. A first section deals with the learning theory and principles which are inherent in the approach, without which the ideas that follow are not very enlightening. A second section contains exercises for looking at conflict, change, influence and power, trust and communication, negotiating and creativity. A final note deals with the use of closed-circuit television (CCTV) in learning how to negotiate.

Some Relevant Learning Theory

The only reason for looking at theory is to see what it tells us about how we should practise. A number of approaches has been made to determine how learning should take place. For example, Bloom and his colleagues have suggested that there are a number of 'domains' or different areas of learning which require different treatments or learning methods.[46] In Figure 7 a fifth area of self-knowledge has been added by Tom Boydell,[47] a colleague of mine.

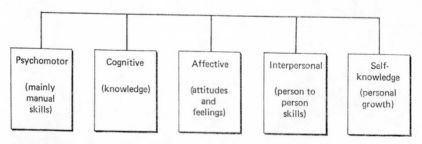

Figure 7: Areas of Learning Behaviour

The implication is that learning in each area requires different methods. For example, whilst lectures might be appropriate for achieving cognitive objectives, they are hardly sufficient for psychomotor or interpersonal skills. This approach to classifying areas of learning in order to select learning methods more appropriately has been used extensively by industrial training boards.

In practice, however, this method does not completely solve the problem of choosing learning methods, because most human behaviour cannot be slotted so conveniently. Consider for example negotiating, which is a complex behaviour spanning more than one area:

Knowledge of procedures, rules and regulations at various levels, issues at stake, etc.	Cognitive area
Feelings and beliefs about the issues; your case; other side's case; 'fairness', 'justice', etc.	Affective area
Ability to express self clearly; to respond appropriately to other side; to develop trust and understanding with own team and other team	Interpersonal area
Knowledge of own behaviour under different conditions; strengths and weaknesses; likes and dislikes, etc.	Self-knowledge area

So we can see that every area but one is important in developing the complex ability or skill of negotiating. It is perhaps fair to suggest that some areas are more important than others. Kniveton[48] and Rackham[49], for example, both stress the importance of social skills which are roughly equivalent to the interpersonal area here. This is to be welcomed in one way because of teachers' tendency to 'teach', that is, talk at learners. Most teachers, especially if they have been trained, behave as if learning consists of the transmission of knowledge from them to the relatively passive learners. Learning social skill, involves, like any other skill, practice and activity by the learner, so this stress moves us in the right direction.

I believe, however, that it is an oversimplification to say that negotiation is a social skill, and that therefore we should use those methods appropriate, for example role play, simulation, discussion, and so on. To designate it a skill in this way still implies that the teacher knows the answers and that all the learner has to do is to follow this direction and he will arrive in due time in safety and security. Learning to negotiate involves more than just the mastery of some social skills. This is so, not only in horizontal terms (that is, other areas of learning behaviour), but also in vertical terms, the level or depth of learning which may involve all areas. Table 4 illustrates these levels, using the analogy of a craftsman learning to use his tools.

Table 4: Levels of Learning[50]

No.	Level	Description
1.	Memory	The learner can recognize, identify and describe the purpose of a tool
2.	Understanding	The learner understands how and why the tool works and what to do to use it
3.	Application	The learner can use a given tool in a limited number of situations in which the selection of the appropriate tool is made by someone else
4.	Transfer	In a wide range of new, unique situations the learner can select and use the appropriate tool from his complete repertoire; if necessary he can modify existing tools or manufacture his own new ones to meet the needs of each unique situation as it arises

These levels imply a deepening of skill, insight and knowledge as we move from no. 1 to no. 4. Harrison has used Kelman's three categories of influence (see p. 102 above) – compliance, identification and internalization – to describe the same process in colleges. The same implication of permanence, of centrality to the person, is apparent in his article.[51] In the development of ability to negotiate I suggest that we are trying to operate at level no. 4 rather than at level no. 1. Level no. 4 introduces some important words like 'new', 'unique' and 'manufacture' which place great demands on us as teachers if we want to couch our objectives in these terms. How do you train, teach, help someone to learn about things that haven't happened yet? Levels nos 1–3 assume that there are 'right answers' that the trainer can eventually either pass on to the learner or confirm for the learner, once discovered. Of course there are many such important things to learn, from the two times table to the grievance procedure. These are the laid down, standard procedures into which learners are initiated and inducted. If all learning was of this kind then we would have few problems. However, there is an important area of learning where there are no correct behaviours or right answers: most of the interpersonal, affective and self-knowledge areas, for example, and indeed any higher cognitive learning.

Kniveton has called this the problem of 'teaching judgement'.[52] I would not call it 'teaching' because of the connotations of giving the 'right answers' and the inequality of the teacher-student relationship. Abercrombie has defined judgement as 'decision or conclusion on the basis of indications and probabilities when the facts are not clearly ascertained'.[53]

Knowledge is necessary, but not sufficient. Knowledge is the tool bag which can be assembled from learning at levels nos 1, 2 and 3, but which does not alone accomplish anything. To any job, task or work there is a discretionary element. However great our knowledge there is an area of unknown where we guess or act on the basis of judgement. Complete knowledge would remove the need for judgement or creativity. Jacques points out how worrying this sensation of not knowing is, but how inevitable: 'Moreover, it is also of the essence of work that, having decided how to set about a task, and having completed it, you can never be sure that if you had decided to do it another way you might not have done it better or more quickly. You just do not know.'[54]

Level no. 4 learning is concerned with this discretionary element. Comparing level no. 4 with levels nos 1, 2 and 3, there are some obvious differences in the learning process and methods used.

There is a tendency for methods to be more structured at level no. 1 than at level no. 4; similarly feedback increases as we move through level no. 1 to no. 4. If this is accepted, lectures, which are highly structured and involve virtually no feedback, should be most useful at level no. 1. Since lecturing is used more than other teaching methods, it is probable that it is often used incorrectly for the achievement of objectives beyond level no. 1.

Secondly, as we move towards level no. 4 it gets harder to specify learning outcomes – or even to recognize them when manifested – and therefore more difficult to select correct methods. The tutor's margin of error due to uncertainty and ignorance grows, so he needs to relinquish his 'expert' role and develop a learning community of equals where the search for learning is a shared cooperative enterprise.

Thirdly, levels nos 1–3 assume that correct tools, principles, procedures and rules are available; that they can be taught by a teacher to students with the aid of various techniques. Level no. 4 is characterized by a state of uncertainty on the part of the teacher and the student. There are no 'right' answers and therefore no correct teaching techniques. We often say of this level, 'These are things which cannot be taught, they can only be learned'. Learners are often in a state of ambiguity, anxiety and perplexity, and the teacher's role is similar to that described in the 'learning community' approach described below (pp. 121ff.).

Another difference is that learning at levels nos 1–3 tends to follow the traditional sequencing rules of theory→practice, part→whole, and simple→complex learning. Level no. 4 often turns these on their heads, distils the theory from the experiences of practice, discerns the parts by comprehending the whole, and so on. At the first three levels, the learning methods chosen decide the nature of the learning; at level no. 4 the nature of the learning dictates the method. The standard case study or role play is never used, although you may recognize elements of these in the unique learning design necessary for each different learning experience.

This approach is often termed 'experiential learning' which means helping learners to learn from their own experience. In industrial relations we should avoid giving the 'right answers', not least because, let's face it, we just don't have them. Our students often know more than we do, that is, unless we take refuge in the comforting labyrinths of trade union history or the satisfying technicalities of macro-economics.

Eric Batstone recently gave a paper called 'The Meaning and Experience of Work' in which he made two significant points for teachers of industrial relations.[55] The first one was that we do not know what our students need to learn; we must let them teach us; education is a reciprocal process. Secondly, if education is to be effective, the workers must educate the educators and *negotiate* over the content and process of their education.

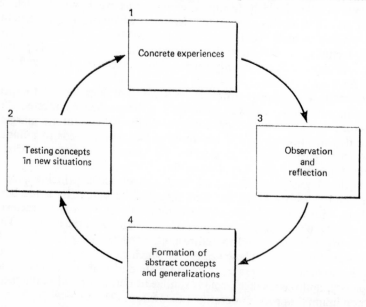

Figure 8: The Learning Cycle[56]

So what role does this leave for the teacher or trainer? Figure 8 (opposite) shows the 'experiential learning' cycle.

Actually this cycle applies to all learning, but traditional teaching tends to start at the bottom (no. 3 here), putting in theories, models, concepts, and hoping the learners will do the rest. Experiential learning starts from the actual, here and now, experience of the learner, causes him to reflect and observe, and to form, each his own, perhaps unique concepts and test them in his own way.

The idea of 'negotiated learning' is implicit in this process, and nowhere more so than industrial relations. In order to ensure that the learner's needs are met a continuous evaluation and negotiation of what is learned needs to go on. The teacher is not responsible for the learner learning, but the learner is, and the teacher is there to help.

In Sheffield the concept of a 'learning community' has been developed to achieve this purpose. The twin principles are that each person is responsible for his own learning, and that each person has the responsibility of offering himself as a resource to any other member of the community. (Further details of the learning community can be found elsewhere.)[57]

In the mainstream educational system, cocooned by examinations and certificates, teacher and taught connive in a conspiracy of complete, organized 'knowledge'. Learning is relatively anxiety-free, teachers behave as expected. In a learning community teachers violate traditional expectations and may provoke such anxiety in doing so that no learning is possible. I have found that in this sort of situation the teacher must manifest what I call 'overt care'. Learners will be highly suspicious of a teacher who claims not to know the answers, and anxious when they have to look for themselves. They will do this, and thereby 'learn how to learn' if they trust the teacher and feel that he is genuinely concerned for their learning and for them as people. This is a largely emotional matter and the teacher must learn to show and express his emotions fully. In due time, if the community grows, then learners will provide this security, warmth and care for each other.

The following exercises and learning methods I have used whilst trying to follow this learning community approach. They have to be taken in that light, but nonetheless most of them could be introduced on a conventional programme. It is quite proper to mix experiential learning exercises with sessions based on lectures or discussions, and often has great effect.

Although these exercises are presented in sections, this is only for administrative convenience. The classifications are approximate, mean different things to different people, and contain learnings well beyond the boundaries of particular categories. The best exercises are those developed and suggested by the learning group, but the teacher will help if he or she has some basic designs handy. Remember that ideally what you do should be negotiated. The other point to make is that these exercises are the tip of a huge iceberg. (Some books containing others are given on pp. 278–9.)

Exercises for Increasing Trust and Communication

These come first because increased trust and open communication go together, and both are necessary for significant learning. These exercises have a dual purpose, then: to learn about communication and to develop the learning community.

EXERCISE 1: GETTING TO KNOW YOU

At the beginning of a session or even during one, this is excellent for opening people up and illustrating the Johari Window (see Figure 6, p. 108).

1. Ask the group to form pairs, choosing people not well known to each other.

2. Tell them they have twenty minutes (they may take more in practice) to get to know the other well enough to introduce him to the group. (This can be an alternative to the old method of introductions by going round the room with each person introducing himself, or it can be used during a session, where the instruction is to find out *more* about the other person which the group has not seen.)

3. Let them find suitable corners in the room and remind them to change round after ten minutes (so that both find out about the other, if they are doing it that way).

4. After twenty minutes (or whatever time allowed) have the round of introductions.

5. Using the Johari Window, discuss the type of information found, for instance the 'safe', about job, job history, family, hobbies, etc., and the more 'risky', about politics, religion, likes and dislikes, etc.

EXERCISE 2: LISTENING AND RESPONDING

To practise listening and 'hearing' (see pp. 105 ff.) Takes about forty-five minutes, and should be done in threes.

1. Divide into threes and find a private spot.

2. Designate members A, B and C.

3. Each person chooses a controversial topic to speak on; current live issues are best, such as 'We need a statutory incomes policy', 'Trade unions are responsible for inflation', 'Extra-marital sex is responsible for the increasing breakdowns in marriage'.

4. For the first round of 5–10 minutes, A is speaker, B is responder, C is referee. When the group wants to move on but in any case after ten minutes, rotate so that B becomes speaker, C responder and A referee. Rotate for third and final round.

5. At the start of each round the speaker must start with a statement on his topic. When he has finished the responder *must*, without notes, *summarize in his own words what the speaker has said.* When he has done this *to the speaker's satisfaction,* the responder makes a statement which the speaker must summarize before replying. (An alternative design is to allow the responder to summarize only and then let the speaker carry on making statement no. 2 without argument from the responder. This is easier to do, but less realistic.)

6. Discuss in the full group the dangers and pitfalls in listening and talking, for instance:

the different meanings of words,

the emotional content of words and phrases,

forgetting and storing,

paraphrasing, showing own frame of reference and perception,

the difficulty of getting the 'message' across.

EXERCISE 3: COMMUNICATING WITH AND WITHOUT FEEDBACK

Takes about 45–60 minutes.

1. Get two volunteers, A and B.

2. Give sheet no. 1 (Figure 9, p. 124) to A and place him in a chair with his back to the group and holding it in such a way that no one can see it. Instruct the group *that no one is allowed to ask questions or make any noise at all.* They are to take down A's message.

3. Time how long A takes; ask him to estimate how much of the message has got over to each person; each group member to estimate how much of the message they have right.

4. Give B sheet no. 2 (see Figure 9), placing him facing the group but with the sheet hidden. Instruct the group to ask any questions or stop B if and when they wish. Members of the group are to take down B's message.

5. Repeat no. 3 above for B.

Show group the correct message; ask them to mark both messages.

6. Draw up a table on a flip chart or board to show each group member's estimated and actual results for both A and B. Discuss the effects of feedback on communication, for instance:

it slows it down,

it improves accuracy in 'getting it over',

it raises individual perception problems,

it improves understanding.

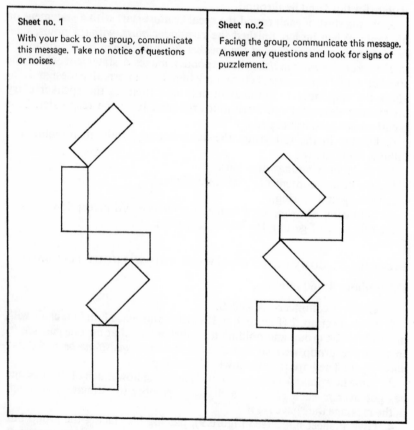

Sheet no. 1

With your back to the group, communicate this message. Take no notice of questions or noises.

Sheet no.2

Facing the group, communicate this message. Answer any questions and look for signs of puzzlement.

Figure 9

EXERCISE 4: GIVING PERSONAL FEEDBACK

For a small group, this aims to develop the idea of giving and receiving feedback, which is so vital to full communication.

1. Ask each group member to respond to the following questions (or some of them, since some are more 'risky' than others).

   (a) Who are the two members who speak most?
   (b) Who are the two members who speak least?
   (c) Which two have most influence on the group?
   (d) Which two are most 'open'?
   (e) Which two would you choose to go on a long train journey with?
   (f) Which two do you talk to most?
   (g) Which two do you talk to least?
   (h) Which two are most keen to get down to work?
   (i) Which two like to joke and fool about most?
   (j) Which two like to avoid conflict and strong differences?
   (k) Which two have helped most when conflicts have arisen?
   (l) Which two have clashed most strongly in group meetings?

Obviously you can add questions to the list to suit your own purposes.

2. Take each question in turn and find the people who are the chosen ones by consensus. Discuss the implications for them as people and the group.

Note that when using exercises of this kind, which touch people far more than a role play will, the teacher should exercise great care and judgement over how much people can take. In actual fact the group usually takes care of its own; this is one of the learning community objectives.

This is all there is space for here. There are hundreds of exercises for developing communication skills. Communication here has been treated as an interpersonal rather than an organizational process and this is deliberate. Some insight into organizational communications will be developed from later exercises on negotiating and consulting. In interpersonal communications these exercises try to use the principles of (a) emphasis on small groups, especially twos and threes; (b) being open and honest about oneself; (c) being honest with others about their effect on you. If you observe these principles, almost any exercise will do as a vehicle.

Exercises for Looking at Conflict and Change

EXERCISE 5: DAYDREAMING[58]

This exercise is designed to bring out the various approaches to conflict resolution and can be used to illustrate Figure 3 (p. 97). It takes perhaps thirty minutes.

1. Ask the participants to get as comfortable as possible and take their

coats and shoes off, for example. They should sit on the floor and close their eyes.

2. Now ask them to put themselves into the daydream you are about to describe, to imagine that they are actually going through it. Then in a slow and relaxed voice, say something like, 'You are walking through the shop (office, school, etc.) when you see some way off the person who you are most in conflict with at the moment. You realize that you have a few seconds to decide what action to take. As he or she comes closer a number of possible actions flash through your mind. Decide now what these are and what the consequences of each of them are.'

3. Hold the silence for at least two minutes, then tell them that it's over, and the person has gone. 'Come out of your daydream and open your eyes when you're ready.'

4. Get each person to spend a few minutes writing down the possible actions and their results. Stress that we're talking about approaches and that it is not necessary to reveal details of personal situations.

5. List the group's responses on the board or flip chart and examine them along with the model in Figure 3 (p. 97). Discuss different personal approaches and the results and satisfactions gained from these.

EXERCISE 6: ROLE NETWORKS

This exercise is designed to introduce the idea of role conflict and the stresses this can produce. It can be used together with the material on conflict foci (pp. 93 ff). It takes about $1\frac{1}{2}$ hours.

1. Divide the group into pairs and give each person a large sheet of paper and a pen or crayon. Tell the group that each pair is to work on one person's role network at a time, spending about twenty minutes on each.

2. One of each pair describes his network whilst the other draws it for him on the sheet of paper. A cross or symbol in the middle represents the person, whilst all the people or departments or organizations who make demands upon or who supply things for that person are drawn on the perimeter (see Figure 2, p. 94).

3. 'Role senders' can be drawn near or distant depending upon their force or importance; for instance, if the person is a shop steward, his members will be a stronger force than, say, the company personnel officer.

4. When the network has been drawn, list under each role sender the demands he makes upon the central role. Note where these demands conflict with one another.

5. Repeat for the other half of the pair. By letting each person draw the other's network and list the demands made, the exercise also provides practice in helping.

6. Discuss the completed networks in the whole group, paying special attention to the conflicting demands.

EXERCISE 7: PREPARING FOR CHANGE

This exercise can follow on from Exercise 6. Although it is presented here as an exercise to be done in pairs and threes, it can be done in two groups or departments. The exercise takes about two hours, but can be split between nos 4 and 5.

1. Everyone should choose another partner. Each person should think of a situation that really concerns him or her that he or she would like to improve. (If Exercise 6 has been done, then one of the relationships with a particular role sender could be used.) The problem must be a *real* one which concerns or worries the person.

2. Any situation or relationship can be seen as a balance between demands and responses, pushes and pulls, forces for and forces against.[59] The partner writes down the demands made on the person and the responses he makes *as things stand at present*.

For a shop steward dealing with his supervisor, these could be represented thus:

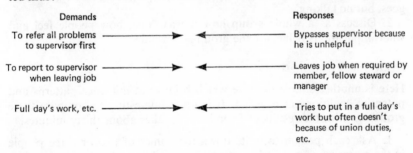

Demands	Responses
To refer all problems to supervisor first	Bypasses supervisor because he is unhelpful
To report to supervisor when leaving job	Leaves job when required by member, fellow steward or manager
Full day's work, etc.	Tries to put in a full day's work but often doesn't because of union duties, etc.

Figure 10

3. Now plot the demands and responses *in the desired state*, that is, what demands would you like the supervisor to make on you, and what responses would you ideally like to be making. Again the partner questions and writes down the desired demands and responses for the other.

4. Repeat for the other half of each pair. Pairs can repeat after no. 2, and again after no. 3, rather than doing both stages at a time.

5. Now form the group into threes, breaking up each pair if possible. Person A is to be the one with the problem, B is the helper and C is observer. For fifteen minutes B tries to help A with his problem, whilst

C observes. After fifteen minutes, C gives five minutes' feedback to B about his helping behaviour. Then rotate so that C becomes the one with the problem, A tries to help him, and B observes. Rotate again to complete the round. Everyone is 'helped', tries to help and observes.

6. In a whole group discuss what sort of behaviours were helpful and what were unhelpful. What sort of changes were possible and what sort of strategies could be adopted? What lessons were learned about changing situations?

7. Get each person to write down what he or she has learned most or what he or she is going to do as a result of the exercise. These can be pinned up on a board or put on a table.

Exercises for Looking at Power and Influence

EXERCISE 8: STATUS RANKING

This is a very useful and not too threatening non-verbal activity which can be done in a few minutes.

1. Instruct the people in the group to line up in the centre of the room in order of influence on the group, *without speaking*. Any other behaviour goes, but no talking.

2. Discuss as a whole group how it was done, how people feel and what implications it has for the group as a whole.

EXERCISE 9: SOCIOGRAM

Here is another simple exercise which brings out influence patterns and potential coalitions in a group. It is quite interesting to compare these groupings with the results of Exercise 8. It takes about thirty minutes.

1. Ask each person to write down the names of two or three people in the group who have had most influence on him or her.

2. On a large sheet of paper or the board, indicate all the group members and draw in the influence lines. Can you see any coalitions, pairings, sub-groups? How do these affect the behaviour of the full group?

Exercises for Practising Conflict Resolution and Negotiating

EXERCISE 10: WINNER TAKE ALL

This is an excellent exercise for illustrating the win/win, win/lose, lose/lose strategies of negotiating. I usually ask each person to put in a stake first in order to increase the conflict. It takes about an hour.

1. Divide the group into two (or two sets of two if the group is larger than sixteen). Put them in separate rooms (they should not be able to see or hear each other).

2. Give each group the rules, as follows. Designate Group no. 1 and Group no. 2. It is extremely important to state that the winners are the group with the highest, positive score.

3. *The Rules*

The game is played on the following matrix:

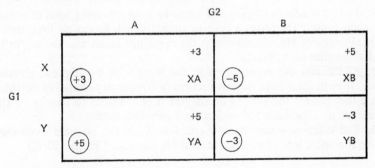

Figure 11

It is played between two groups, G1 and G2. Each team has complete freedom as regards goals, strategy, etc.

The rules of the game are as follows:

(a) The game consists of fifteen Trials.

(b) Each Trial consists of a decision by Group no. 1 added to each decision by Group no. 2.

(c) The decision of Group no. 1 may be either X or Y. The decision of Group no. 2 may be either A or B.

(d) Both decisions are taken simultaneously and in secret. There is immediate feedback at the end of each Trial.

(e) The result of each Trial is thus a combination of both groups' decisions, for example XA:YB.

(f) The circled numbers on each square of the matrix refer to Group no. 1: the uncircled numbers to Group no. 2. Thus if Group no. 1 decides on Trial 2 to play Y and Group no. 2 decides to play A, the complete decision YA will result in a gain of 5 to Group no. 1 and a loss of 5 to Group no. 2. The decision A results in a gain for both groups. The decision YB results in a loss for both groups.

(g) On Trial 8, values in the matrix are doubled but revert to normal for Trials 9–13.

E

(h) On Trial 14, all values in the matrix are doubled.

(i) On Trial 15, all values are squared; however, the minus signs remain minus.

(j) Between Trials 7 and 8 the opposing groups can send an envoy to negotiate for four minutes, but he cannot commit his groups to a strategy in advance.

(k) Before Trial 15, the groups can negotiate again on a group basis for seven minutes.

4. The tutor acts as umpire and needs to keep a running total of scores for each group. He tosses a coin to decide which group go first, thereafter alternating. He communicates the combined result and the scores to each team after each round.

5. At the end the money goes to the team with the highest, positive score. If both sides have negative scores (as frequently happens) the tutor can either pocket the money or suggest it be donated to charity or the caretaker as a penance for ending in a lose/lose bind.

6. The discussion can be concerned with all the possible outcomes, using the spectrum of conflict resolution methods (see pp. 97 ff.)

EXERCISE 11: ONE-ON-ONES

These are short one-to-one exercises, and are in fact role plays suitable for CCTV recording and play-back. They are again done in trios or in front of the whole group. They can be used to practise influence and conflict resolution styles and to generally illuminate many of the points made in Part 1 about communication and negotiating.

Divide the group into threes; give each three copies of the briefs for all three one-to-ones (see below) and three copies of the video observation sheets (see Table 5, p. 133).

Let the threes take their own time rotating the observer, management and union roles, with plenty of feedback time. If you are using CCTV, then the threes will probably have to move round as well, to allow others a turn.

1a. Management spokesman to convenor: 3 minutes
You are in the final stages of a critical negotiation. The union is acting very militantly and pushing you towards the limit of your authorized offer, but you don't want a strike. You are in a bad situation because the offer which you thought would be the acceptable one has just been rejected out of hand by the convenor, without even conferring with his colleagues. When he told you to go back for more, you lost your cool and told him to

go to hell. Now a real impasse has been reached and neither party is willing to make the next move.

You have just met the convenor in the toilets. There is no one else around and you have three minutes to get negotiations going again.

1b. Convenor to management spokesman: 3 minutes

You are in the final stages of a tough negotiation over wage rates. You and your committee are not looking for a strike, but in the last session you assumed a very militant posture to scare the company and make them really dig deep. Unfortunately you carried things just a little too far. The company made a proposal and in line with the role you had been playing you attacked this proposal and dismissed it, making the management spokesman look small in the process. You told the management spokesman to go back and get some more and he blew up and told you to go to hell. You are both out on a limb now; neither party is willing to make the next move.

You've got to talk to the management spokesman privately so you follow him into the toilets. No one else is there. You have three minutes to get negotiations going again.

2a. Management spokesman to union full-time official: 7 minutes

You are near the end of a long negotiation on a package which includes an increase in hourly rates. This is your first negotiation as main spokesman for management and you do not know the full-time official very well. Thirty minutes before the final session is due to commence you meet the official in the lift. You manage to persuade him to take a short walk down the corridor with you as you sense he is interested in talking.

The situation is this; you've got 5p an hour as your last offer. The union have just come down to 9p. Average settlements in your industry have been running around 6–8p. You have an authorization to settle for 6p across the board but if you really need it, you can go as high as 7p. The company cannot afford a strike and you do not want to make a mess of your first job as senior negotiator.

Your task is to make the settlement now.

2b. Union full-time official to management spokesman: 7 minutes

You've just bumped into the chief management negotiator whom you have not had many dealings with before. He persuades you to take a walk down the corridor to discuss the present situation. In thirty minutes' time you will be commencing the final bargaining session to try to settle the hourly wage rise which is part of your current negotiations. The last management offer was 5p an hour and you finally came down to 9p. You know that the average settlements for this type of work have been in the range of 6–8p, but you reckon that you can get 8p out of this relatively inexperienced man. However, you don't want a strike and you would prefer to settle the deal now.

3a. Personnel officer to senior steward: 4 minutes

The senior steward has just been in your office laying the law down about a man who is being formally warned for persistent late arrival. You know that the procedure has been followed in warning the man, but that he is a very popular person and a former shop steward. However, you're surprised at the chief steward's anger and indignation; he scarcely gives you a chance to answer him, but warns you that further action to dismiss this man will be met by a very militant reaction from the shop floor.

You are very worried by this because you have sensed in the past that your relationships with this steward have not always been smooth and that perhaps you have not understood each other very well. He seems to strike you as an aggressive, irritable man who easily flies off the handle.

You go down on to the shop floor to look for him and find him by the vending machine. He is on his own and you decide to try to clear the confusion up because you must maintain management's rights to dismiss a man after the full procedure has been followed. On the other hand, you obviously do not want to sour relationships. You have four minutes to attempt to reopen this area.

3b. Senior steward to personnel officer: 4 minutes

Just an hour ago you blasted the personnel officer for giving a written warning to one of your best friends. You know that Jack has been late a few times for work but that this is because of a personal problem which he is not anxious to have made public. You do not like the personnel officer very much. He rubs you up the wrong way. He seems to be a very persistent and obstinate person who is always somehow prying into you to find out what makes you tick. You often seem to get aggressive with him but you do not always understand why this is because you don't regard yourself as an aggressive person generally.

As a result of the meeting with him, you stuck your neck out more than a bit and promised militant action if any further steps were taken following Jack's written warning. You're not sure whether your members will back your words.

As you're standing by the vending machine the personnel officer approaches you. You wait for him a little sullenly.

Table 5: Video Observation Sheet

---

1. Communications: verbal

How clearly did you communicate? Why?   How clearly did he appear to
                                         communicate? Why?

2. Communications: physical

Did you feel you communicated anything   Did he communicate anything
physically by your stance, distance apart,   physically, considering the same
expression, eyes, etc.? If so, what and how?   elements? If so, what and how?

3. Trust

Do you feel he trusted you? Why?   Did you trust him? Why?

4. Interpersonal

How would you describe yourself during   How would you describe him
the exercise?   during the exercise?

After the trios (or groups) have worked their way through the one-to-ones, a full group can discuss the various strategies in influencing negotiating and resisting.

There are many other negotiating exercises. Neil Rackham's controlled pace negotiations allow for the examination via behaviour categories of a real, slow-motion negotiation.[60] (See p. 92 for some of these behavioural categories.) An international negotiating exercise, illustrating inter-group issues as well as strategies and power, is available in package form.[61] More traditional industrial relations exercises are relatively common.[62]

I personally prefer real, live experience to any exercise. The teacher's skill lies in developing the atmosphere in which participants will learn from their own, undiluted experience and in offering ways of structuring and restructuring this experience. For example, negotiations can take place on any live issue of contention, from where we should drink tonight to what should be the programme for tomorrow. After all, most of our negotiating is spent on this sort of issue!

A Note on the Use of CCTV

Videotape provides an 'accurate' record of what happens. It is 'objective' in that it is not mediated or distorted by human perception, although this is an argument against taking it as gospel. It does provide a unique experience of watching oneself behave and the effect this has upon others. It does this in a way which is impossible to do when involved. Think of the slow motion replays on 'Match of the Day' which give a good idea of how CCTV can delineate the action.

Video playback fits into the reflecting and observing part of the experiential learning cycle described earlier in Part 2. If you remember, this went as follows:

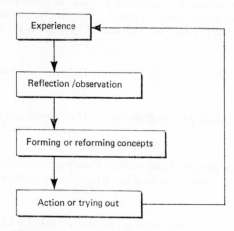

Figure 12

Many people find observing and reflecting on their own behaviour extremely difficult and CCTV can be very helpful here. On the other hand, it can frequently be more trouble than it is worth. If the technology gets in the way of the learning, then you may think twice about it.

Some of the advantages of using CCTV are as follows:

1. All information, verbal and non-verbal, is stored and is available for later use. No other method can do this.

2. The non-verbal behaviour of people is particularly important in our interactions. We are often saying one thing and indicating another. CCTV shows this superbly.

3. There is no perceptual bias, distortion or selection with CCTV: it records all and makes denial difficult or less easy.

4. It allows study of an interaction from outside. Those involved can look back 'objectively' on their performance.

5. Taken together with observers' comments, CCTV provides an ideal mix of objective and subjective feedback on behaviour.

6. Videotape acts as a mirror. Each person can decide what he is willing to accept and what to attend to. He can do this privately without any other person forcing him to look at something he thinks is important.

7. CCTV is good fun, and it also encourages awareness and consciousness of behaviour. Once the inhibiting effects of this are overcome, it is an indispensable aid to learning.

Its disadvantages are:

1. The technology can distract from the learning, especially if the participants are operating the equipment or seeing themselves for the first time.

2. If a real error is captured on the tape, insensitive replay of this can really rub it in. Video-recorders are honest but they don't discriminate like human observers.

3. There will be too much data to use if the recording goes on for very long; this creates selection problems.

4. General ignorance and fear of technology may be inhibitive. They may also lead to distractions in camera work, poor selection of playback, bad timing, etc.

5. There may be lack of skill in integrating CCTV playback into learning objectives and process: for instance, how much? when? where?

6. It is time-consuming. If you have a thirty-minute negotiation and then play it back, that's well over an hour gone.

The use of CCTV, including camera work and feedback, is a skill in itself. For those interested, a recent series of articles goes into more detail than is possible here.[63] However, a few rules of thumb might help.

1. When choosing equipment consult an AVA specialist. Things move quickly in this field and equipment is getting smaller, more flexible and cheaper. You need at least one videotape recorder, one camera, one monitor and a couple of microphones. It is possible to buy this equipment now for less than £1000.

2. When using the equipment it is often better to fix the camera rather than distract with wobbly close-ups and break-neck 'zooms'. A skilled cameraman can be very helpful with his various techniques, but there is a consequent danger of the technology becoming obtrusive and distracting.

3. Take short recordings, such as ten minutes or less. The one-on-ones are designed for this purpose. If you record a longer session, try to select the significant episodes to play back, and intersperse discussion and comment.

4. With a large group, you have to plan how best to use the equipment.

It is rather boring for twenty people to watch two performing. Careful planning of recordings and feedbacks is necessary.

5. Above all, don't be seduced by all that white-hot technology. CCTV is a tool which can take up needless time and energy if not used sparingly. I personally like to arrange for small groups of between two and six to use the CCTV one at a time in order to get full value. With larger groups I prefer human observers, often using observation sheets like the one included in Exercise 11 above.

Notes

1. Frankenberg, R., *Communities in Britain* (Penguin, 1966).
2. Toffler, A., *Future Shock* (Pan, 1972).
3. Rackham, N., 'Controlled Pace Negotiation as a New Technique for Developing Negotiating Skills', *Industrial and Commercial Training* (July 1972).
4. This has been developed from Pondy, L. R., 'Organisational Conflict: Concepts and Models', in Thomas, J. M., and Bennis, W. G., *Management of Change and Conflict* (Penguin, 1972), pp. 359–79.
5. Coser, L., *The Functions of Social Conflict* (New York: Free Press, 1950).
6. Kahn, R., *et al.*, *Studies in Organisational Stress* (New York: Wiley, 1964), p. 65.
7. Coser, *op. cit.*
8. Deutsch, M., 'Productive and Destructive Conflict', in Thomas, J. M., and Bennis, W. G., *op. cit.*, p. 381.
9. Kahn, R., *et al.*, *op. cit.*, p. 65.
10. March, J. G., and Simon, H. A., *Organisations* (New York: Wiley, 1958), p. 112.
11. See for example Fordyce, J. K., and Weil, R., *Managing with People: A Manager's Handbook of Organisation Development Methods* (Addison Wesley, 1971).
12. See for example Goodwin Watson, 'Resistance to Change' in Bennis, W. G., Benne, K. D., and Chin, R., *The Planning of Change* (New York: Holt, Rinehart & Winston, 1968), pp. 488–98.
13. Machiavelli, *The Prince*, Everyman edition (Dent, 1940), pp. 43–4.
14. Festinger, L., *A Theory of Cognitive Dissonance* (New York: Harper, 1957).
15. Jamieson, D. W., and Thomas, K.W., 'Power and Conflict in the Student–Teacher Relationship', *Journal of Applied Behavioural Science*, Vol. 10, No. 3 (1974), pp. 321–36.
16. Blake, R. R., and Mouton, J. S., *The Managerial Grid* (Houston, Texas: Gulf Publishing Co., 1964).
17. Bartos, O. J., *The Process and Outcomes of Negotiations* (New York: Columbia University Press, 1964), pp. 236–70.
18. Pedler, M. J., and Cooke, P. J., 'Industrial Relations Training in the USA', mimeograph, Sheffield Polytechnic, 1974.
19. Collins, B. E., and Raven, B. H., 'Group Structure: Attraction, Coalitions, Communication and Power', in Lindzey, G. and Aronson, E., *The Handbook of Social Psychology* (Addison Wesley, 1969), Vol. 4, p. 160.
20. Collins and Raven, *op. cit.*, pp. 166–8.
21. *Op. cit.*, p. 334.
22. Kelman, H. C., 'Processes of Opinion Change' in Bennis, Benne and Chin, *op. cit.*, pp. 222–30.
23. *Op. cit.*, p. 331.

24. Deutsch, *op. cit.*, p. 394; Walton, R. E., 'Two Strategies of Social Change and Their Dilemmas' in Thomas and Bennis, *op. cit.*, p. 490.

25. *Op. cit.*, pp. 395–6.

26. *Ibid.*, p. 392.

27. Fox, A., *Industrial Sociology and Industrial Relations*, Research Paper No. 3, Donovan Commission (HMSO, 1966).

28. On communication see also *The Activist's Handbook* in this series.

29. Hovland, C. I., Janis, I. L., and Kelley, H. H., *Communication and Persuasion* (New Haven: Yale University Press, 1953).

30. Kniveton, B. H., 'Industrial Negotiating: Some Training Implications', *Industrial Relations Journal*, Vol. 5, No. 3 (autumn, 1974), pp. 27–37.

31. *Op. cit.*, p. 34.

32. Rapoport, A., *Fights, Games and Debates* (University of Michigan Press, 1960).

33. *The Games People Play* (Penguin, 1968), p. 18.

34. See for example, Jongward, P., and James, M., *Winning with People* (Addison Wesley, 1973).

35. *Op. cit.,* and Rackham, N., *et al.*, *Developing Interactive Skills* (Wellens Publishing, 1972).

36. Lynd, H. M., *On Shame and the Search for Identity* (New York: Harcourt Brace, 1958), pp. 45–7.

37. Luft, J., 'The Johari Window' quoted in Schein, E. H., *Process Consultation* (Addison Wesley, 1969), pp. 21–6.

38. From Deutsch, *op. cit.*, p. 386.

39. Alan Fox has an interesting discussion of the various types and models of trust in *Beyond Contract: Work, Power and Trust Relations* (Faber, 1974), pp. 66–84.

40. Walton, R. E., and McKersie, R. B., *A Behavioral Theory of Labor Negotiations* (New York: McGraw Hill, 1965), p. 283.

41. Referred to as 'factional conflict' by Walton and McKersie, *op. cit.*, p. 283.

42. Referred to as 'boundary conflict' by Walton and McKersie, *ibid.*, p. 283.

43. Kniveton, *op. cit.*, p. 37.

44. On information required, for example, Gottschalk, A. W., 'The Negotiating Process', in Naylor, R., and Torrington, D., *The Code of Personnel Administration* (Gower Press, 1973) is much more detailed; Kniveton, *op. cit.*, goes into some detail on social skills.

45. Argyris, C., 'Today's Problems with Tomorrow's Organisations', in Thomas and Bennis, *op. cit.*, p. 180.

46. Bloom, B. S., *et al.*, *A Taxonomy of Educational Objectives: Vol. 1, The Cognitive Domain* (Longmans, 1956).

47. Unpublished paper.

48. Kniveton, B. H., 'Industrial Negotiating: Some Training Implications', *Industrial Relations Journal*, Vol. 5, No. 3 (autumn 1974), p. 31.

49. Rackham, N., 'Controlled Pace Negotiation', *Industrial and Commercial Training* (June 1973).

50. These levels and the illustrative analogy were developed by Tom Boydell.

51. Harrison, R., 'Classroom Innovation: A Design Primer', in Runkel, P., Harrison, R., and Runkel, M., *The Changing College Classroom* (Jossey-Bass, 1969), pp. 302–42.

52. *Op. cit.*, p. 37.

53. Abercrombie, M. L. J., *The Anatomy of Judgement* (Hutchinson, 1960).

54. Jacques, E., in an essay entitled 'Learning for Uncertainty' in *Work, Creativity and Social Justice* (Heinemann, 1970), p. 120.

55. At the Sheffield University Extra-Mural Department's Conference on 'Adult Education and Industry', 4–6 April 1975.

56. Kolb, D. A., Rubin, I. M., and McIntyre, J. M., *Organizational Psychology: an Experiential Approach* (Englewood Cliffs, New Jersey: Prentice Hall, 1971), p. 28.

57. Pedler, M. J., 'Learning in Management Education', *Journal of European Training*, Vol. 3, No. 3 (1974).

58. Adapted from 'Conflict Fantasy' in Pfeiffer, J. W., and Jones, J. E. (eds.), *Annual Group Facilitators' Handbook 1974* (La Jolla, California: University Associates, 1974), pp. 22–3.

59. This way of analysing problems is known as 'force field analysis' and was first developed by Kurt Lewin. See for example, Fordyce, J. K., and Weil, R., *Managing with People* (Addison Wesley, 1971), pp. 106–8.

60. The complete exercise, with examples, can be found in *Industrial and Commercial Training* (July 1972), pp. 266–75.

61. 'War and Peace', available from the Learning Resources Unit, Management Studies Dept., Sheffield Polytechnic, Sheffield.

62. See for example, Karl Hedderwick's in *The Industrial Tutor*, Vol. 1, No. 6 (March 1972).

63. Bristow, J., and Bradshaw, R., 'Effective Use of Videotape for Feedback for Developing Social Skill and Relationships', a series of five articles in *Industrial Training International* (January–June 1975).

Section IV

The Framework of Collective Bargaining

The word 'framework' illustrates the difficulty of describing collective bargaining in Britain. To call this a 'system' falsely suggests a tidy, institutional arrangement, and also causes confusion because of other uses of the word, such as in the phrase 'systems theory'. The word 'pattern' is possible, but it is vague; 'framework' is nearer the mark because it indicates that there are some guidelines and fixed points, but not too much rigidity, rather something upon which structures have to be built and connections made.

This can still be an unrealistic concept for the active trade unionist if the 'framework' confines itself to institutions. Even the informal system, as it was called by the Donovan Commission, with work-place stewards building up company and national combine committees, may have an 'institutional' air about it. In reality, the framework is complex and multi-dimensional, in which institutional and organizational forms are permutated in a variety of ways, and are interwoven with history, law, rules and regulations, technology, politics, social cross-currents and the impacts of personalities.

For these reasons, it is difficult to set down the framework in any satisfactory diagrammatic form, as any diagram tends to stress the institutional side and automatically gives the framework a false rigidity. Figures 13 and 14 illustrate these difficulties, and are sometimes used by tutors with some explanation of the relationships shown.

The three essays in this section are related to different parts of the bargaining framework: Doug Gowan traces some of the institutional patterns and shows how they developed over time and what some of the thinking is behind them – a picture of bargaining units from the point of view of the trade union. Geoff Woodcock describes some of the major organizations developed by employers, and J. E. Mortimer brings in 'the third side', now much more in the open, the Government and its roles in the framework. (Eds.)

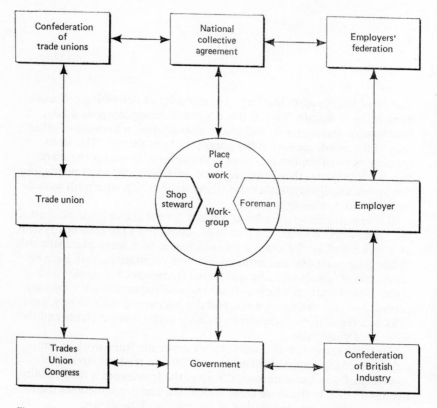

Figure 13

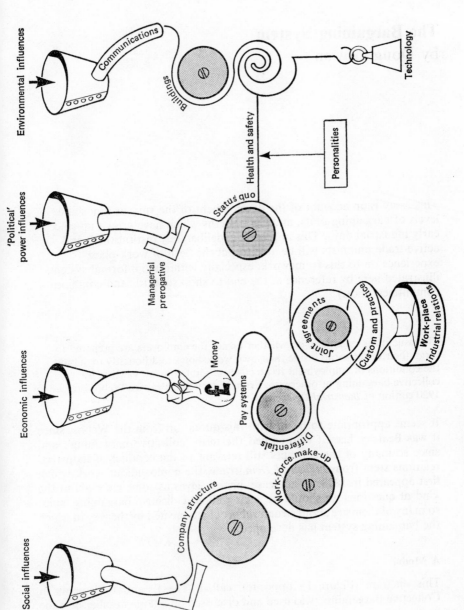

Figure 14: The Heath-Robinson Work-Place Industrial Relations System

The Bargaining System
by Doug Gowan

This essay is an account of the development of the various kinds and
levels of bargaining units, and the patterns which have grown up since
early industrial days. This approach is deliberately institutional, and
active trade unionists will be able to put the flesh of work-place
experience on to this framework, especially within the informal system,
illustrated here by reference at the end to shop stewards and combine
committees. (Eds.)

The issue turns essentially on whether or not the employers are prepared to
forgo their dictatorship inside their own workshops, and honestly to submit
the conditions of employment to an effective joint control, whether by
collective bargaining or otherwise. From Sidney and Beatrice Webb, Preface to
1920 edition of *Industrial Democracy*.

It seems appropriate to begin with this quotation from the Webbs, since
it was Beatrice herself who coined the term 'collective bargaining', and
since so many of the concepts still relevant to the conduct of industrial
relations stem from *Industrial Democracy*, the compendious work which
first appeared in 1898. In any case, history gives us some clues about the
kind of questions we should be asking about collective bargaining, since
so many of them are about structural problems created by the way in which
the bargaining system has developed.

A Model

This diagram (Figure 15 opposite), called 'The Essential Elements in
Collective Bargaining', was used and discussed on a large number of trade
union courses in 1970 and 1971, at the time when the Conservative
Government's Industrial Relations Bill was in its Parlamentary stages.

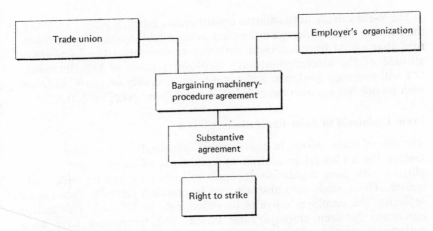

Figure 15

The purpose of the diagram was to remind trade union students of the importance of the freedom to arrive at suitable procedures, to negotiate on terms and conditions of employment, and to strike in the event of a failure to agree.

Without these freedoms, so the argument went, there could be no effective collective bargaining, which has as part of its definition 'voluntary agreement' on 'terms and conditions of employment'. Legal restrictions on procedure agreements, or the right to strike, as provided for in the 1971 Industrial Relations Act, would jeopardize the ability of unions to enter freely into agreements.

Taken to extremes, putting restrictions on collective agreements so that they would not apply to the individual contract 'agreed' between master and workman would mean trying to reverse a hundred years of developments in the influence of collective bargaining.

The diagram does, however, provoke other questions that are fundamental to discussions of collective bargaining:

How are trade unions and employers *organized* to enter into bargaining arrangements?

What factors determine the *level* at which bargaining takes place: workshop, district, company or industry?

What *authority* do the procedural and substantive agreements have over trade union members and employers?

In one form or another these questions crop up at every stage in twentieth-century industrial relations literature.

The Webbs made authoritative contributions on each point. They saw the purpose of the collective agreement as the establishment of a 'common rule' that would have sufficient authority to counteract the *laissez-faire* attitude of the nineteenth-century employer typified in the statement: ' "I will pay each workman according to his necessity or merit, and deal with no one but my own hands." ' (*Industrial Democracy*, 1898, p. 177)

From Unilateral to Joint Regulation

The aim of trade unions, in conventional industrial relations jargon, is to replace the unilateral regulation of conditions of employment by employers with joint regulation through collective bargaining with trade unions. This sounds very abstract, but in practical terms it often means replacing the employer's works or office 'rule book' with a collective agreement between employer and union. The terms that have been collectively agreed will in most cases be inserted into the individual employee's contract with his employer, as shown in the Figure. The terms of the agreement are 'implied' in the individual contract.

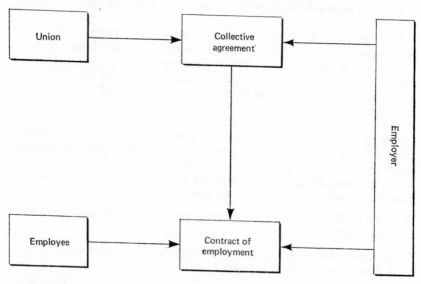

Figure 16

The question for unions is whether there are any subjects which are left outside the collective agreement and which are still in effect controlled solely by the employer through his own rules. In some factories or offices there is still a direct clash between the terms of agreement and an employer's rule book.

Even where a union has managed to secure that all *written* terms and conditions of employment are subject to collective bargaining and agreement, there will often be many working arrangements that in effect govern the behaviour of the employees. These are usually known as 'custom and practice'. The Webbs took it somewhat for granted that trade union objectives in collective bargaining were to extend the 'common rule' to whole industries.

Leaving aside for a moment the question of what is an 'industry', to a certain extent this was a reflection of current thinking on 'industrial unionism'. Collective bargaining at workshop level had in fact pre-dated trade unions, and coexisted with them. The point was to extend the principle of eliminating differential treatment of each class of employees, as in primitive workshop bargaining, and restricting it to *district* and *national* levels. The model in 1898 looked like this:

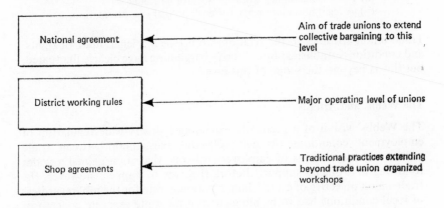

Figure 17

At this date is was still not certain whether the 'method of collective bargaining' was to be the most effective in spreading equality of conditions of employment over the country, since it had a strong contender in 'the method of legal regulation'.

The Effects of Legislation

It would be a mistake to underestimate the part played by legislation in bringing about social changes in favour of workers and their trade unions in trade union policies over the last 150 years.

The 'Rules and Standing Orders' of the TUC contain the following under *'Rule 8: Duties of General Council'*:

8(a) **The General Council shall transact the business in the periods between each Annual Congress, shall keep a watch on all industrial movement, and shall where possible coordinate industrial action.**

(b) *They shall watch all legislation affecting labour and shall initiate such legislation as Congress may direct. . . .*

The TUC revised the format of its Standing Orders in 1925, under Clause 2, 'Objects', as follows:

2 Objects
(a) The objects of the Congress shall be to promote the interests of all its affiliated organisations and generally to improve the economic and social conditions of the workers. . . .
(b) (2) Wages and hours of labour –
    (a) A legal maximum working week of 44 hours
    (b) A legal minimum wage for each industry or occupation.

Trade union attitudes to the relationship between a legal 'floor of rights' and conditions established by collective bargaining have clearly fluctuated, but this is beyond the scope of this essay.

The Webbs and After

The Webbs' vision of a gradually extending industry-wide regulation of employment conditions through collective bargaining between trade unions and associations of employers was one that soon gained a wider following and official support. Before this was to happen, however, the trade union objective of establishing a national 'rate for the job' regardless of local conditions had to be mingled with the quite separate concern of employers and Government to establish effective conciliation machinery to reduce or eliminate industrial disputes, if necessary backed by legislation (such as the Conciliation Act of 1896).

Whitley and Bargaining Machinery

The two tendencies came together in the Whitley Committee's Report of 1917. The impact of war had, as so often in the twentieth century, forced a radical rethinking of attitudes that had not proved possible in economic and political crises in peacetime. The official chronicle of these events was

the old Ministry of Labour's *Industrial Relations Handbook*[1] which saw
things this way:

During the war trade union membership greatly increased, and the unions
acquired a new status as the Government of the day took them into
consultation to an increasing extent. War conditions called for greater
flexibility in production and steps had to be taken to avoid stoppages of work
arising out of trade disputes. . . . National arbitration gave encouragement
to the regulation of wages on a national basis, and after the war wage changes
in many industries continued to be made on a national basis and through
centralised organisations. In spite of the legal prohibition of stoppages of
work and the acceptance of compulsory arbitration, areas of unrest developed
throughout the country at the mid-period of the war. These seemed to have
a common origin in what was called the Shop Stewards' Movement, which
found its inspiration in the theory of industrial unionism. The essence of this
was devolution of authority to the workshop and the establishment of
workers' control therein on militant lines with the ultimate object of securing
control of industry generally. . . . This situation developed a number of serious
aspects. . . .

Serious indeed. The step taken by the Government was to set up a Committee on the Relations between Employers and Employed, the Whitley
Committee. Its terms of reference are worth recalling:

(1) to make and consider suggestions for securing a *permanent improvement
    in the relations between employers and workmen*; and
(2) to recommend means for securing that *industrial conditions* affecting the
    relations between employers and workmen shall be systematically reviewed
    by those concerned with a view to improving conditions in the future.
    (Italics added for emphasis.)

The idea of a 'permanent improvement' in relations between employers
and employees which might be *brought about by structural changes in
collective bargaining* was novel in 1917. Earlier thinkers on the subject,
such as Mundella in the nineteenth century, had tended to stress 'conciliation' between masters and workmen. But the practical recommendations
of the Whitley Committee were:[2]

(a) that joint industrial councils should be formed in well-organised industries;
(b) that works committees representative of the management and the workers
should be appointed in individual establishments;
(c) that the system of statutory regulation of wages in badly organised trades
should be extended; and
(d) that a permanent court of arbitration should be set up.

It was implicit in the proposal for an extensive system of joint industrial councils that District Councils would be set up to carry out similar functions under the guidelines set out by the National Joint Council.

The New Whitley system thus looked something like this:

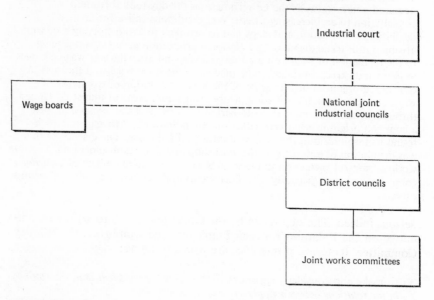

Figure 18

This in outline was the 'formal system' of industrial relations that was to figure so prominently as an object of criticism in the Donovan Report almost fifty years later. It was based on the premise that employers and workers should organize themselves *industry by industry*. Thus the proposed system depended on the capacity of unions and employers to *organize effectively* at industry level, and to *apply authoritatively* the agreements reached there at work-place level. The idea of a 'common rule' concerning terms and conditions of employment was still of crucial importance to trade unionists, but was less so to employers for whom national concili-ation machinery was less pressing in the relative quiescence of the postwar slump. The fear that a 'levelling up' of wage rates might occur certainly crossed their minds.

In the same immediate postwar period, employers' organizations were regrouping and the T U C was reorganizing itself. Both these were responses to the prospect of Lloyd George setting up a National Economic Council, which never happened. In the T U C, G. D. H. Cole's recommendations which led to the new General Council did have some effect: his plan to group unions by industries to encourage them to form industrial unions was put into practice. But industrial unions did not and have not emerged as a result of those initiatives. Whitleyism, except in the Civil Service, generally failed to influence the rest of industry until after the Second World War, when it developed in the nationalized industries. In local government where NALGO had pushed for the system since 1918, Whitleyism did not win through until 1946 following a judgment in the House of Lords which stopped the opposition of local authorities.

Employers' Associations and Bargaining Machinery

Clearly the problem of organization *on the part of the employers* was the major factor hindering the development of a formal national collective bargaining structure in local government. This is hardly surprising, given the longstanding *laissez-faire* antipathy to collectivism in general, and trade unionism in particular. A hint is given in the Donovan Report, which put forward a useful analytical principle that we might use to help us see why this should be so and to give us a partial answer to one of our earlier questions. It said:

as a general rule, the scope of arrangements made for joint negotiation in any particular industry may be said to be determined by the manner in which the employers have organised themselves. For example, in the engineering industry there is only one employers' organisation negotiating with many unions and associated for the purpose of a Confederation.[3]

It is difficult to understate the importance of this principle even though its implications were not fully carried through into the Report's recommendations.

Seventy employers' associations submitted evidence to the Donovan Commission, which was charged to report on trade unions and employers' associations. This seems a large number, but there are 172 employer organizations; the largest, apart from the Engineers, are the National Federation of Building Trades Employers with about 750000 employees, the British Printing Industries' Federation with 250000 and the Shipbuilders' and Repairers' National Association with 90000 employees (though this one will soon disappear under nationalization). Many are concerned both to represent groups of employers in negotiation with unions and also to give advice on commercial matters. Some associations directly arose out of the need of employers to respond collectively to trade union action, and have remained largely negotiating bodies. The Iron Masters of the North of England, of Lincoln and of the Midlands were early examples, succeeded by the British Steel Corporation. The Engineering Employers' Federation emerged as the force it still is from the great lock-out of 1897. But employers' associations today often regard themselves as advisory and educational bodies in the sense of encouraging among their members more positive action in industrial relations both in relation to the unions and to government policies.

It may seem perfectly obvious today that unions must negotiate with employers at the point where management has negotiating power to effect changes on employees' behalf. This may be at the level of the plant, company, industry or nation. But the decision on the employer's side about where negotiating power lies may well have been made precisely in order to confront most effectively (or often to divide and conquer most effectively) the unions' strongest positions of power. Before nationalization for example, many steel employers negotiated on a company basis, knowing full well that the main unions in the industry had no corresponding, company structure.

Union Objectives

What about the influence of trade union objectives on bargaining structures? Clearly the form of bargaining procedures and units has a direct effect on the coverage of the 'common rules' that unions seek to spread across their membership. But many different influences have gone into the making of bargaining units, including the organizational background of the unions themselves.

Historically, it was the practice for each trade to negotiate separately for its members in any work-place; and when process workers, in iron and steel making, for example, semi-skilled workers in manufacturing industry, labourers, clerical workers and technical supervisors and managerial staff all in turn became organized, a wide range of negotiating rights was established for separate unions in many companies and industries. Industrial unions like the NUM which represent all manual workers in an industry, though not the deputies and supervisory staffs, are rare. Attempts to establish industrial unions in the steel industry and on the railways failed. The reasons for such failures were as much the genuine special common interests of work groups as the conservation and inertia of the vested interests of separate union organizations. A great mass of separate bargaining units has thus come to exist on the ground throughout industry.

Side by side with this, and despite this, unions came increasingly to bargain for their members at national level in Joint Councils with the employers as in the Whitley model. Basic rates and hours of work were agreed collectively for workers in particular industries often as the result of a federated group of unions like the Confederation of Engineering Unions negotiating with the Engineering Employers' Federation. In what were once called the 'sweated trades', where works were widely dispersed and hard to organize, national wage boards (succeeded by wages councils) set the rates of pay and hours of work.

The point, however, that it was the general objective of trade unions to extend proper collective bargaining to recalcitrant industries and employers did not escape Governments, who had seen this as a potential source of industrial disputes. The wartime Order 1305 and the subsequent Order 1376, while banning certain kinds of industrial action, required unorganized employers to recognize terms and conditions of employment negotiated by others.

The Terms and Conditions of Employment Act

This type of provision was later codified in the Terms and Conditions of Employment Act, 1959, which in the well-known Section 8 allowed a union to claim:

(a) that terms or conditions of employment are established in any *trade or industry, or section of a trade or industry,* either generally or in any district . . .

(b) that the parties to the agreement, or to the proceedings in which the award was made, are or represent organisations of employers and organisations of workers, or associations of such organisations, and represent (generally or in the district in question, as the case may be) a substantial proportion of the employers and of the workers in the trade, industry or section. . . .

(c) that as respects any worker of the relevant description *an employer engaged in the trade, industry or section* (or, where the operation of the agreement or award is limited to a district, an employer so engaged in that district), *whether represented as aforesaid or not,* is not observing the terms or conditions (hereinafter referred to as 'the recognised terms or conditions'). . . .

The Secretary of State may take any steps which seem to him expedient to settle, or to secure the use of appropriate machinery to settle, the claim and shall, if the claim is not otherwise settled, refer it to the Industrial Court. (Emphasis added.)

The emphasis in the Section is on extending the representativeness of collective bargaining, although it should be noted that there is no clear prescription of *nationally* negotiated terms as those that are relevant to the claim. The Industrial Court (later the Industrial Arbitration Board) in fact allowed many claims based on locally negotiated wage levels significantly higher than national minimum rates, at least until they were directly opposed on this point by the Pay Board's lawyers during the period of the 1970–4 Conservative Government's Phases II and III Incomes Policies.

Wages Councils Industries

The procedure provided by Section 8 of the 1959 Terms and Conditions of Employment Act did, however, exclude wages councils industries. In this sector the trade union movement backs the proposals in the Employment Protection Act of 1975 to transform wages councils as appropriate into 'statutory joint industrial councils'. In 1976 there were still nearly three million employees in the wages council sector. But the functions of these new industrial relations animals are not as yet clearly defined.

These sections of the Employment Protection Act thus mark the latest phase in the historical attempts by trade unions to extend the formal machinery of collective bargaining to virtually the whole range of employment situations.

Company Bargaining: The 'New' System?

Up to this point we have considered some of the 'formal' aspects of collective bargaining, and the pressures that have led to its gradual extension over most of British industry. But the circumstances in which trade unions organize today are of course very different from those the Webbs commented on. The entrepreneurial capitalism of the nineteenth century has given way to the monopolistic and oligopolistic powers of domestic and international companies; the public sector has expanded to cover a broad sector of the work force; previously integrated 'industries' have split or merged with others; and American and other companies controlled from abroad have set up factories with every intention of constructing an industrial relations system inside them 'just like at home'. Each of these factors has tended to stress *enterprise* rather than *industry* bargaining. Professor Clegg attempted to categorize it thus:

Firstly, there are the *company agreements of 'non-federated' firms* which negotiate direct with the unions. Where one great corporation covers the whole of an industry its settlements are both industry and company agreements. The National Coal Board and the British Railways Board are two examples. Their company agreements are independent enclaves within the boundaries of the relevant industry agreements. Among them are such well-known companies as Ford, Vauxhall and ICI. Secondly, there is company bargaining in federated firms. Some federated firms negotiate formal agreements which supplement industry agreements, and elsewhere understandings or arrangements may be made between company and union spokesmen at informal meetings.

Where a company consists of more than one plant there is a distinction between company and plant bargaining. Some non-federated multi-plant firms prefer to allow each plant to negotiate its own agreements with the unions in place of a single company agreement.[4]

To these categories we should add one for companies that refuse to enter into any form of bargaining arrangement with trade unions.

Evidently the model has lost any pretence of simplicity, and what we have now is a series of alternative forms of collective bargaining machinery, often running in parallel. If we attempt to simplify Clegg's dense formulation of the situation even further, we might end up with this diagram:

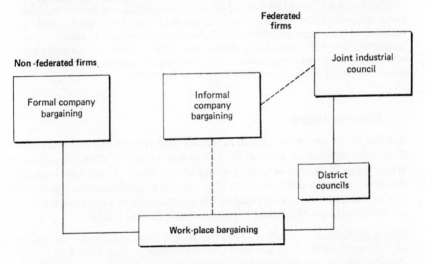

Figure 19

Note that the 'formal company bargaining' category on the left-hand side of the diagram includes huge corporations such as the NCB and the Ford Motor Company. 'Informal company bargaining' on the right-hand side can range from irregular discussions between union representatives and company spokesmen to institutionalized bargaining arrangements for dealing with certain terms and conditions of employment, such as a company pension scheme.

In some cases the development of company bargaining separate from industry-wide negotiating machinery has been the result of the inflexibility of Joint Industrial Council machinery, and in others of a positive desire by a company to pursue independent industrial relations policies often aimed at reducing the influence of unions. Thus some companies, such as Courtaulds, have withdrawn from JIC machinery.

The TUC's own industrial relations guide makes the following points about the fact that the main influence in the form of negotiating machinery is often employer organization:

84 Employers' associations have important functions in concluding industry-wide agreements with trade unions and advising member companies on developments in industrial relations. They should therefore . . .
   (b) *revise their constitutions where necessary to facilitate company-level bargaining* . . . it was mentioned that the senior management of individual companies too often ignore the need to develop and implement industrial relations policies, partly because of the manner in which employers' associations and trade unions conclude agreements at industry level. While these agreements have been suitable and sufficient for both parties in some industries, they have been supplemented in others by the trend towards plant and shop floor bargaining to which the constitutions and the organisation of some employers' associations have been slow to adapt.[5]

The Donovan Analysis

The Donovan Report was much more unhappy at the structural weaknesses that were appearing in the formal industry-wide system of collective bargaining. Not only was bargaining at the level of industry losing its authority over the determination of terms and conditions in any particular work-place, but the continuance of the system itself in its present form was an apparently psychological barrier to more radical change:

The decentralisation of collective bargaining has taken place under the pressure of full employment which has been almost continuous since 1938. Full employment encourages bargaining about pay at the factory and workshop levels. . . . In Britain it has brought special consequences because of the way in which our industrial organisations have reacted to it. Among these reactions has been a decline in the authority of employers' associations. . . .[6]
   The formal and informal systems are in conflict. The informal system undermines the regulative effect of industry-wide agreements. The gap between industry-wide agreed rates and actual earnings continues to grow. Procedure agreements fail to cope adequately with disputes arising within factories. Nevertheless, the assumptions of the formal system still exert a powerful influence over men's minds and prevent the informal system from developing into an effective and orderly method of regulation. The assumption that industry-wide agreements control industrial relations leads many companies to neglect their responsibility for their own personnel policies. Factory bargaining remains informal and fragmented, with many issues left to custom and practice. The unreality of industry-wide pay agreements leads to the use of incentive schemes and overtime payments for purposes quite different from those they were designed to serve.[7]

Who was to blame for this state of affairs?

If we follow our earlier principle, employers' organizations must be criticized first for a failure to adapt, but trade unions were also in line:

Trade unions have, like employers' associations and managers, helped to sustain the façade of industry-wide bargaining, but cannot bear primary responsibility for the decline in its effectiveness. However, certain features of trade union structure and government have helped to inflate the power of work groups and shop stewards.[8]

'Inflate' here is clearly an emotive word, for it has clearly been the policy of many British unions in recent years to increase the authority and influence of shop stewards and union members (see *The Organized Worker* in this series).

The Donovan Report has also been criticized for producing an analysis of industrial relations on the basis of the situation in a selected number of private sector industries, notably engineering, building and printing. Industry-wide bargaining in the mining industry, for example, would certainly not now be regarded as a 'façade' with the achievement – against substantial management opposition – of a national day wage structure, thus achieving a 'common rule' for the industry. The same could be said of bargaining arrangements in many other parts of the public sector. Trade union attempts to force employers to organize themselves for the purposes of collective bargaining with unions in the wages council sector have been described earlier. Nor are comparisons with the American system of homogeneous company bargaining particularly helpful, since the most notable feature of American industrial relations is the absence of collective bargaining arrangements for most employees.

Often discussions on 'collective bargaining structures' turn out on inspection to be discussions of the substantive results of the bargaining process. The 'decentralization of bargaining', for example, has obvious implications for the operation – or failure – of incomes policies:[9]

over the last thirty years there has been a decline in the extent to which industry-wide agreements determine actual pay. In 1938 there was only a modest 'gap' between the rates which they laid down for a normal working week and the average earnings which men actually received. By 1967 the two sets of figures had moved far apart . . . the tables record a remarkable transfer of authority in collective bargaining in this group of industries. Before the war it was generally assumed that industry-wide agreements could provide almost all the joint regulation that was needed, leaving only minor issues to be settled by individual managers. Today the consequences of bargaining within the factory can be more momentous than those of industry-wide agreements.[10]

Other Developments

Three other developments have affected and are likely to affect the form of bargaining units: the growth of shop steward combine committees in multi-union plants and companies; the impact of planning on bargaining; and the growth of Government intervention.

SHOP STEWARD COMBINE COMMITTEES

This development is very much part of the 'informal system'. In many work-places in which there is more than one union with negotiating rights, shop stewards' committees have been formed which are often made up of the convenors of the different unions. In large companies, such committees may send representatives to an overall combine committee set up for the company. There may also be formal industry-wide committees formed by individual unions. Also, occasionally, a negotiating committee may be formed with representatives from many unions so that one company or industry can deal with the problem of the multi-union structure. Convenors can be included in this unit, as they are in the Ford National Joint Negotiating Committee.

The Donovan Commission had recommended 'factory-wide agreements' as the remedy for the disorder caused by the conflict between the formal and informal systems. The Labour Government's White Paper 'In Place of Strife' in 1969 proposed a register of the collective agreements of those three hundred companies which had a labour force of over five thousand. The TUC conferences, after the publication of the Donovan Report, raised, in particular, the question of the relationship between multi-union committees in large plants and companies and the national and district officials responsible for the main union negotiations. Various reports of the Commission on Industrial Relations on the problems of specific companies generally included advice that employers should formulate company-wide policies and joint works committees should be established to cover all matters requiring negotiation or consultation. This implied that unions had to reorganize themselves to work together for bargaining purposes on a company and even a site basis.

By 1975 only fourteen out of 150 large UK companies had 'recognized' combine committees, and within federated employers' firms management has shown little interest in recognizing them. There are problems in any case when combine committees have no organizational status in the trade unions' formal bargaining process; attempts to set up bargaining positions can be bedevilled by the lack of communication and procedural routes across the system. Here is an example of this from a conference report to the Vickers Combine Committee in July 1975.

The attempt by the Vickers Board to introduce a new pension scheme throughout the Group, provides a graphic illustration of my general argument. The new proposals were put out in Vickers factories in May 1974. The Barrow Confederation District Committee asked the National Confederation in a letter before that body at their meeting on 24th June 1974 to arrange national discussions with Vickers to improve the pension proposals. The Confederation then asked the Districts containing Vickers establishments their views on the matter and at the National meeting held on the 8th of August the District replies indicated that a meeting with Vickers at national level was what they wanted. The Confederation Executive then decided to ask each Union concerned what they desired on the matter. On the 17th of October the Confederation General Secretary reported on the replies from the Unions and, despite the AUEW Executive pressing for a meeting of works representatives with Vickers and the views of the Districts wanting a meeting, the matter was noted and to date there has been no approach by the shop floor national Unions to Vickers for a meeting. The Vickers Combine Committee as well as writing to the company direct for a meeting have also expressed to the national unions their desire for such a meeting to take place but in both cases at present with no result.

There can be problems too in the relations between combine committees and separate plant stewards' committees, as this comment by the Lucas Aerospace Combine Committee reveals.

We think at the moment that we are the only effective permanent combine committee in the country. Such a committee needs reliable lines of communication with the autonomous shop stewards' committees, and it must be based on mutual trust. You only develop this trust through joint struggle. There were some problems at first – one or two of the autonomous committees had justifiable fears about whether a combine committee might not be an elite, one or two others thought it might take some of the power away from themselves. Our activity is always two-way: each autonomous committee has one vote on the combine committee, irrespective of the number of people they represent. They all have a share in working out joint decisions which are recommended back to be applied in all the plants.

In these variations in the form of bargaining units, unions are often trying to respond to the actions of employers who deliberately may seek to divide and conquer by negotiating separately with workers from different occupations, departments and plants. The most serious of the trade unions' difficulties here is demonstrating the importance of unity in the face of these practices, and creating the organization to give effect to this unity.

PLANNING AND BARGAINING

This is a further factor to be considered when looking at the formal ways in which employers and workers organize themselves for bargaining purposes. When the Donovan Commission was examining the 'myth' of formal industry-wide bargaining, the new structure of little Neddies and ITBs was being erected *on an industrial basis*. But since then the problems of defining what is an 'industry' have grown more rather than less acute. The largest firms are growing larger, and vertical integration from raw materials to the marketing of finished products is proceeding at the same time as the development of horizontal conglomerates. A typical firm might plan its product over a span of half a dozen of the subdivisions of the Standard Industrial classification.

Technological change has compounded this process. If EMI develops its research in the field of high energy detection for military and other applications to produce an X-ray 'body scanner', to what industry is it attributable? If Unilever develops a new computerized word-processing system to deal with its own administrative problems, and then markets it as a software package? Clearly in these examples what is relevant to planning discussions is the company as an innovator. Hence the emergence of the concept of the unions making 'planning agreements' with the major firms is more and more significant to the economy.

Table 6: Share of Largest Firms in Net Output (per cent)

	1935	1958	1963	1968
50 firms	14·9	24·7	27·9	32·4
100 firms	24·0	32·2	37·4	42·0
200 firms	n.a.	41·0	47·9	52·5
Share of Largest Firms in Employment (per cent)				
50 firms	15·0	21·2	24·3	29·4
100 firms	22·0	27·7	32·6	37·8
200 firms	28·0	35·5	42·0	47·1

Source: *Lloyds Bank Review*, October 1974

If we add to planning agreements the legislation on disclosure of information in the Employment Protection Act, the new arrangements for statistics from the *New Earnings Survey* to be published for certain large companies, and the current debate on worker representation on supervisory and management boards, the effect is a dramatic new emphasis on trade union organization on a company basis. The significance of these changes should not be underestimated, nor should the problems they pose for trade unions. The trade union movement has national and regional objectives, but increasingly the industrial strategy to achieve them will depend on action at company level.

THE GROWTH OF GOVERNMENT INTERVENTION

As J. E. Mortimer's essay reveals (pp. 188–208), Government intervention and planning is affecting the framework of those collective bargaining units which have been established so far. For example, the TUC became a sort of 'bargaining unit' when it 'negotiated' with the Government the 1974 'Social Contract' and the 1975 £6 limit. Similarly, over prices, the CBI has been drawn into the framework. As Government intervention increases, this 'macro-bargaining' clearly becomes much more important to workplace trade unionists.

It is always, therefore, particularly necessary to examine the motives of advocates of collective bargaining reforms. For unions, an important factor is still the achievement of the 'common rule', which now is not just the fixing of basic rates of wages, but the standardization of best practice across an industry. The real pressure to achieve this kind of objective will increasingly not be directed towards achieving formal changes in bargaining structure – these as we have seen are dependent on the capacity of employers to organize themselves – but towards developing the skills, knowledge and awareness of full-time and lay trade union officers, and the services available to them in achieving their objectives. This in itself will generate faster development in the joint regulation of British industry.

The challenge posed by trends towards participation and industrial democracy, towards successive social contracts and incomes policies, towards involvement in health and safety policies, towards facing multinational companies, demand an imaginative response from the unions.

Notes

1. HMSO, 1961, p. 21.
2. *Industrial Relations Handbook*, p. 21.
3. *Royal Commission on Trade Unions and Employers' Associations*, para. 22.
4. Clegg, H. A., *The System of Industrial Relations in Great Britain* (Blackwell, 1970), p. 223.
5. TUC, *Good Industrial Relations: A Guide to Negotiators* (TUC, 1971), pp. 28–9.
6. Para. 74.
7. Para. 149.
8. Para. 1016.
9. See Clegg, H. A., *How to Run An Incomes Policy* (Heinemann, 1971).
10. Para. 57.

Key Management Institutions
by Geoffrey Woodcock*

Within the bargaining framework, employers have developed their institutional forms, some of which may be in reaction to union structures. This essay describes some of the major national organizations which have emerged and their historical development: Chambers of Commerce, the Confederation of British Industry, trade associations, combined associations. Detailed examples are provided of the structure and workings of the CBI and the Engineering Employers' Federation. The essay concludes with reflections and theories about these institutions and an assessment of their power and influence.

This information should be helpful to trade unionists, but they will also need to know the particular character of their own plant, company and industry's employer, who may either have little or no connection with other employers' organizations, or if he has, may pay little attention to their advice or their plans.

There are very few accounts of the bargaining strategies or internal bargaining structure of private companies, though we may have more with fuller disclosure of information in the future. One of the books in the series, *Information at Work* by Michael Barratt Brown, should help trade unionists to find out more.

They may then go on to find out too about the links which employers have, not just with the national organizations mentioned, but between each other, across national and political frontiers, in cartels, monopolies, oligopolies, and through the maze of interconnections. It is interesting to note the contrast which may exist between a divided trade union movement inside a firm, an industry, a country or an international unit,

*The writer wishes to acknowledge the assistance received from his colleague, Bob Houlton, the officials of employers' associations, in particular the Engineering Employers' Federation and a number of its constituent associations, the Liverpool office of the CBI, the Merseyside Chamber of Commerce and Industry, and the Management and Supervisory Studies Division of the St Helens College of Technology.

when 'United we stand' might be thought to govern union actions, and the employer who is much more conscious of organization, although he might in fact be expected to be governed by competition and divisiveness. Ernie Johnston refers to this solidarity of employers in his book in this series, *Industrial Action* (p. 83). (Eds.)

Introduction

John Jackson is a manager in a medium-sized manufacturing company in the Midlands. The convenor and shop steward know him quite well from their encounters over the negotiating table and from informal meetings. They feel that they have him weighed up and they keep an eye on him as he moves around the factory. But there is a side to John Jackson's life as a manager that rank-and-file trade unionists rarely, if ever, see. Mr Jackson is involved in a number of employer and management organizations which exist to protect and advance his interests and those of the company. In their own way these organizations are as important as trade unions. Since they help to mould our industrial society, it is vital for trade unionists and industrial tutors to understand how they work and what they do.

TYPES OF ORGANIZATION

What kind of organization is John Jackson involved in outside the factory? Over a period of two months he will probably attend meetings as a company representative at the local Chamber of Commerce, the Confederation of British Industry, an employers' association and a trade association. On his own behalf he may also attend meetings of the British Institute of Management and the Institute of Personnel Management.

These organizations elect representatives and delegates to a wide number of other organizatons. So John Jackson may be a representative on a whole network of bodies, as Figure 20 (p. 162) indicates.

WHY DO THESE ORGANIZATIONS EXIST?

There is no single simple answer to this question, but three hard-headed business reasons stand out. First, there is always a need for accurate information. Second, companies need to defend their interests. Third, companies have interests in common, so they combine together to promote their interests. Let us look at these reasons in more detail.

F

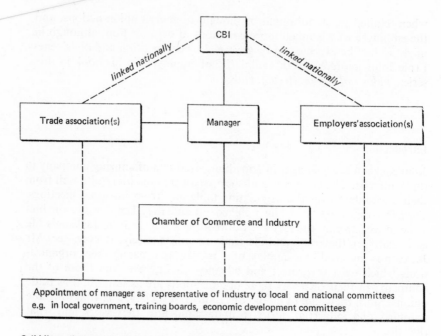

Solid line : direct link between manager and organization
Dotted line: links through and between organizations

Figure 20

Information

Management organizations provide information on a range of business matters, for instance, advice and briefing documents on the latest legislation, international affairs affecting industry, the interpretation of an industrial relations agreement, raw material fluctuations, the movement of costs in an industry and export opportunities.

Defence

This particularly applies to industrial relations, which is usually the responsibility of an employers' association, through which financial and organizational assistance is provided to resist 'unacceptable' wage claims or changes in working conditions. Such organizations also send representatives to the local authority or the Government when a company or industry is threatened by changes in, say, investment, or regional or industrial policy.

Promotion

Management organizations act as interest or pressure groups in order to promote companies, an area of employment or a sector of industry. They will arrange stands at exhibitions where literature is displayed to encourage recruitment and public relations techniques are used.

As an effective manager, our John Jackson serves his firm's interests by plugging into this network of management institutions. Through them he acquires valuable intelligence to assist internal decision making and planning. By encouraging these outside relationships he makes useful contacts with customers, suppliers, rivals and the local business and political establishment.

This essay describes the development, organization and activities of some management institutions and assesses their place within the industrial relations system and in our society.

The Major Management and Employers' Institutions

CHAMBERS OF COMMERCE

Local Chambers of Commerce represent the manufacturing, finance and service industries in their community. They are the most broadly-based organization of those which managers attend as representatives. Chambers of Commerce[1] are best known for promoting overseas trade for their locality and for helping members with export and other local trade matters. They are linked together nationally through the Association of British Chambers of Commerce. Despite this they carry less weight in national than in local affairs.

THE CONFEDERATION OF BRITISH INDUSTRY

The second association of industries is the CBI. Although the CBI has a well-developed regional structure, it operates very much as a national organization, so that it is called the TUC of manufacturing industry. There is a considerable dual membership of the CBI and Chambers of Commerce and their operations also overlap. For these reasons, Governments have maintained that it would be tidier to have one organization to represent all private and public enterprises. But, as with trade union rationalization, such reforms take a long time to bring about.[2]

The CBI was itself the product of the merger in 1965 between the British Employers' Confederation, the Federation of British Industries and the National Association of British Manufacturers. The two major partners, the FBI and the BEC, had agreed in principle to the merger as long ago as 1946.

These organizations have different areas of influence. Chambers of Commerce may represent to the local authority the interests of a local firm on a variety of issues such as development area status, housing for key workers, improving road access, special sewage or waste disposal facilities, or new industrial training courses at the local technical college.

On the other hand, it would be the CBI that would raise with the Government the case for an increase in investment allowances, a change in the taxation of 'expenses', or an anti-dumping tariff.

TRADE ASSOCIATIONS

Trade associations specialize in the trading interests of companies. They may deal with technical matters, legal questions, advice on costing and estimating, sales promotion and exhibitions, education and training and the public relations of the industry. In the engineering sector, for example, there are about seventy trade associations which include the Engineering Industries' Association, the Society of Motor Manufacturers and Traders and the Ironfounders' National Federation.

EMPLOYERS' ASSOCIATIONS

Employers' associations are concerned mainly with the labour relations of their members. W. E. J. McCarthy (now Lord McCarthy), Director of Research on the Donovan Commission, defined employers' associations as: 'organisations of employers of labour which seek to assist, influence or control the industrial relations decisions of member firms; we are not concerned with organisations who are *only* engaged in trading and commercial activities.'[3]

There are many different sorts of employers' associations.[4] For example, the Donovan Commission received written evidence from seventy employers' associations ranging from the CBI, the Engineering Employers' Federation, the Shipbuilding Employers' Federation and the National Federation of Building Trades Employers, on one hand, to the Federation of Master Organ Builders, the National Federation of Master Window Cleaners and the Stourbridge Crystal Glass Manufacturers' Association on the other. The evidence presented to McCarthy and Munns[5] shows that not only were these organizations' size and complexity markedly different, but so were their scope and influence, a 'result of the differing needs and preferences of the firms that belong to these associations'.

Sometimes all the members want is a common forum where views and experiences of industrial relations problems may be shared. In other cases there is a desire for a range of specialist services, including the operation of a disputes procedure and the settlement, at national level, of what are in effect minimum wage levels for the industry. Very occasionally there is a wish among member firms to go further than this, i.e. to develop an organisation which takes effective joint action to solve common problems, including the negotiation of effective rates of pay that operate throughout the industry.[6]

COMBINED ORGANIZATIONS

The Donovan Report noted that most of the organizations (as distinct from companies) affiliated to the CBI were combined organizations. 'Of the 108 organizations in membership of the CBI, 75 combine the functions of employers' associations.'[7] The *Report* noted that the number of combined organizations was growing, citing the examples of bodies representing the chemicals, rubber manufacturing, and shipbuilding and ship-repairing industries. The *Report* strongly backed combined organizations because it was unrealistic to separate 'industrial relations from commercial matters'.

When a manager takes part in the affairs of these institutions, which might broadly be categorized as 'employer bodies', he is performing his role as a representative of his *firm's interest*. We will now discuss *management organizations* which serve *managers' individual or career interests*. These may be described as 'qualifying' or 'professional' institutions.

MANAGEMENT ORGANIZATIONS

Most of these are concerned with the training and professional accreditation of managers. Sometimes training is acquired on the job, through an apprenticeship, being articled, or as a trainee in combination with 'sandwich courses', block or day release, evening classes, or correspondence courses. Examples are the Institute of Cost and Management Accountants and the Chartered Institute of Secretaries for administrators and company secretaries. Engineers qualify through examinations and after gaining practical experience become members of professional bodies such as the Institute of Mechanical Engineers. There are also specialist institutions such as the Institute of Marketing, the Institute of Work Study Practitioners, the Institute of Purchasing and Supply, the Institute of Transport.[8]

Some professional management institutions, like the Institute of Supervisory Management, provide a ladder up from the shop floor or office desk.

Another is the National Examinations Board in Supervisory Studies (NEBSS) which was established on the initiative of the Department of Education and Science in 1964. NEBSS operates by choosing an approved college, usually a technical college, through which it develops courses for supervisors. Supervisors who gain a Certificate in Supervisory Studies and holders of Ordinary National Certificates or Full Technological Certificates of the City and Guilds can take courses which will enable them to become members of bodies such as the Institution of Works Managers.

Most of these organizations use the word management in their title, for example the Institute of Administrative Management, the British Institute of Management or the Institute of Personnel Management. They award full membership only to those applicants who, as well as passing the examinations, have actually been senior managers for a specified period.

The British Institute of Management and the Institute of Personnel Management

The BIM is the largest general organization; there are over 50000 individual members and some 12500 organizations are company members. It organizes the usual branch activities and conferences, and publishes documents, papers and journals such as *Management Survey Reports, Management Information Sheets, Management Checklists,* the quarterly *Management Review and Digest* and the monthly *Management Today.*

The Institute of Personnel Management, with about 18000 members, plays an important role in management education and the formation of attitudes about the relations between management and unions. Academics see personnel managers as performing two roles in management. First, they diagnose problems. Second, they advise the other members of the management team and apply their knowledge of the behavioural or social sciences, particularly sociology and psychology, to industry. The IPM's aim (see its brochure) 'is to encourage and assist the development of personnel management by (i) spreading knowledge and information about its practices; (ii) promoting investigation and research; (iii) [it] establishes and maintains through training and other services high standards of qualification and performance.' Like the BIM it provides information, advisory and library services for its members and arranges national, regional and local branch conferences, courses and meetings. It also publishes books and leaflets, a monthly journal called *Personnel Management* and a *Digest* for members and subscribers.

The activities of the BIM and the IPM are similar in style and sometimes overlap since the BIM, as a general organization, includes in its functions personnel and industrial relations. They have the problem common to most voluntary organizations, which is that branch involvement is minimal. These qualifying or professional institutions also suffer another disadvantage when compared with employer bodies. Many of their members regard them purely as a means of progressing up the career ladder; this attitude is very similar to that of many members of trade unions. Branch activity is not usually part of the work life of a manager. Thus branches are under severe competition from other voluntary organizations which may have more relevance to a manager's career, such as the Masons, the Rotary Club or the Golf Club. Attendance at meetings of employer bodies, in contrast, is considered to be part of the work-load of a manager, being of more direct usefulness to the employer and to the manager in his role as an employee and not as an individual. It is important to note that the membership of all qualifying institutions is sought by *individuals* who are, or aim to be, managers.

Although many professional and management institutions can play an important part in influencing relationships between unions and management, the predominant organizations in this area are the employers' associations. We will therefore concentrate, like the Donovan Commission, on 'the largest single industry organisation of employers in the United Kingdom', namely the Engineering Employers' Federation, and the Confederation of British Industry, of which the EEF is a constituent member.

The Historical Development of Employers' Associations

Informal associations between employers, according to Adam Smith,[9] were common in the eighteenth century. As workers combined together to form trade unions during the Industrial Revolution they faced great difficulties and opposition. The employers counter-attacked by founding their own combinations, sometimes formally and sometimes informally.

These associations became more formalized during the nineteenth century in response to improvements in the organization and action of national trade unions. During the last decade of the nineteenth century and in the early years of the present century most of today's key employers' federations were created, including those in the building, engineering, printing, shipping and shipbuilding industries.

As a result of this union activity, particularly the aggressive 'new unionism',[10] some associations and federations held conferences with unions. By the start of the First World War procedures had been negotiated with the trade unions for dealing with disputes both locally and nationally.

The first combinations of engineering employers were usually temporary and based upon an industrial town or area. The crucial period for the development of the employers' organizations in the engineering industry was the period 1896–8 culminating in the 'great lock-out' which lasted from July 1897 to January 1898. The membership of the Employers' Federation of Engineering Associations grew from 180 to 702 firms as the result of this action.

The lock-out was a clear victory for the employers who dictated the terms of the 1898 settlement. It was also a victory for the Federation as an institution for it secured for itself a permanent role in industrial relations in engineering. It was a well-established and very tough negotiator. It confirmed its reputation in 1922 by another lock-out, lasting thirteen weeks, over the right to manage. Again the Federation was victorious and dictated the settlement, a restatement of the 1914 York Memorandum. This was a disputes procedure based on stages at works, local and national level. It became known as the 'rocky road to York', because it was there that disputes reached the national level, although they were often referred back to the local level where they should have been decided initially.

To this day the unions feel the status quo provisions[11] embodied in this agreement were accepted because of the unions' weakness. During the 1960s this felt injustice re-emerged as a prominent issue, with the procedure for resolving disputes, which had become clogged with cases during this period. Proposals for recasting the conference stages were proposed first by the EEF in 1967 and again in 1969. These negotiations eventually broke down, hampered, as Wigham[12] argues, by the political climate of 1970 – the Conservative victory and the preparations for the Industrial Relations Act in 1971. In September 1971 the Confederation of Shipbuilding and Engineering Unions gave three months' notice to end the procedure agreement for manual workers and the last Central Conference took place under the old arrangements at York in December 1971 when a record case list was completed.

Although a new clerical procedure agreement came into effect on 1 November 1973, it was not until March 1976 that a new 'procedure for the avoidance of disputes' was finally concluded with the manual unions. This provided for new domestic and external stages of procedure. The new agreement stated that 'in the event of any difference arising which cannot be immediately disposed of, then whatever practice or agreement existed prior to the difference shall continue to operate pending a settlement or until the agreed procedure has been exhausted.'

Martin Jukes QC (Director-General of the Federation, 1966–75) distinguishes three distinct phases in the development of the Federation.[13] These are the counter-attack phase, the negotiations and consensus phase and the dynamic phase. Historically the first two phases, as he himself admits, are not separate in time, but he does contend that in this inter-mingling 'it would be realistic to say that the former was more typical'. He considers that the conflicts of 1897–8 and 1922 illustrate 'that from thesis and antithesis emerges a synthesis'.[14]

The thesis of authoritarian management control is countered by an antithesis which may find its expression in different ways such as demands for joint control by trade unions, for demands for workers' control, for demands that frankly amount to industrial anarchy, but from this conflict of thesis and antithesis emerges the acceptance of the industrial system as a pluralistic system in which each has its place.

Jukes regards the negotiation and consensus phase as being in many ways 'the most characteristic of the operations of industrial federations'. He thinks that the little-known document written in 1927 for the EEF, 'Thirty Years of Industrial Conciliation', is significant, even in its choice of title. Its author points out that 'No credit appears to be given for the amount of conciliation that has taken place during the past years.'

The dynamic phase (a term taken from behavioural science) is seen as the increasingly important emphasis on the social sciences and innovation and experiment in industrial relations.

This analysis of the development of the EEF and other employers' associations may be criticized for its use of 'phases'. It is difficult to separate the 'counter-attack' phase from the negotiation and consensus phases, since at any moment the external conditions and personalities influence the dominance of one style to the detriment of the other. The later dynamic phase has become a further variable, and it too has had its cycle as the emergent ideology. In 1976 initiatives on labour matters tended once again to be in the hands of the Government and the EEF appeared to be entering into a period of internal consolidation and external defensiveness.

The Organizational Structure of Employers' Institutions

The outline structure of selected employers' associations (Figure 21, p. 170) provides a sketch of the arrangements within some industries in Britain. Because there is much diversity, the CBI itself and one of its major con-stituent members, the EEF, will be focused upon in more detail.

THE CBI

Any broad-based confederation of industrial and commercial interests will tend inevitably to be inflexible. It is likely to react ponderously and be lacking in innovation and enterprise. The image of an employers' cart-

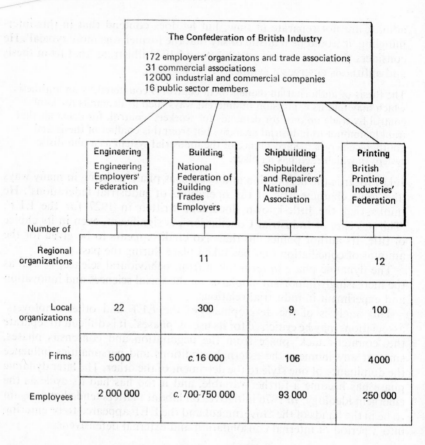

The Confederation of British Industry

172 employers' organizatons and trade associations
31 commercial associations
12000 industrial and commercial companies
16 public sector members

	Engineering	Building	Shipbuilding	Printing
	Engineering Employers' Federation	National Federation of Building Trades Employers	Shipbuilders' and Repairers' National Association	British Printing Industries' Federation
Number of Regional organizations		11		12
Local organizations	22	300	9	100
Firms	5000	c. 16 000	106	4000
Employees	2 000 000	c. 700-750 000	93 000	250 000

Figure 21:   An Outline Structure of Selected Employers' Associations [15]

horse to match Low's cartoon representation of the TUC becomes a real possibility.

The membership of the CBI includes corporate members like employers' associations and trade associations, as well as individual companies in manufacturing and transport. This means that there has to be wide representation on the governing body of the Confederation. In addition, the nationalized industries and commercial affiliates from banking and insurance have been encouraged to become involved in the CBI's activities. Therefore it is not surprising that the Governing Council of the CBI consists of over 400 members. Sir Ralph Bateman admits that before he became President he 'held the view that a Council of over 400 would inevitably be an unwieldly and ineffective body. Experience has demonstrated to me, however, just how sensitive a barometer of membership feeling it is.' Although the sole authority for policy-making remains with this Council and the standing committees which serve it, Sir Ralph created a President's Consultative Panel in July 1974 to advise him on his role as the elected head of the organization. The Council has thirty standing committees,[16] many with panels and sub-committees which provide involvement in the CBI's affairs for 'well over a thousand representatives of companies, trade associations and employers' organisations'. (In 1976 the TUC had a more compact General Council, and in order to keep its size down has until recently excluded from its membership representatives of certain unions such as ASTMS.)

The strength of the CBI lies in the member associations and larger companies and there is an inevitable bias towards London. In order to counteract this tendency the CBI has twelve regional councils consisting of 24–48 individuals elected by members in each region. These regional councils are serviced from ten regional offices, whose staff keep in touch with members locally, making up to a thousand visits each month to companies in their areas.

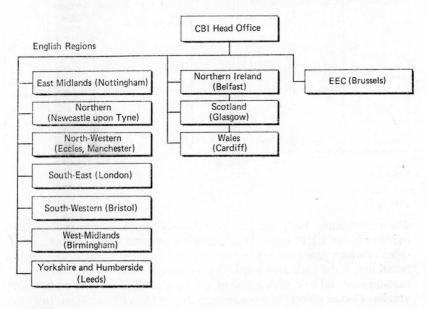

Figure 22

The head office has a permanent staff, consisting of a Director-General, three Deputy Directors-General, one of whom is responsible for Social Affairs, a Chief Economic Adviser, eight Directors and the Secretary. An organization chart of the CBI head office is shown below (Figure 23).

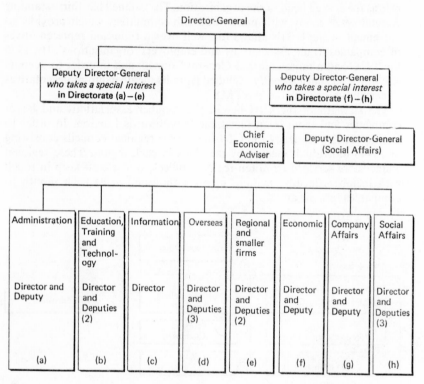

Figure 23

THE EEF

The coordinating body for employers' associations in the engineering industry is the EEF, which is a federation of autonomous associations, some of which guard their independence fiercely. Thus the basic organizational unit is the local area employers' association which employs either a part-time official or a wide range of specialist staff, depending on its size, and has elected officers and committees drawn from its members. In 1976 there were twenty-two associations affiliated to the Federation, which have a total of approximately 5000 members who between them employ about 2 million workers (about 60 per cent of the potential members in terms of numbers employed). The EEF's evidence to the Royal Commission stated that the 'associations are organisationally virtually autonomous but . . . no step affecting the objects or interests of the Federation shall be taken by any association without previous consultation with the Management Board of the Federation.'

The EEF is managed by a General Council which consists of ex-officio members (office-bearers, etc.) and elected members; executive action is taken by the Council through a Management Board which meets monthly. The election of members to the General Council has traditionally been based on each association's wage bill. Until 1975 the members of the Management Board were appointed by the General Council in numbers related to the nine federated regions and their wage bills, with a maximum from any region of four, but the 1975 changes in the constitution provide for direct representation from associations. Each region formerly had a Regional Committee which had little executive power, but if required these may now continue to act on an ad-hoc basis as a coordinating and consultative body between the associations within each region. There are many other committees, which are shown on Figure 24 (p. 174).

The structure of the Federation primarily consists of the local association committees from which are elected the General Council and the Management Board with its sub-committees.

It is interesting to note the changes since the chart was published in 1965. By 1974 the number of member firms had increased from 4500 to 5000 and the number employed was nearer 2 million than $1\frac{1}{2}$ million. During this decade the local associations were encouraged to combine resources and have been reduced to twenty-two from thirty-nine. This resulted in the number of Regional Committees being reduced from eleven to nine even before the 1975 changes. The number of standing committees has remained static; or only their titles have changed.

The Director-General is appointed by the General Council. He is responsible for the appointment of headquarters' staff, apart from the two senior Directors, whose appointments are made by the Management Board, of which the Director-General is a member. Martin Jukes regularized certain advisory groups and added a group to which the chief labour relations managers from about thirty of the largest members are invited.[18] The structure of the staff organization at headquarters was published for the first time in the 1968/69 Annual Report. Before this time the elected officers and the Director appear to have laid little emphasis on the internal organization of the EEF's 'civil service' departments, apart from circular letters announcing new appointments and responsibilities.

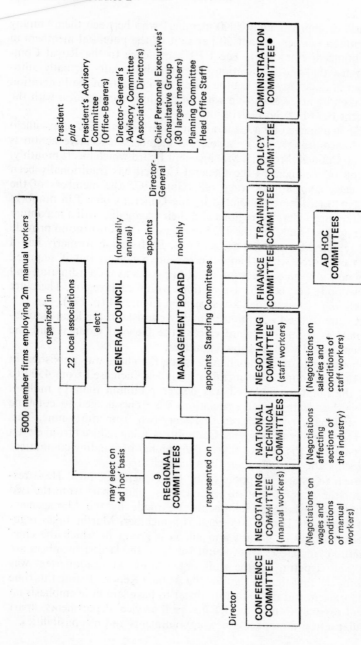

President
plus
President's Advisory
Committee
(Office-Bearers)

Director-General's
Advisory Committee
(Association Directors)

Chief Personnel Executives'
Consultative Group
(30 largest members)

Planning Committee
(Head Office Staff)

5000 member firms employing 2m manual workers

organized in

22 local associations

elect

GENERAL COUNCIL

(normally annual)

appoints

Director-General

MANAGEMENT BOARD

monthly

appoints Standing Committees

may elect on
'ad hoc' basis

9
REGIONAL
COMMITTEES

represented on

Director

CONFERENCE
COMMITTEE

NEGOTIATING
COMMITTEE
(manual workers)

(Negotiations on
wages and
conditions
of manual
workers)

NATIONAL
TECHNICAL
COMMITTEES

(Negotiations
affecting
sections of
the industry)

NEGOTIATING
COMMITTEE
(staff workers)

(Negotiations on
salaries and
conditions of
staff workers)

FINANCE
COMMITTEE

TRAINING
COMMITTEE

POLICY
COMMITTEE

ADMINISTRATION
COMMITTEE ●

AD HOC
COMMITTEES

● This committee has fallen into disuse.

+ There is also a special organizational structure to cover the outside erection contracts of constructional engineering companies.

Figure 24: The Organization of the Engineering Employers' Federation[17]

Administration before 1967 was largely in the hands of the Secretary. The narrowness of the organization is reminiscent of the office structure of a local association or trade union office, and little regard has been given to the larger scale of the operations and to the potentially wider sphere of activities.

The change to a flatter staff structure took place as the result of external suggestions, a consultant's recommendation and the appointment of two new directors, one in charge of a Research Department, and the other in charge of Advisory Services. The Federation staff organization in January 1975 is shown below (Figure 25).

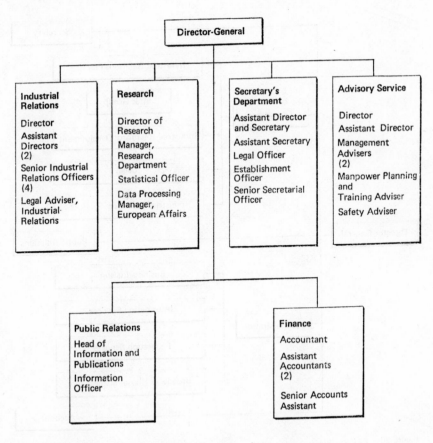

Figure 25: EEF Staff Organization, 1967-75

The dynamic phase described earlier by Martin Jukes is reflected in the organizational structure of the Federation from 1967 to 1975 with its emphasis on the innovatory departments of research and advisory services as well as the traditional negotiating and administrative functions. With the retirement of Martin Jukes and the appointment in 1975 of a former management consultant, Anthony Frodsham, as the new Director-General, a period of consolidation, even retrenchment, seems likely. There is evidence of this in the 1976 management structure of the Federation's headquarters staff (Figure 26 below).

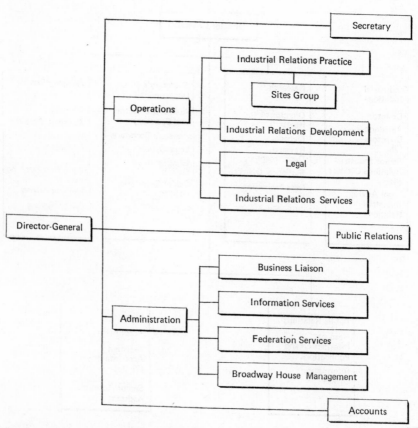

Figure 26: EEF Staff Organization, 1976

It may be noted that the research and advisory services departments no longer exist and that most of their various sections, such as training, safety and statistics, have been regrouped with changed titles under directors in charge of operations and administration. Reference has already been made to the emerging mood influencing internal consolidation in the Federation. It appears that some of the reforms and activities which will be described in the next section have yet to take firm root.

The Activities of Management Institutions and Their Methods of Operation

The services offered by management institutions vary a great deal in quality and comprehensiveness. Some larger professional bodies provide, for example, information, a library, educational courses and publishing. Many smaller ones merely provide a means of gaining a qualification with perhaps a newsletter or magazine and some attempts at branch activities. The traditional professions focus mainly upon the technical aspects of their work. It is primarily the specifically management institutions which are devoted to the formation and changing of management attitudes and the information and ideologies upon which these are based. Managers acquire the most effective corporate experience perhaps in the regional or national conferences, when individuals receive group support. Foremost in this sphere is the large annual conference held at Harrogate by the Institute of Personnel Management. This large-scale event run by a professional institution is most relevant to the bargaining context since it brings together leading academics, trade unionists and practitioners in this field.

The range of activities of employers' associations was investigated for the Donovan Royal Commission by V. G. Munns, and the findings were published in Research Paper No. 7.[19] Munns placed these into categories called 'industrial relations' and 'other main activity'. The industrial relations activities he grouped into: '(1) The representation of employers' interests in dealing with trade unions, including the negotiation of wages and conditions of employment, and the handling of disputes between employers and workers'. (para. 24) This category includes the negotiation of national and local wage rates and other conditions of employment, such as holidays and 'fringe benefits' for both manual and staff workers and the servicing of disputes informally and formally through agreed disputes procedures.

He also included in the industrial relations category '(2) Assistance to members in dealing with their own management/labour problems' (para. 24). Under this heading, he gives such activities as contacts with union officials on behalf of members and general advice and assistance on industrial relations matters which might include a certain amount of consultancy.

The other main activities performed by employers' organizations described by Munns are, for example, the important function of the representation of employers' interests to Government; the provision of information services to members by, for example, meetings or circulars; the collection of statistics and information; assistance in manpower matters (help with recruitment and selection, training, education, safety, health and welfare and with manpower planning problems such as are associated with labour supply and demand and its efficient use).

The examination of the organizational structures of the CBI and EEF provides a guide to their activities.

The CBI, like the TUC, has no formal control over its members. It can only advise and, at most, 'lean on' its members.[20] Many of its activities are necessarily limited to coordinating members' interests and representing these nationally and internationally. Ideally, just as it is possible for a Government to obtain organized labour's view from the TUC on a proposal, it should be possible to seek industry's view from the CBI. CBI departments provide support for the committees and the briefings for the CBI's membership of the National Economic Development Council, which usually meets under the chairmanship of the Prime Minister. Thus the CBI responds to Government initiatives and also, through its panels and committees, suggests changes in policy and legislation.

The activities of employers' associations do not fit in with the public's image, which is still largely derived from a reflection of its historical development purely as a defensive group formed as a means of balancing the growing power of the trade unions. Those connected with the engineering industry, however, stress that they observed or experienced during the late 1960s what they believed to be an attempt to initiate a new phase in industrial relations. This was predicted by Arthur Marsh when he wrote about the EEF: 'It is to be expected that younger, active managements and officials should attempt, in their own minds, to recast the future of the Federation. Associations are moving, slowly in some cases and more rapidly in others, to the view that they ought to adopt a more positive role in educating their members in management problems and in the issues involved in public questions. . . .'[21]

The first example of this was regarded to be the 1964 four-year 'package deal'. This was proposed by the EEF itself and was seen as the first concrete evidence to indicate that the employers were assuming responsibility for initiating change. Martin Jukes described this new outlook of employers' associations as the 'dynamic phase of industrial relations'.[22]

The factors which seem to have brought about this change of attitude were a combination of circumstances which acted as catalysts to accelerate the prevailing mood in some employers' groups which Marsh described in the quotation above. First, there was the Government's decision to constitute a Royal Commission on Trade Unions and Employers' Associations which encouraged self-examination and required evidence for the Commission. It was also stimulated by the Research Papers.

Second, there was the stimulus of the prices and incomes policy of the mid-1960s, when the Government and the Prices and Incomes Board were insisting that wage increases above the norm be based on equivalent savings in costs by changes in working practices and increased productivity, and that across the board annual national wage settlements should be replaced by local or plant bargaining.

Third, the personal influence of the office-bearers and officials of the EEF was most important. Since 1963, primarily through the initiative of a President, Sir Stephen Brown,[23] the organization has appointed a reforming Director-General and has made fundamental changes in its organizational structure and created research and advisory departments.

Although many of V. G. Munn's comments in the Research Paper referred to apply to employers' associations in general, a careful study of his text provides specific examples of the activities of Engineering Employers' Associations or of Federation Headquarters which can be related directly to EEF functions. For instance, whilst the activities of employers' associations, such as the EEF, do not fully protect their members from the effects of strike action, Munns regards their claim that they reduce its extent as justified. Further, he maintains that 'they are also trying to improve the failings of their own members in management techniques and the handling of industrial relations problems; and the importance of this consultancy and advisory function towards its own membership is increasing relatively to corporate action in defence of its members against organised labour.'

Consultancy is seen as the natural way to help members, who since they are voluntary cannot normally be subjected to more than the minimum of control. Work study and management consultancy services have evolved to meet the requirements of members in their efforts to improve productivity. For instance, the West of England Engineering and Allied Employers' Association has provided facilities for some years for the training of management and supervisory staff in work study, 'so that piecework prices can be negotiated on a sounder basis or measured day-work introduced'. This sort of service has been extended by some of the larger associations or regions.

In addition, indirect action 'designed to improve the state of industrial relations' has been taken by a number of associations. Munns considers that this 'is likely to be more effective in the long term than attempts to deal with individual strike situations'.[24] Munns describes the EEF's function in the engineering industry as that of 'stimulating the consideration of problems and providing support on request'. Evidence of this was shown by the expansion of the Federation's Statistical Department under a newly appointed Research Director in 1969 and in the enquiries on wage drift, planning of manpower resources and research into methods of productivity bargaining and payment systems.

There is a danger of taking a snapshot of an organization at any one point in time, since organizations evolve as the result of contact with the wider social and economic environment. In addition, there is a limit to how much change and initiation by the leadership is acceptable to members. Some employers believed that the new-fangled activities described above were quite unnecessary, while others regarded them as an opportunity to drag some reactionary employers into the twentieth century. Perhaps these differences of perspective on the role of the EEF have contributed to the current period of consolidation, which gives some members time to adopt to the 'cultural shock' of this transition, though it might be argued that the 1976 organizational changes provide evidence not only of consolidation and retrenchment but even of reaction and regression to the former dominant attitudes of defensiveness.

The full range of activities of the EEF is similar to those described in general for employers' associations by Munns. The objects of the EEF are laid down in its consitution under nine headings which may be classified into two categories of industrial relations activities: collective bargaining and assistance and advice to members. Collective bargaining involves the representation of employers' interests in dealing with trade unions, including the negotiation of wages and conditions of employment of both manual and staff employees, and the handling of disputes between employers and workers by the use of a mutually agreed set of disputes procedures and by informal contacts and representations.

In practical terms the assistance and advice may first of all be obtained from the local association officials, who attempt to solve individual cases. This is often in the form of informal contact by telephone and may include interpretation of national agreements with the unions, or of Government legislation on such matters as redundancy payments, industrial safety, training, aspects of 'social contracts' or forms of 'incomes policy'. In the larger associations specialized consultancy or management education may be provided. The local official or specialist may consult with Federation Headquarters. This may result in further action such as representation to the Government or bodies such as the Industrial Training

Boards. In addition, the local association will have access to various information, computer and statistical services, and research, manpower and productivity specialists.

Both the national negotiations and the disputes procedures as performed in recent years have been subjected to severe criticism from many quarters, including the Royal Commission, the unions and the employers themselves. Reference has already been made to the fact that the disputes procedure for manual workers was under suspension from 1971 to 1976. The normal procedure was that the Association's Industrial Relations Officers provided the negotiating expertise vis-à-vis the appropriate Union Secretary at the first two stages of works and local conferences. These have now been replaced by the external conference stage. The arrangements for the final stage, of the monthly Central Conferences – for manual workers at York and for staff workers at London – were made by headquarters staff, who organized the meeting of employers' panels and unions' national officials in 'courts'. As has already been mentioned, criticisms have usually been levelled at the length of time of the operation of the 'procedure' and also at the status quo provisions involving managerial prerogatives, which it is alleged were agreed by the unions in 1922 'after a national defeat at the hands of the employers'.

The new agreement for manual workers reflects this dissatisfaction since it provides that, unless there are questions concerning the interpretation or application of a national agreement, the procedure shall be regarded as being exhausted at the external conference stage. The monthly York rituals will thus be replaced by discussions on national agreements normally 'within seven working days' and by 'an agreed forum with representatives of the Federation and the Confederation which will meet from time to time as required to consider matters of mutual concern to the parties' (quotations from the actual agreement).

In describing and assessing the activities and operations of management institutions the following questions arise. How representative are such bodies of their constituents or potential constituents? How effective are they in achieving their objectives? What is their future? The final section of this essay will attempt to assess their power and influence.

An Assessment of Power and Influence

The professional bodies have traditionally regarded pressure group activity, as such, to be not the 'done thing'! Sufficient influence has generally derived from the status of the profession and the high regard attached to its leading members by the establishment. It is perhaps an indication that these attitudes have become outmoded and ineffective that Sir Fred Catherwood, Chairman of the BIM from 1974, initiated the 'professional forum'. This originated from the ad hoc quarterly meetings of the presidents of the larger professional institutic ns. The planned forum would be a body 'which comprehends all the professions, where different disciplines can meet and argue and in which final conclusions can be debated widely and publicly with the authority which only such a comprehensive body can give'.[25]

In April 1975 Sir Fred underlined the need for a cohesive professional voice in Britain: 'A trade union on strike has the backing of the whole trades union movement and the support of a hundred years of trades union tradition. There is no comparable body for the p ofessions. Our backing can only come from the service to society. W e cannot solve our own problems at the expense of society. We can only look after ourselves as an incidental result of making gains for all.'[26]

It is too early to evaluate the potential of this loose amalgam of professions. Much will depend on its ability to demonstrate its usefulness. It is possible that the BIM itself will attempt to assume this role, since at the time of going to press a General Meeting of BIM members was being asked to approve an additional representative role for the BIM which would put into effect the resolution passed at the 1976 BIM National Convention which called upon the Institute to 'organize itself to enable direct consultation to take place with the Government on all matters affecting managers before legislation is put into effect', and 'to establish practical methods by which responsible interests . . . may consult with and discover the views of professional management . . .' There is far more evidence upon which to draw in assessing the power and influence of employer bodies. In so doing, it is tempting to draw direct analogies between the TUC and the CBI in their relationships with the Labour and Conservative parties, respectively, and Governments formed by these parties. This should be resisted since the link between the CBI and political parties is more tenuous. The official view was elaborated in the internal document, 'The CBI's Role and Purpose', in which it was stated that: 'Though much of what the CBI does and advocates has important political implications it is non-party political. Its job is to speak up for its members' interests; it will welcome support for those interests from any quarter.'

The document elaborates upon the various priorities of the CBI's purposes, which are:

(i) to uphold the market system and the profit motive that sustains it.
(ii) to bring home to the public at large that no other system offers comparable opportunities for growth with such freedom of choice and action for the individual.

(iii) to oppose further encroachment on the private sector wherever this is inconsistent with the proper functioning of the market system.

(iv) to press for greater freedom from Government interference for the existing nationalised sector and permit its proper commercial development. . . .

These are statements which would hardly be regarded as exactly in the mainstream of socialist or radical thinking, and, although the CBI is non-political, it follows that members of the Conservative party are more likely to be in harmony with such priorities. The broad composition of the CBI, representing the whole of British industry including, at present, all the nationalized industries apart from the Post Office, gives rise to possible difficulties in political relationships and influence; it may, however, provide an entrée to influence in other political parties. In describing its role the CBI believes that: 'Although the conditions in which public sector corporations operate are often different in certain respects, the efficient operation of nationalised industry is of vital importance to the private sector, and, differences of structure and philosophy apart, there are many areas where their interests are interrelated.' It is in this search for common ground to accommodate the public sector that the CBI, which describes itself as 'the champion of all that is best in modern capitalism', is in difficulty.

The impression recently has been that Government influence and 'interference' have primarily been directed at the trade unions, but an examination of employers' organizations and discussion with officials and members provides evidence of the same activity on the other side of industry. Not only are there Acts of Parliament such as the Trade Union and Labour Relations Act, the Health and Safety at Work Act, together with the employment protection and industry legislation, but there are also the government agencies such as the Advisory, Conciliation and Arbitration Service and the Price Commission.

The members believe that the degree to which employers' bodies are allowed freedom to operate and react to external influences and internal pressures, is the key to their effectiveness. With the extension of plant bargaining, the smaller members, in particular, need to feel the support of the employers' associations in the exercise of any power they may have over the unions. There is the traditional fear of being 'picked off' in a dispute. The EEF has received considerable publicity about its Indemnity Fund which provides financial help to firms during strikes.

The Donovan Report believed that employers' associations could still have an important role in giving advice on negotiation, in training and information services, and in representing their members' interests to Government departments. The Report is remembered primarily for its recommendations on reforms in collective bargaining and in trade union organization, but it did also point out the need for change in employers' associations. It suggested that the functions of employers' and trade associations should be combined. It encouraged the amalgamation of smaller associations, and specifically suggested certain structural and representational changes within the EEF.

Since then much has been written about the widening role of employers' associations in general and the EEF in particular. A new dynamic era was promised, and in a comprehensive range of services and activities the future would be secure. Yet paradoxically the return to a degree of defensiveness in the face of the external conditions and internal pressure already described has assured the immediate future of employers' associations. The medium-sized and smaller members specifically need the guidance of experts in the complexities of labour relations legislation. The larger members still value the representative functions of employers' associations in their relationships with Governments. The view of outside commentators is that the structure of management institutions is every bit as untidy as union structure. There is of course some dual membership between qualifying institutions and trade unions; chartered engineers and chemists often also belong to white-collar unions such as ASTMS or IPCS. But perhaps the greatest complexity is within the membership of employer bodies. Many companies belong to at least one trade association (there are sixteen in the foundry industry sector of engineering alone), perhaps the local Chamber of Commerce and Industry, the CBI and corporate membership of the BIM, and in addition may belong to one or more employers' associations to cover industrial relations.

It would require a fresh start to achieve some semblance of order in the demarcation of employer bodies. Only slow progress should be expected in rationalization since many associations are every bit as proud of their independence and traditions as some of the smaller unions. They are generally wary of take-overs sponsored by head offices and they have to weigh the advantages of independence and specialization against efficiency and the possible lack of responsiveness to smaller members.

There has always been some controversy in employers' bodies about the power and influence of the smaller members compared with the large corporations. In the CBI, for example, the smaller members have been given special status by the formation of a Smaller Firms Council. This is seen as a safeguard against the submerging of the smaller members, companies who were most likely to have been members of the National Association of British Manufacturers, and was done in order to stave off the undue growth of a Smaller Businesses' Association formed from the dissatisfied rump of the NABM. In contrast, the EEF has been more successful in involving the small and medium-sized members and it has been feared that the larger members have not been participating at a sufficiently senior level. This factor has been accommodated by making more vice-presidents and forming the Chief Personnel Executive's Consultative Group. Both groups have become involved in advice and policy decisions.

These observations point to deep-seated stresses in employers' organizations which need to be skilfully managed in order to achieve any consensus. There has always been the problem of regional differences, for instance the Midlands are known for their independence in EEF circles. It has also been difficult for the large and the small and the strong and the weak to agree in pay negotiations. For example, motor manufacturers in the Federation have tended to be 'freebooters', and they and other strong units may pay wage rates without considering the impact upon their fellow members.

How much power and influence can such a seemingly fragmented structure provide? Formal links through such bodies as the CBI and the informal connections created by interlocking memberships of company representatives in employer bodies of varying types can be important. Perhaps the role of the individual will help us to assess the extent of power and influence of this section of society; for certainly since the decline of the lock-out as a sanction in collective bargaining it is unlikely that the power of association, of itself, will have much influence in the bargaining context or in Government circles.

The key individuals in the employer bodies, the office holders and senior officials, in my view provide the clue to how much influence these organizations may exert in the decision making processes in Britain and Europe. A number of investigations of top decision makers, politicians and the leaders of industry[27] suggests that it might also be instructive to examine the names and companies represented in the leading offices and committees of employer bodies. Much of the effective influence in national decision making of each association seems to rest in their ability to attract sufficiently 'weighty' captains of industry to their vice-presidencies, councils and committees. This factor appears to be very important in the case of our chosen example of an employers' association, the EEF. Here not only is influence in the right quarters sought, but the membership and involvement of the large companies in the engineering industry are maintained, whose attachment to the EEF, historically, is weakest. These include GEC and British Leyland, for example, who might feel that they have sufficient influence on their own without an employers' association.

On the other side of the equation, Governments and decision makers in our society, aware of the possible influence of management institutions, are probably also anxious to assert their independence of such interest groups or lobbies. Employer bodies are constantly being forced to adjust to Government interventions, in legislation, in changing patterns of public ownership, and in the creation of new public institutions such as tribunals and the Advisory, Conciliation and Arbitration Service. Professional bodies also are likely to be affected by decisions made in the sector of further and higher education.

The above remarks should remind us that institutions in our society are constantly subjected to pressures and change, so that any description can only be a snapshot, as we have said. Thus power and influence ebb and flow, so that observers of management must keep up to date with events. As one senior official of an employers' association put it when he was informed about this essay being written: 'What a time to be writing about that subject – everything is in a state of change!' That statement could have been made at any time in the last decade about industrial relations. At the moment there appears to be no prospect of a period of stability.

Notes

1. Chambers of Commerce should not be confused with either the Junior Chamber of Commerce, which is one of a number of social and fund-raising groups similar to the Rotary Club, the Round Table or the Lions, which cater for businessmen, or the Chamber of Trade which represents local retailers.

2. Lord Devlin conducted a Commission of Inquiry (report published 1973) into the state of industrial and commercial representation in Britain. Mr (now Sir) Ralph Bateman, President of the CBI, commented in its 1974 Annual Report: 'Follow-up action continued on the Devlin report. . . . Meetings between myself and the Director-General and our opposite numbers at the Association of British Chambers of Commerce were held and we all hope that closer cooperation will continue to develop in 1975 at both national and local/regional level.'

3. Research Paper No. 7, Royal Commission on Trade Unions and Employers' Associations (HMSO, 1967), p. ix.

4. See the Department of Employment, *Directory of Employers' Associations, Trade Unions, Joint Organisations* (HMSO, 1960).

5. McCarthy and Munns' Research Paper No. 7 to the Royal Commission is the most useful research document yet published on employers' associations.

6. *Ibid.*, p. x.

7. *Report of the Royal Commission on Trade Unions and Employers' Associations* (HMSO, 1968), Cmnd. 3623, para. 745.

8. For an exhaustive list see Priestley, B., *British Qualifications* (Kogan Page, 1973), 4th edn.

9. Smith, A., *The Wealth of Nations* (Pelican, 1974), pp. 169–70.

10. See Pelling, H., *A History of British Trade Unionism* (Penguin, 1963), pp. 93–122.

11. Status quo in this instance is taken to mean that while a question is going through procedure 'work shall proceed meantime on current conditions', that is, conditions *after* the change being challenged. Some exceptions included general alterations in wages or working conditions which were already the subject of agreements. The proposed wording

from the unions to cover status quo was as follows: 'It is accepted by the trade unions that management have the right to manage and to expect all normal management decisions concerning the efficient operation of the establishment to be implemented by workers immediately, except that any decisions which alter the established wages, working conditions, practices, manning, dismissals (except for gross industrial misconduct) or redundancy to which the workpeople concerned object, shall not be implemented until the local conference procedure has been exhausted.' Employers regarded this as giving a single trouble-maker the right to block management decisions before a local conference resolution.

12. See Wigham, E., *The Power to Manage: A History of the Engineering Employers' Federation* (Macmillan, 1973), p. 238.

13. Jukes, M., *The Role of the Industrial Federation in the 1970s* (Industrial Education and Research Foundation, 1969); also in Barrett, B., Rhodes, E., and Beishon, J., *Industrial Relations and the Wider Society* (Collier Macmillan, 1975), pp. 103–8.

14. *Ibid.*, p. 5. The observant reader will note that Jukes' historicist and dialectical approach is in the Marxist tradition.

15. From Armstrong, E. G. A., *Industrial Relations: An Introduction* (Harrap, 1969), p. 58, amended. Armstrong's sources: written evidence of the CBI to the Royal Commission, Research Paper No. 7, Royal Commission on Trade Unions and Employers' Associations, as amended by information from the Ministry of Labour Directory of Employers' Associations, and from the organizations themselves.

16. Perhaps the most important of these for industrial relations would be the Committees on Employment Policy, Industrial Relations and Manpower, Labour and Social Affairs, and Wages and Conditions.

17. From Marsh, A. I., *Industrial Relations in Engineering* (Pergamon, 1965), p. 56 (amended).

18. See Wigham, *op. cit.,* pp. 218–21.

19. *Op. cit.*

20. In evidence to the Donovan Commission 'rebels' or 'independents' were referred to as 'rogue employers'. In the engineering industry some have also been described as motor industry 'freebooters' (see Wigham, E., *op. cit.,* p. 199).

21. Marsh, A. I., *op. cit.,* p. 71.

22. Jukes, M., *op. cit.,* p. 5.

23. Wigham, *op. cit.,* pp. 212–13.

24. Munns, Donovan Commission, Research Paper No. 7, p. 77.

25. See *New Scientist*, Vol. 64 (1974), p. 732.

26. *Guardian*, 14 April 1975.

27. See, for example: Lupton, T., and Wilson, C. S., The Social Backgrounds and Connections of 'Top Decision Makers', *The Manchester School*, Vol. 27, No. 1 (January 1959), pp. 30–51; Guttsman, W. L., *The British Political Elite* (MacGibbon & Kee, 1963); Barratt Brown, M., 'The Controllers of British Industry', from Coates, K., *Can the Workers Run Industry?* (Sphere, 1968), excerpts of which may be found in Urry, J., and Wakeford, J. (eds.), *Power in Britain* (Heinemann Educational Books, 1973).

The Government and Collective Bargaining
by J. E. Mortimer

It is important to have a clear account of the growing involvement of Government in the bargaining context and framework, and this description by J. E. Mortimer of the development of Government intervention since 1961 illustrates the upward curve of the graph.

What is also important is to distinguish the different roles that Government may play in bargaining. This essay is mainly about its role as industrial relations and economic policy-maker, combined with its role as law-maker, regulation-maker and creator of institutions from the National Incomes Commission of 1962 to the more recent Advisory, Conciliation and Arbitration Service of 1975. There are other roles: as employer; as fixer of minimum rates through wages councils and of wage limits through incomes policies; as setter of codes and fair practices; as creator of a bargaining atmosphere through a taxation and social wage policy and minimum standards; as influence on working conditions, through health and safety regulations, security of employment, training and re-training. Many of these roles are described in another book in this series, *Trade Unions and Government*.

Should the involvement of Government continue to be as intense, as there is every chance it will, then every active trade unionist will need to adjust his work-place thinking to allow for this expansion of influence and for its impact on all the other parts of the bargaining context. (Eds.)

Introduction

Between 1961 and 1976 successive Governments, whether Labour or Conservative, found it necessary to intervene with an incomes policy in the process of collective bargaining. The main periods of intervention can be readily distinguished. They were:

1961–4 (Conservative), the introduction of a 'pay pause', the publication of a White Paper 'Incomes Policy: The Next Step', the setting up of the National Incomes Commission and the National Economic Development Council.

1964–70 (Labour), the joint statement of intent, the setting up of the National Board for Prices and Incomes, a succession of White Papers on prices and incomes policy, legislation for the control of prices and incomes.

1970–4 (Conservative), de-escalation in the public sector followed by the publication of detailed codes for the regulation of prices and pay and the setting up of a Pay Board and a Prices Board.

1974–6 (Labour), the operation of the 'social contract' in its original form and then in modified form, together with legislation for the control of prices and charges.

Both of the main political parties when out of office have declared their opposition to any kind of statutory intervention on pay. Thus, to take examples from more recent General Elections, the Conservative Party programme in 1970, after the experience of the Labour Government's prices and incomes policy, said: 'We utterly reject the philosophy of compulsory wage control.'

In October 1974 the Labour Party manifesto stated:

At the heart of this manifesto and our programme to save the nation lies the Social Contract between the Labour Government and the trade unions, an idea derided by our enemies, but certain to become widely accepted by those who genuinely believe in government by consent – that is, in the democratic process itself as opposed to the authoritarian and bureaucratic system of wage control imposed by the Heath Government and removed by Labour.

The considerations which have led successive Governments to introduce incomes policies have been remarkably similar. They are concerned with difficulties connected with the balance of payments, the rate of economic expansion, the level of investment in industry, the weakness of sterling as an international currency and the tendency for incomes to increase more quickly than productivity.

These problems are not confined to or peculiar to Britain. The persistence of inflation has been characteristic of all the advanced Western capitalist countries. Some have felt the problem more acutely than others but none has secured price stability simultaneously with full employment. In every advanced Western country there has been, at times, pressure for the use of limited resources, for instance for consumption, investment, social services, overseas spending and military purposes. At other times, when there has not been an excess of demand, prices have, nevertheless, continued to rise because of the upward trend of costs, for example, from wages and salaries, import prices, and from the under-utilization of productive resources in periods of recession leading in turn to higher unit costs.

Conservative Policy, 1961–4

In July 1961 the Chancellor of the Exchequer, Selwyn Lloyd, announced a series of measures to meet what was described as a crisis in the economic situation. These measures included an appeal for a general pay pause. This, it was said, would be enforced by the Government for public employees. The Chancellor pointed out that wage increases were outstripping the rise in productivity. The TUC reacted critically to the Government's measures. The Government appeared to believe, it said, 'that the main need is to reassure foreign speculators that the value of their sterling holdings will be maintained, whatever the cost in terms of lower living standards and the sacrifice of economic growth' (TUC General Council statement, 26 July 1961).

At its September annual Congress the TUC carried a resolution refusing to accept the Chancellor's appeal for wage restraint. An emergency resolution was also carried which deplored the intention of the Government to impose its will upon public employees. It singled out for special criticism 'the Chancellor's interference with arbitration machinery'.

The Government sought to reinforce its policy by direct influence on wage negotiations affecting public service workers and by referring back for consideration proposals for wage increases submitted by certain statutory wages councils. In February 1962 they issued a White Paper 'Incomes Policy: The Next Step' which argued that increases in incomes should be kept within the $2\frac{1}{2}$ per cent by which national productivity was expected to grow. The White Paper also said that arguments that had in the past been used to justify higher pay, such as comparability and increases in the cost of living, productivity and profits, should no longer be regarded as providing of themselves a sound basis for an increase.

The trade unions replied to this policy with constructive opposition. They urged the Government to reverse the decline in economic activity. Deflation at home, they said, was no proper answer to Britain's balance of payments deficit. Policies should be adopted for expanding output and, if necessary, the Government should limit by export quotas or fiscal measures the consumption at home of products which could be sold abroad. The TUC also suggested that selective import controls should be introduced.

In the summer of 1962 the Government announced its intention to set up a National Incomes Commission. This, it was hoped, would provide a more permanent means for dealing with the problem of relating the growth of incomes to the growth in productivity. The attainment of such a realistic relationship was, in the Government's view, the major pre-requisite for achieving faster economic growth.

The Commission was established in November 1962. Its terms em-powered it to examine specific pay questions referred to it by the parties immediately concerned, for instance, employers and unions, or matters relating to pay and conditions referred to it by a Minister. The Commission was required to have regard for the national interest and certain other criteria including: 'the desirability of keeping the rate of increase of the aggregate of monetary incomes within the long term rate of increase of national production.'

The TUC opposed the establishment of the NIC and regarded its purpose as misconceived. At the 1962 Congress a strongly worded resolution, moved by the Transport and General Workers' Union, was adopted condemning the actions of the Government on incomes policy and rejecting the National Incomes Commission. Affiliated trade unions did not cooperate with the NIC and it was largely ineffective.

However, another development during the early 1960s affected the relationship between the Government and the unions and had a longer-term significance. In a review of the economic situation conducted in December 1960 the General Council of the TUC said that the persistent weaknesses of the economy, namely the balance of payments and de-ficiencies in the volume and pattern of investment, could only be re-medied if the Government was prepared to formulate a long-term view of the country's requirements. This would inevitably lead the Government into forecasting and planning. During the subsequent exchanges lasting for a number of months on the Government's policies on the economy and on pay, the TUC continued to press its view about the need for planning.

In August 1961 the Chancellor of the Exchequer suggested to the TUC that substantial gains could be made by the proper coordination of econom-ic policies in cooperation with employers, trade unionists and indep-endent persons. If suitable machinery could be established it would be possible to assess the prospects of a group of the most important industries and to indicate what action was needed to bring them into balance with each other and with the needs of the economy. In a subsequent letter to the TUC the Chancellor stated that he considered it necessary to establish new and more effective machinery for the coordination of plans and fore-casts for the main sectors of the economy. He proposed, therefore, that a National Economic Development Council should be established with himself as chairman. Other members would include Ministers, repres-entatives of the trade unions and of the management of private and public industry. Reponsibility for final decisions about matters of Government policy would remain with the Government, but the views expressed by the Council would carry great weight. The Council would have a full-time staff under a director who would act under the general direction of and be responsible to the Council.

In its initial response the General Council of the TUC was cautious. It explained that though the trade union movement favoured longer-term planning, the ability of the TUC to make a contribution largely depended upon whether trade unionists believed that the Government was sincere in its advocacy of planning and whether the unions were able to influence Government policy.

Discussions continued for a number of weeks but finally in January 1962 the General Council decided to cooperate, or, to use its own words, it was 'decided that they should put to a practical test the question whether participation would give them genuine opportunity of influencing the Government's policies in ways which would help unionists'.

At the 1962 Congress the General Secretary of the TUC, George Woodcock, when speaking about the General Council's decision to join the National Economic Development Council, emphasized that the need for economic planning and the problems of incomes policy could not be separated. The TUC, he said, would not be afraid of discussing what part wages could play in a plan for genuine progress providing all other relevant matters were also open for discussion.

Later in the proceedings of this Congress a motion was moved urging the trade union movement not to participate in the National Economic Development Council. The critics said that they were not opposed to economic planning, but there was no likelihood of the Conservative Government embracing a policy of planning designed to raise living standards, to bring about a more equitable distribution of wealth and income and to strengthen the national economy. The Government's incomes policy, the critics emphasized, could not be divorced from the question of the trade union movement's participation in the National Economic Development Council. One of the critics pointed out that in the introduction to the Government's White Paper 'Incomes Policy: The Next Step' it was stated 'in pursuing this policy the Government are expecting to receive valuable assistance and advice from the National Economic Development Council'.

Opponents of the motion said that if adopted the motion would commit the trade union movement to following a negative policy. By participating in the NEDC the trade union movement might be able to influence policy in a direction which would be helpful to the interests of trade union members. The resolution was defeated.

At the 1963 Congress a special statement on economic development and planning was presented by the General Council. It recalled that the British trade union movement had been in the forefront of the advocates of economic planning because the movement was convinced that planning would promote expansion and thus help create the conditions in which trade unions could perform more effectively their primary job of securing full and satisfying employment and getting real improvements in wages and working conditions. The TUC statement, however, saw economic planning very largely as a process of securing voluntary agreement between various interests. To this extent the statement regarded planning more as an exercise in cooperation within the existing capitalist system than as a means of transforming capitalism into socialism. The TUC statement said; 'The success of planning will depend on the extent to which groups of interests in our society are prepared to make their attitudes and actions conform to the needs of the community as a whole as expressed in an agreed plan which would secure optimum use of the nation's resources.'

Supporters of the policy argued that this was a policy of realism. Critics argued that it was based upon the illusion that big business would subordinate its interests voluntarily to the needs of the people. The TUC considered that the policy rested largely on voluntary cooperation. The TUC statement argued that 'the advantage of this method (a development of the NEDC model) is that it recognizes that planning, to be effective, must be largely based on consent. The more that representatives of industry at all levels are involved in creating a plan, the more committed they will be to implementing it.'

The statement on economic development and planning did not avoid the problem of prices and incomes. It acknowledged that prices and incomes could not be excluded from the discussions of the NEDC. It emphasized, however, that a prices and incomes policy would succeed only if everybody concerned was convinced that it was a necessary part of a wider programme for the growth of real incomes, and that restraint by one section of the community would not merely result in a gain to other sections. One of the necessary factors of economic growth, said the TUC, must be an expansion of real purchasing power.

Labour Policy 1964–70

The newly elected Labour Government in 1964 stressed that what was needed was not only an incomes policy but a policy which would also embrace productivity and prices. It suggested that such a policy would be possible if it were set within the context of economic expansion.

The Government approached the employers and the unions and the result was a joint statement of intent on productivity, prices and incomes. This was agreed in December 1964. The content of the statement was that the Government's economic objective was to achieve and maintain a rapid increase in output and real income combined with full employment. The social objective was to ensure that the benefits of faster growth were distributed in a way that satisfied the claims of social needs and justice. The major objectives of national policy were to raise productivity and efficiency so that real national output could increase. It would then be possible to keep the general level of prices stable and to keep increases in wages, salaries and other forms of income in line with the increase in productivity.

The TUC summoned a special conference of executive committees of affiliated organizations to consider this new development of policy. The report of the General Council, which was in support of the joint statement of intent, was endorsed by 6 649 000 votes as against 1 811 000. The General Council said that the economic circumstances of the country and the wider interest of workpeople had established the imperative necessity of the measures proposed by Government. In reaching this conclusion the General Council was guided by two major considerations. In the first place, the Government had declared its clear commitment to a plan for the revival of the British economy. It would thus be possible to provide an increase in real incomes combined with full employment. Secondly, its social objective was to ensure that the benefits of faster growth were distributed in a way that satisfied the claims of social needs and justice.

This attempt at a prices and incomes policy lasted from 1964 until 1970. The policy was developed in considerable detail and described in several White Papers. A National Board for Prices and Incomes was established and Prices and Incomes Acts were passed by Parliament in 1966, 1967 and 1968.

In spite of the care with which the policy was launched, the very wide support it enjoyed, and the good work done by the National Board for Prices and Incomes, the policy eventually broke down. The question why it broke down is fundamental for an understanding of the problems of an incomes policy. The intended framework for the policy was that there should be expansion, which would make it possible to achieve rising living standards. The plain fact was, however, that during the period of the policy Britain's economy did not expand as rapidly as was envisaged in the joint statement of intent. On the contrary, it continued to grow sluggishly and indeed for a period there was no growth at all. There was very little margin for higher real incomes.

In 1965 and during the first part of 1966 wages and salaries continued to increase at a faster rate than national output. In the middle of 1966 the Government introduced a prices and incomes standstill followed after six months by a period of severe restraint. The norm for wage and salary increases was put at nil, and there was a ceiling for increases of not more than 3½ per cent except where it could be shown that there had been exceptional increases in productivity. In fairness it has to be said that wages and salaries did not fall behind prices during this period. This, however, was due more to pressure from below for higher pay than to the operation of the policy within the lines set out in the White Papers.

The deficit in the balance of payments was not overcome until late in the life of the prices and incomes policy. The necessary stern measures to deal with it at an early stage, either by drastic cuts in overseas spending as, for example, for military purposes or by devaluation, were not taken. When devaluation did eventually take place in November 1967, it led inevitably to price increases. It was accompanied by various curbs and restrictions designed to reduce the balance of payments deficit.

Towards the end of 1969 there were signs of serious unrest about the effect of the policy on certain groups of low-paid workers. The revolt was led by dustmen, who broke through the policy. A White Paper published in December 1969 directed special attention to the plight of the lower-paid workers. What was needed, it said, was a real improvement 'in the position of those low paid in the context of particular situations, of particular needs, and of particular systems of pay negotiation'.

During 1970 there was an upsurge in wage and salary claims. Pay increases were higher than before, and it became clear that the formal policy had broken down. Millions of people felt that there had not been any recognizable improvement in their standard of living for a number of years. There was also a General Election impending and neither Government nor Opposition considered it politically opportune to urge that wage and salary claims and settlements should be kept at a level commensurate with the increase in national output.

The main lesson of the period 1964–70 was that the success of a prices and incomes policy depends not only on the terms of the policy and the machinery with which it is implemented but on the economic framework in which it has to operate. Economic expansion provides the basis for higher living standards. If this expansion does not take place a prices and incomes policy will inevitably run into difficulty.

The achievement of the 1964–70 Labour Government was that during its six years of office it converted a substantial balance of payments deficit into a substantial surplus. This was secured, however, by means which made it impossible to fulfil the expectations aroused by the 1964 joint statement of intent.

One other important development during the period of office of the two Labour Governments between 1964 and 1970 had a direct bearing on the relationship between collective bargaining and the State. It started with the appointment of a Royal Commission on Trade Unions and Employers' Associations in 1965. The Commission, under the chairmanship of Lord Donovan, reported in 1968. The terms of reference of the Commission called for an examination of the role of trade unions and employers' associations not only in promoting the interests of their members but also 'in accelerating the social and economic advance of the nation'. There had been a good deal of discussion in the press and among commentators, not all of which was inspired by genuine concern for good industrial relations, about the effect on Britain's economic performance of disputes and unofficial strikes.

The analysis of industrial relations presented in the Donovan Report drew heavily from the experience of the engineering industry. It said that Britain had two systems of industrial relations: one, the formal system embodied in the official institutions, and the other, the informal system, created by the actual behaviour of trade unions and employers' associations, of managers, shop stewards and workers. The Report said that the existing system had a number of important advantages. It was flexible and provided a high degree of self-government. On the other hand, it had a number of serious disadvantages. There was a tendency towards extreme decentralization which sometimes degenerated into indecision and anarchy. This in turn bred inefficiency and a reluctance to change. All these characteristics, said the Report, became more damaging as the rate of technical progress increased and as the need for economic growth became more urgent. One of the important conclusions of the Report was that 'the central defect in British industrial relations is the disorder in factory and workshop relations and pay structures promoted by the conflict between the formal and informal systems'. The Commission urged that there should be more orderly factory-wide agreements, and that industry-wide agreements should be limited to those matters which they could effectively regulate. The Commission recommended certain changes in the law affecting industrial relations, but their main emphasis was on the need for reform within an essentially voluntary system. This reform was to be assisted by an Industrial Relations Commission.

The trade union movement welcomed many of the conclusions and recommendations of the Donovan Commission but also criticized the extent to which its views had been influenced by the experience of the engineering industry. Many trade unionists in other industries said that the general conclusions drawn by the Donovan Commission were not valid for their particular industries or services. Nevertheless, the trade union movement generally supported the view of the Donovan Commission that changes and reform should be made broadly within the framework of the voluntary system of industrial relations.

The Government's proposals for new legislation following the Donovan Report were published early in 1969 in a White Paper entitled 'In Place of Strife'. The proposals contained a number of surprises. There were various suggestions to assist unions and promote trade union objectives, but there were also proposals which the unions strongly disliked and which appeared to be at variance with the findings of the Donovan Report on the need for reform within an essentially voluntary system. The Government proposed to take discretionary powers to require a union to conduct a ballot before a strike which in the Minister's opinion threatened economic damage. These powers were to be backed by the threat of financial penalties. The Government also proposed to take discretionary reserve powers to impose a conciliation pause in certain disputes. Again these powers were to be backed by threat of financial penalties. Another proposal was that the Secretary of State for Employment should have power in disputes between unions to impose financial penalties on an employer or union which refused to comply with a recommendation by the Commission on Industrial Relations that a union should be excluded from recognition. Yet another proposal was that trade unions should be obliged to register and that they should be required by statute to ensure that their rule books covered certain defined subjects.

The General Council of the TUC in its reply to the White Paper said that some of the proposals of the Government could in principle help to improve industrial relations, but it was opposed to other proposals. It issued a statement emphasizing that its objections to these proposals were very strong.

In April 1969 the Government announced that it had decided to introduce into the current session of Parliament a short interim Bill to deal with some of its main proposals in 'In Place of Strife'. The Government considered that the immediate problem was the unofficial strike. The interim Bill was to include provisions for enforceable recommendations in certain circumstances concerning the recognition of trade unions, inter-union disputes and the ordering of a conciliation pause in unconstitutional stoppages.

The trade unions' opposition to the Government's proposals continued to grow and a special Congress was convened in June 1969, at which this feeling was strongly endorsed. A motion affirming the trade union movement's unalterable opposition to the imposition of financial penalties on trade unions and workpeople was adopted by 8 252 000 votes to 359 000. The General Council was also authorized by a very large majority to take further action in order to assist in the improvement of procedures and the settlement of disputes.

There was a succession of meetings between the Prime Minister and the TUC at which the TUC continued to express its strong opposition to the Government's proposals. Inside Parliament it also became clear that there was a substantial number of Labour Members who would not support the Government's proposals in the division lobby. In the circumstances a compromise was inevitable. The Government withdrew from the line which it had intended to take and in return the General Council agreed to a solemn and binding undertaking to give urgent consideration to disputes which led or were likely to lead to an unconstitutional stoppage of work involving directly or indirectly large bodies of workers and to give advice to the union or unions concerned with a view to promoting a settlement. In cases in which the General Council considered that there should not have been a stoppage of work before the procedure was exhausted it undertook to place an obligation on the union or unions concerned to take energetic steps to secure an immediate resumption of work. The undertaking was set out in detail in an annex to an agreed statement between the Government and the General Council.

At a later stage the Government decided to introduce a new Bill on industrial relations which did not include any penal clauses. This Bill was generally supported by the trade union movement but before it could proceed through its various stages in Parliament there was a General Election and the Labour Government was defeated.

Conservative Policy, 1970–4

With the election of a Conservative Government in 1970 a new phase in the development of incomes policy commenced. At the outset the Government took the view that its influence on pay should be exerted primarily through the negotiations for which it had a direct responsibility. This meant that it should seek to influence negotiations in the public sector. This, it believed, would then affect negotiations and settlements in the private sector. In this way inflationary pressure would be reduced without the necessity of a formal incomes policy or statutory intervention in the collective bargaining process.

The policy, however, was soon in difficulties. Some of the workers in the public sector were low paid, including large numbers of manual employees in local authorities. The Government did not conceal its displeasure when an independent inquiry provided a higher settlement for local authority workers than the amount favoured by the Government. Electricity supply workers were also involved in a dispute, and this led to the setting up of a Court of Inquiry which also recommended increases rather larger than those offered in negotiations.

Later, early in 1971, there was a dispute affecting postmen. Again it became clear that the Government was seeking to hold down the level of settlement in the hope that this would affect the conduct of collective bargaining over a much wider area. Early in 1972 the Government's policy suffered a serious setback following a miners' strike. The underlying problem in the mining dispute, said the TUC General Council, was 'the Government's negative attitude and . . . its attempt to impose rigid restrictions on collective bargaining in the public sector'. The Government was unable to impose its policy on the miners and, ultimately, following the report of a Court of Inquiry and further negotiations, a settlement was secured on terms far higher than those it had originally contemplated.

The unions representing public sector employees protested strongly against the Government's policy. They felt that it was operating unfairly against the public sector. They argued that if the Government wanted to pursue an incomes policy it should do so openly and not seek to impose it on one group of workers in the hope that negotiations elsewhere would be influenced by example.

The Government's view was that the problem of inflation was very serious and that action was needed to deal with it. In the 1970 General Election campaign the Conservative leaders had conducted a vigorous attack on the rising cost of living, particularly during the closing phase of the Labour Government. The Conservative Government continued to adhere to its opposition to a formal incomes policy but argued that it had a special responsibility to influence negotiations in the public sector. The Government pointed out that the rate of cost inflation in the United Kingdom was affecting export prices and making the balance of payments surplus extremely vulnerable. The Government's view was that it was essential that pay settlements should be de-escalated.

In the summer of 1972 there was an exchange of views between the Government, the CBI and the TUC about the measures needed to stimulate expansion, ensure full employment and overcome inflation. By the late autumn it was clear that the Government and the TUC would not be able to reach agreement on a policy for the management of the economy and on 6 November the Prime Minister announced that the Government had concluded that it was necessary, in the absence of agreement, to bring in statutory measures on prices and incomes. This, however, would take time and in the meanwhile there was to be a standstill on prices, rates, dividends and pay. Under the second stage of the policy, announced later, a Price Commission and Pay Board were established whose main functions were to implement a price and pay code drawn up by the Government. The TUC convened a special Congress in March 1973 which adopted a General Council report opposing the Government's policy. The Congress also adopted a resolution calling upon the General Council to lead coordinated action in support of affiliated unions in dispute. The resolution also invited unions to join in a day of national protest and stoppage against wage control and the increases in food prices.

The Government's price and pay policy subsequently went through various phases, and detailed codes for price and pay control were developed. The policy continued to be opposed by the trade union movement. A resolution was carried at the 1973 TUC stating that statutory price control must be accompanied by measures to increase social justice and to promote economic expansion in order to ensure a planned growth of real incomes.

The final breakdown in the policy came at the beginning of 1974. The miners were pressing for substantial improvements in wages, but the Government insisted that the pay code should be observed. There was a strike in the mining industry and the TUC urged the Government to permit the National Coal Board to negotiate a settlement. The TUC said that the miners should be treated as an exceptional case and that repercussions in other industries could be contained. The Government asked the Pay Board to undertake an examination of the claim of the miners for a pay increase larger than that permitted in the pay code. A three-day week was in operation in industry and the Government was in difficulty. It decided to call a General Election. The Government was defeated in the election and a new Labour Government was returned with a very narrow majority.

During the period of office of the Conservative Government the controversy about economic policy and the control of prices and incomes was overshadowed by the controversy about the 1971 Industrial Relations Act.

The Conservative Party had made it clear in its election programme in 1970 that if returned to office it would introduce a comprehensive Industrial Relations Bill. This, it said, would 'provide a proper framework of law within which improved relationships between management, men and unions can develop'. The Conservative Party said that its aim was to strengthen the unions and their official leadership by providing some deterrent against irresponsible action by unofficial minorities. The next Act, it promised, would lay down what was lawful and what was not lawful in the conduct of industrial disputes. The framework of law would also provide for agreements to be binding on both employer and unions. A new Registrar of Trade Unions and Employers' Associations was to ensure that 'rules were fair, just, democratic and not in conflict with the public interest'. The Conservatives said that their Act would provide for the holding of a secret ballot in case of a dispute which would seriously endanger national interest and for a 'cooling-off' period of over sixty days.

The Industrial Relations Act 1971 followed broadly the lines promised in the Conservative Party election manifesto. It was denounced by the trade union movement in very strong terms. When the Bill was going through Parliament the TUC organized a national petition against it, held a national rally at the Albert Hall, convened one of the largest ever protest demonstrations in London and arranged a house delivery of a leaflet in cities and large towns. Nearly two thousand full-time trade union officials attended training programmes for the campaign of protest. In a report to a special Congress on the Industrial Relations Bill the General Council said that 'the fiction that the British economy is being threatened by industrial disputes pervades the Government's whole approach'. The General Council argued that a number of provisions in the Bill was designed to limit the right to strike and to enforce these limitations by the Courts.

A number of 'unfair industrial practices' was listed in the Act. These gave rise to legal liabilities. The TUC strongly opposed the legal requirement that a union must register before it could call itself a trade union and thus enjoy certain limited advantages. The Government's aim, said the General Council of the TUC, was 'to impose an alien concept of authority on the internal workings of trade unions'. The Registrar, it pointed out, would have very substantial powers to determine and alter trade union rules in return for certain curtailed and limited forms of legal protection. The Commission on Industrial Relations and the Industrial Court, said the General Council, would also have powers to devise and conduct ballots of trade union members and of workpeople in relation to a number of issues such as recognition which were crucially important to trade union organization and practice. The statutory right not to join a trade union would, said the TUC, encourage those who were were hostile to trade unions or who might have a grievance against a union which they were unwilling to pursue through the union's machinery. The TUC also opposed the presumption in the Act that any agreement would be legally binding unless an express provision to the contrary was included in the agreement itself. It pointed out that this was completely contrary to the normal practice of British industrial relations.

In its report to the special Congress held in March 1971 the General Council strongly advised affiliated unions not to register under the Act. It recommended that 'before any union decides to apply to be entered on the provisional register, or to take any steps to remain on the provisional register, or thereafter to seek full registration, it shall inform the General Council of its reasons for doing so, and give the General Council the opportunity to express a view'. Some unions, led by the Amalgamated Union of Engineering Workers, argued that this was not enough. They urged that unions should be required not to register. The General Council's recommendation was accepted by the relatively narrow majority of 5055000 votes to 4484000.

At the 1971 TUC held in September the decision of the special Congress on this issue of registration was reversed. A composite resolution, moved by Hugh Scanlon on behalf of the engineering section of the AUEW, was carried by 5625000 votes to 4500000. The resolution instructed the General Council to support all unions in their fight against the legislation and in turn to instruct affiliated unions not to register under the Act.

In a railway dispute in the spring of 1972 the Government used its power under the Industrial Relations Act to apply to the National Industrial Relations Court for an order requiring the railway unions to stop their industrial action. None of the three railway unions appeared before the NIRC to answer the Government's application for a cooling-off period. The application was granted and the cooling-off period took effect. It did not achieve anything and at the end of the cooling-off period the unions' industrial action was resumed. The Government then applied to the National Industrial Relations Court for a ballot of railwaymen. The result of the ballot showed overwhelming support for the unions. Nearly 130000 railway workers voted in support of the three unions and only 23000 voted against. This was the only occasion on which the Government sought to use the Industrial Relations Act for the imposition of a cooling-off period and a ballot. The Act had been shown to be ineffective. Indeed, if anything, its effect was to strengthen rather than to weaken the resolve of the majority of railwaymen to support the claim submitted by their respective unions.

In July 1972 five dockers were imprisoned in Pentonville following their refusal to comply with an order of the National Industrial Relations Court about 'blacking' at the Midland Cold Storage Company in Hackney. Their imprisonment resulted in immediate stoppages of work in the docks, printing, transport and some other industries. The TUC decided to ask for a meeting with the Prime Minister, at which the TUC pressed the Government for urgent action to secure the release of the dockers. The TUC pointed out to the Prime Minister that the Industrial Relations Act was worsening industrial relations; that the policy of registration had failed; that strike ballots had failed as had been illustrated in the railway dispute, and that the National Industrial Relations Court was creating widespread hostility. The objectivity of the entire judiciary was thus being brought into question by the actions of a special court which was widely regarded as politically motivated.

No progress was made in these discussions and towards the end of July the General Council decided to call on all affiliated unions to organize a one-day stoppage of work and a demonstration on Monday 31 July for the release of the five dockers. The effect of this call for a one-day general strike was immediate. On 26 July the dockers were released from prison.

The unions had differing views about appearing before the National Industrial Relations Court. The special Congress had decided that 'affiliated unions shall not co-operate with the NIRC and the CIR'. The General Council subsequently decided, however, that where action was being taken against a union or its members the union should have the right to defend itself or its members before the NIRC or an industrial tribunal. An uncompromising line was taken by the Amalgamated Union of Engineering Workers. On the occasions when it was taken to the National Industrial Relations Court for alleged unfair industrial practices it refused to recognize the authority of the Court. It was particularly incensed at the Court's intervention in a case concerning trade union recognition at a small engineering firm in the home counties. The employer claimed that he was being subjected to an unfair industrial practice because the union refused to call off the dispute after it had been referred to the CIR. Fines were imposed on the AUEW and, when it refused voluntarily to pay, its funds were sequestrated. The effect of this procedure was to provoke bitter feeling within the union, and a series of strikes took place in many engineering factories.

Halfway through the period of office of the Conservative Government, the TUC and the National Executive Committee of the Labour Party agreed to establish a liaison committee which in due course laid the foundation for what came to be known as the 'social contract'. The committee was established in January 1972. The committee decided that it should seek to find areas of agreement on the related questions of industrial relations and the management of the economy. It started by calling for the immediate repeal of the Industrial Relations Act, the introduction of new legislation for the voluntary reform of industrial relations and the establishment of an independent conciliation and arbitration service.

In February 1973 a joint statement was issued by the TUC and Labour Party liaison committee entitled 'Economic Policy and the Cost of Living', which emphasized that the problem of inflation could be properly considered only within the context of a coherent economic and social strategy. This strategy should be designed both to overcome Britain's grave economic problems and to provide the basis for cooperation between the unions and the Government. The statement called for direct statutory action on prices to influence the whole climate of collective bargaining, a new approach to housing and rent, a large scale redistribution of income and wealth, greater spending on social priorities and an immediate commitment to a pension of £10 a week for a single person and £16 for a married couple. The statement stressed that all these policies had to be underpinned by agreed policies on investment, employment and economic growth.

Labour Policy, 1974–6

The newly elected Labour Government of 1974 announced its intention to fulfil the policies outlined in 'Economic Policy and the Cost of Living'. The Government said that the Industrial Relations Act would be repealed and would be replaced by new legislation providing for voluntary collective bargaining and the voluntary reform of the system of industrial relations. It said that a new independent conciliation and arbitration service would be established. After three weeks in office the new Labour Government introduced its first Budget which provided for an increase in pensions to £10 for a single person and £16 for a married couple. Tax changes were also introduced to help the less well off through increased allowances. Higher income tax rates were imposed on the better off. Some tax loopholes from which the wealthy had benefited were also closed. The Chancellor announced that the Government would introduce a wealth tax and also a gifts tax. Extra money was allocated for food subsidies and a decision was taken to freeze rents. The National Industrial Relations Court and the CIR were abolished and so too was the Pay Board. A Royal Commission on the Distribution of Income and Wealth was subsequently established, and at a later stage an Employment Protection Act was passed to extend the legal rights of workers and trade unions.

The trade union movement welcomed the actions taken by the Government in fulfilment of the social contract. The General Council issued a statement of policy on 26 June 1974 entitled 'Collective Bargaining and the Social Contract' which was subsequently endorsed by the 1974 TUC. Its most important recommendation was that: 'although the ground work is being laid for increasing consumption and living standards in the future, the scope for real increases in consumption at present is limited, and a central negotiating objective in the coming period will therefore be to ensure that real incomes are maintained.'

This, explained the General Council, would entail claiming compensation for the rise in the cost of living since the last settlement. Threshold agreements were to be taken into account. The General Council also urged that there should be a twelve-month interval between major increases and that priority should be given to attaining reasonable minimum standards including the TUC's low pay target of a £25 minimum basic rate for a normal working week for those aged eighteen and over. Unions were urged to make full use of the Conciliation and Arbitration Service.

At the 1974 TUC criticism of the policy was voiced by a small number of unions but after debate a critical motion was withdrawn. Critics argued that although some welcome measures had been taken, no real advance was being made towards redistributing income and wealth in favour of working people. Critics also pressed for much more substantial cuts in arms expenditure and for higher investment in industry.

Through the winter of 1974–5 and the spring and summer of 1975 the level of wage and salary settlements more than kept pace with the rise in the cost of living. Prices moved upwards not only as a result of increases in labour costs but also the very much higher prices for oil and raw materials. The rate of inflation climbed to over 20 per cent and was beginning to move towards 30 per cent. Meanwhile Britain's balance of payments was very heavily in deficit.

In the summer of 1975 the Government felt it necessary to take urgent and drastic action. It pointed out that the rate of inflation in Britain was higher than in other competing industrial countries and that Britain was becoming ever more heavily dependent upon foreign creditors. Unless steps were taken to curb the rate of inflation British exports would become even less competitive and foreign creditors would lose confidence in the stability of the British economy. The Government also said that the rate of inflation was contributing to unemployment. Industrialists were losing confidence in the future of British industry. Soaring costs, inevitable under inflation, were eroding the funds necessary for industrial investment. And all this was happening at a time when the economic system in the rest of the Western world was in deep recession.

The Government entered into discussions with the TUC about the economic situation and a voluntary agreement emerged for a limit of £6 a week on wage and salary increases with a cut-off point at £8500 per year. This policy was developed largely at the suggestion of the General Secretary of the Transport and General Workers' Union, Mr Jack Jones, who had urged that there should be a flat rate increase for workers.

At the 1975 TUC the policy of the General Council, set out in a report entitled 'The Development of the Social Contract', was adopted by 6945000 votes to 3375000 votes. The General Council referred to the repeal of the Industrial Relations Act 1971 and the introduction of new legislation favourable to working people and trade unionism. It spoke also of the factors contributing to inflation, including wages. It said that there was an urgent need to bring down the level of inflation and recalled that in the summer there had been considerable pressure on sterling. The General Council called for a reduction in the level of unemployment, higher investment in industry and selective import controls.

The critics on this occasion were more numerous than at the 1974 Congress. They argued that the policy had now been transformed into one of reducing the living standards of millions of working people. Military expenditure was still running, it was said, at a high level and industrial investment at a low level. The Government, it was alleged, had retreated on some important issues including, for example, the weakening of the Industry Act, 1975. The critics pointed to the high level of unemployment and said that a policy of reducing living standards would lead not to full employment but to even more unemployment.

In defending the General Council's policy Jack Jones said that both the General Council and the Government had sought to help the pensioner, the low paid, the housewife and ultimately the country in the battle against inflation. Had the General Council not joined the Government in action to arrest the downward movement of the pound and the severe threat to Britain's financial stability, the country might have experienced an economic setback from which it would not have recovered for generations. The trade union movement, he said, could not afford to destroy the Labour Government.

In the early part of 1976 further discussions took place between the Government and the T U C on the development of the social contract. The Chancellor of the Exchequer announced in his Budget a number of conditional measures for the reduction of direct taxation. These measures depended on trade union agreement for a further extension and reinforcement of the counter-inflation policy. The T U C responded, and after discussion with the Government agreed to a number of guidelines on pay which they then put to a special Congress held in June 1976. They were approved by 9 262 000 votes to 531 000.

The guidelines were for the period 1 August 1976 to 31 July 1977. The General Council said that pay increases during that period should be limited to a percentage increase of 5 per cent on total earnings for all hours worked, with a cash minimum of £2·50 and an upper cash maximum of £4 per week. These figures were to apply to all full-time adults aged eighteen and above with pro rata payments for part-timers and juveniles. The increases were to be payable as an individual earnings supplement. The twelve months' interval between major pay increases was to continue to apply. All other improvements including non-wage benefits, said the General Council, should be kept within the overall pay figure except those for which specific exception had been made, for instance equal pay. Improvements in occupational pension schemes up to the contracting out level provided in the Social Security Pensions Act could also be implemented outside the pay figure.

In commending these guidelines to the special Congress held in June 1976 the General Council said that the Government had continued its broad programme of legislative advance. It pointed to the passing of the Trade Union and Labour Relations Amendment Act which finally repealed the Industrial Relations Act, the introduction of the Employment Protection Act and other measures. In its report to the special Congress the General Council said that the social contract was not a subject for an annual discussion between the Government and the TUC, but was a continuing process based on mutual trust and understanding. The General Council welcomed the assurance of the Government that the aim was to halve the rate of inflation yet again by the end of 1977. It was firmly opposed to any suggestion from the CBI that the price code should be abolished. The General Council outlined its priorities for social policy. It called for speedy action on a wealth tax and said that the 'planned growth of social expenditure and of the public sector must play its part for economic recovery'. The General Council stated that it was strongly urging the Government to reconsider certain aspects of the public expenditure plans and it would vigorously oppose any further public expenditure cuts.

Soon after the special Congress the Government announced that further cuts in public expenditure were to be made. According to reports in the press the TUC representatives expressed their strong misgivings about the proposed cuts and some union leaders said they should be opposed.

Conclusions

A few broad conclusions can be drawn from the experience of the years 1961–76.

Firstly, every Government in Britain, whether Labour or Conservative, has found it necessary – even sometimes despite election pledges – to introduce a formal prices and incomes policy and to influence wage and salary bargaining and price movements. If anything near full employment can be regained it seems unlikely that Governments will be able to act differently in the future. Mass unemployment might make a formal prices and incomes policy unnecessary but it is not an alternative which is socially acceptable.

Secondly, effective price control without some kind of influence on collective bargaining is not possible. Millions of workers are employed in the public sector, such as nationalized industries, local authorities, civil service and the health service and education, and their pay increases always have a bearing on the prices of, for example, gas and electricity, and on fares, rates and taxes. It is unfair to apply an incomes policy only to the public sector. Inevitably, therefore, any attempt at effective price control implies a policy on incomes both in the public and private sectors.

Thirdly, there is no evidence that the statutory control of incomes can be made permanently effective. Imposed controls may sometimes work for a short period but their inflexibility is incompatible with the changes in industry and commerce. Account has also to be taken of the aspirations of people for improvements in their conditions. Even voluntary policies have not worked successfully for very long periods. This, however, is not an argument for no policy at all. A policy for economic growth, price control and incomes is more likely to be successful – at least for a longer period – if the arrangements for incomes rest on consent and goodwill. This means that the arrangements have to be broadly acceptable to trade unionists.

Finally, the problem of inflation should be tackled within the context of a coherent economic and social strategy designed to maintain full employment, to secure a faster rate of economic growth than hitherto, to obtain a balance in Britain's international payments and to pursue objectives of greater social justice. To subscribe to these objectives, however, is not a substitute for a programme to achieve them. The content of such a programme is the central issue of the debate about Britain's economic future.

It is not the purpose of this essay to provide an answer to the question posed in the last of the above broad conclusions. It is sufficient to emphasize that the question is an inescapable one. Is the policy of the present Government on the right lines? It is set out in the statement 'The Development of the Social Contract' and it has the broad, if at times critical, support of the majority of the trade union movement. Should there be a move towards an economic policy favoured by the political Right including much reduced public spending, bigger profits, no further public ownership and reduced direct taxes on all including the better off so as to stimulate effort and enterprise? Or should there be a move towards an economic policy favoured by some of the Left including part of the Tribune group of MPs? This would require more public intervention in industry to provide a much higher level of investment, drastic cuts in military expenditure, selective import controls, the strict regulation of overseas investment and the redistribution of wealth and income in favour of working people.

Within the labour movement the debate is not only about the content of the policy which should be pursued but about the practicability of maintaining in office a Labour Government representing many different shades of opinion. In electoral terms the alternative to a Labour Government is not a government of the more radical Left but a government of the Right.

The future of collective bargaining and, in particular, the relationship between the Government and collective bargaining, cannot be considered in isolation from these other economic issues.

Section V

Bargaining and Workers' Rights

The two essays in this section link the bargaining theme to the account of workers' rights set out in Paul O'Higgins' book. Both authors stress the point that the law merely underpins the control which unions can best achieve through bargaining. That this view is traditional is supported by a typical statement in the TUC's *Annual Report* for 1974 (p. 74):

The General Council consider that statute law can only play a subordinate part in the conduct of industrial relations. The main method is voluntary negotiations between employers and unions, but legislation should ensure that all workers have certain minimum rights and should encourage the development of voluntary collective bargaining and supplement it where necessary.

Trade unionists need the law to help them bargain effectively, but their own role is to develop, through bargaining at 'the frontiers of control' in the work-place, rights which by custom and practice, by agreements and by Parliamentary sanction, may become part of the general context of bargaining. (Eds.)

Bargaining for Rights
by John McIlroy

This essay deals with the new legal rights which are developing, and with their advantages and limitations for the trade unionist. The author describes how unions can make the most use of these rights by bargaining initiatives, and in this way can extend them to cover gaps which the law may have left. He concludes that 'the final guarantee of rights, what makes them work, is union strength and control in the industrial situation'. (Eds.)

Introduction

WORKERS' RIGHTS AND THE LAW

The law has not been used very much in this country to give positive rights to workers in industry. There was not much of a floor of legal rights in industrial relations. Until very recently, when new laws were passed, there was no right in English law to belong to a trade union;[1] there was no legal means by which a union could force recognition on a reluctant employer;[2] if a worker was given the required legal notice his employer could still sack him because he did not like the colour of his eyes.[3]

Trade unionists relied on Government to establish the welfare state and make minimal laws to allow trade unions to exist and operate. But as workers they then preferred to rely on their unions to protect them, not on the State. When the State felt threatened by trade union activities it never hesitated to try to use the law to control them, whether in 1799, 1917, 1927, 1940, 1969, or 1971. When the union movement was strong enough to get favourable legislation passed, as in 1875 or 1906, the judges soon took these protections apart. Trade unions, therefore, had well-grounded suspicions of the law, especially since judges themselves have discretion in interpreting legislation, and indeed are *making* law. Lord Justice Scrutton once remarked, 'It is very difficult sometimes to be sure that you have put yourself into a thoroughly impartial position between two disputants, one of your own class and one not of your own class.'[4] Generations of trade unionists with memories of Tolpuddle, Taff Vale, Pentonville and Shrewsbury would chorus, 'You can say that again.'

Table 7: The New Framework of Legal Rights

Right	Legislation	Enforcement
COLLECTIVE Union recognition	Employment Protection Act, Ss. 11–16, Ss. 121	Advisory Conciliation Arbitration Service; ACAS Central Arbitration Committee; High Court action for breach of contract
To belong to, take part in the activities of, an independent trade union	Trade Union and Labour Relations Act (Sch. I, para. 6) and Amendment Act; changes in Employment Protection Act, 1975, Ss. 53–6, Ss. 78–80	Industrial tribunal; appeal to High Court; Appeal to Employment Appeal Tribunal
Reasonable time off for shop steward duties	Employment Protection Act, Ss. 57–8	Industrial tribunal

Information to help in collective bargaining	Employment Protection Act, Ss. 17–21, Ss. 121; Industry Act, 1975, Ss. 27–36	ACAS Central Arbitration Committee; High Court action; Industry Act fine continuing daily
INDIVIDUAL Not to be unfairly dismissed	Trade Union and Labour Relations Act, Sch. I, Parts 2–4; changes in Employment Protection Act, Ss. 71–3, Part II, paras. 13, 14; Part III, paras. 7, 9, 13	Industrial tribunal with appeal as above
Redundancy pay, consultation, time off to look for alternative work	Redundancy Payments Act, 1965; Employment Protection Act, Ss. 99–107, Ss. 61	Industrial tribunal with appeal as above
Lay-off pay	Employment Protection Act, Ss. 23–33	Industrial tribunal with appeal as above
Health and safety	Health and Safety at Work Act, 1974	Health and Safety Inspectorate prosecution in criminal courts
Information about terms and conditions of work	Contract of Employment Act, 1963; Employment Protection Act, Sch. 16, S. 81	Industrial tribunals
Equal pay	Equal Pay Act, 1970	Industrial tribunal; reference of Agreement to Industrial Arbitration Board
Women and minorities: not to be discriminated against	Sex Discrimination Act, 1975	Industrial tribunal; Equal Opportunities Commission; County Court for injunction
	Race Relations Act	Minister Conciliation Body; Race Relations Board; civil action by Board in County Court
Maternity leave and right to return to your job	Employment Protection Act, Ss. 35–50	Industrial tribunal

The *Economist*[5] found that 76 per cent of judges in the superior courts had been to a major public school, Oxford or Cambridge University, and had then been called to the refined closed shop of the Bar. Their recreations were 'country': huntin', shootin' and fishin'. Of them, 53 per cent belonged to the best known clubs in London including 26 per cent to the Athenaeum. In 1976 two authors, B. Abel Smith and B. Stevens, found that the situation was unchanged and that County Court judges were from similar backgrounds. In December 1974, High Court judges received wages increases of £100 a week under the social contract.

Since 1965 the idea that the law could play a bigger part in guaranteeing basic rights and minimum standards in employment began to prevail. The Industrial Relations Act, an attempt to limit rights and advances in standards of living, meant that the law was in the field. The 1974 Labour Government was willing to trade legal concessions for economic cooperation through the social contract. All this produced the makings of a new legal framework which is more extensive than the Industrial Relations Act and has more chance of actually influencing day-to-day industrial relations because it is accepted by unions. (See Table 7, pp. 212–13.)

If you are an active trade unionist, you need to know about these new legal rights, how they relate to collective bargaining, their good points and their bad points and the problems of exercising them. How far can you build on them and use them as a weapon when bargaining?

These laws often only guarantee peanuts. You need to top up by direct bargaining. The Redundancy Payments Act, 1974, gave a man made redundant after thirty or forty years' service the maximum of £1200. Sometimes the law itself is weak. There is no legal right to reinstatement after an unfair dismissal; the employer only has a duty to take reasonably practicable measures under the Health and Safety at Work Act so that he can argue that a particular safety device is too expensive. To get anything out of some of the new rights you will have to bargain extensively, for instance over equal pay. Their exercise may cause problems: for example, the obstacle course procedure for union recognition in the Employment Protection Act and the lack of safety inspectors to enforce the limited penalties.

Workers should obviously take advantage of a more favourable legal framework; but the final guarantee of these rights is union strength and control in industry. Employers have many rights embodied in the law of contract. But often they cannot use them because the force of the trade unions stands in the way, as in the Industrial Relations Act.

Unions must realize that legal rights should stimulate and encourage bargaining and not lead to relaxation and reliance on the law. No Act of Parliament can guarantee basic rights in the face of restrictive interpretation by a hostile judiciary. The law is distant, expensive, time-consuming, uncertain, often arbitrary. The essential point for trade unions to grasp is the *inefficiency* of the law to meet their purposes. If a determined employer refuses to bargain all the law will do is ensure compulsory arbitration, yet unions want bargaining, not arbitration. 'As a power countervailing management the trade unions are much more effective than the law has ever been or can be.'[6] Legal rights are no substitute; they can be a useful addition within the collective bargaining framework.

WORKERS' RIGHTS AND BARGAINING

How effective can bargaining be in establishing rights? How far can it go? 'There is no barrier except relative bargaining powers to the scope of the subject matter in which the union may interest itself. It can seek to bargain on any matter which is of sufficient importance to its membership to permit it to array a bargaining power adequate to the objective.'[7] How successful you are depends on how strong you are, how much muscle you've got.

Why do certain workers look like Charles Atlases while others regularly get sand kicked in their faces by the bosses? We have to look at a whole range of factors. The employer's market for his product is important. Is it competitive or does he have a monopoly? Is it a sheltered industry or open to international rivals? Are there seasonal fluctuations in demand? Is it a perishable product like a newspaper or is there a longer time-span?

The technology of the work-place and industry is important: the layout of work; the tools and machinery used; the size and concentration of the work force. What about the labour market? Is there a shortage of labour or much unemployment? Is it skilled or unskilled work? How important are labour costs? The overall national economic situation and the distribution of power between classes are also important.

All these objective factors influence bargaining power. But what is crucial is how workers react to them. Growing unemployment may or may not weaken trade unionism, but the way workers read the situation, their aspirations and attitudes, the extent to which they feel able and willing to influence things, these are all important.

It is facile to say that miners' bargaining power is better than nurses' because they have more control over resources and the actions of the other side. Power can only be measured when used and for years the miners did not use their power. The successful exercise of power depends not only on the objective factors described above but also on intensity of feeling, willingness to sacrifice and strategy.

Bargaining power is affected by organization: the role stewards play in shaping the aspirations of their members, their links with other stewards, their relationship with the full-time official and with union bodies outside the work-place. Joint shop stewards' committees can overcome divisions at work, and they provide a framework for solidarity. Combine committees in companies or industries give valuable contacts and knowledge and can provide bargaining support. Members on the district committee or the executive strengthen your work-place organization, particularly during disputes. And don't forget about trades councils. Many workers employed by multi-nationals now see the need for international links.

Bargaining power is the basic guarantee of rights for two-thirds of the work force. The most powerful groups have the most rights. Workers had more rights in the 1960s and 1970s than they had in the 1920s and 1930s. The collective bargaining system does not give workers any cast-iron guarantees. Your paper rights depend on your ability to mobilize power to back them up. Like a house built on shifting sand, today's rights can easily vanish in adverse circumstances. Collective bargaining consists largely of influencing decisions indirectly through a veto and in the past it covered only a few decisions. It does not 'attack management on such basic principles as private property, the hierarchical nature of the organization, the extreme division of labour and the massive inequalities of financial reward, status control and autonomy at work'.[8]

Vigorous trade unionism brings workers up against these basic principles, eads them to question their eternal validity and look for solutions. To really protect ourselves we have to go beyond collective bargaining. We have to eliminate the employer. Any real extension of workers rights will, in the longer term, require workers to take control of the means of production themselves so that industry and society can be run in the interests of the majority on the bases of need and planning, not on the bases of profit and anarchy. This will require not merely constantly pushing for more control in factories and industries; it will require the building of a political challenge at the level of the State. It is only out of the present struggles of workers for more say over their lives that such a challenge can emerge.

We will now look at several areas of bargaining policy, at what collective bargaining has achieved so far and the types of agreements unions have negotiated. We will then examine legal changes and how far the law can help. We should then be able to analyse what objectives trade union negotiators should have in mind for extending workers' rights.

Trade Union Rights

RECOGNITION AND MEMBERSHIP

People opposed to trade unionism never tire of telling us that only a minority of the work force belongs to a union. They have a point. So the job of unions is to see that they don't have a point for much longer, by recruiting people. This is going to bring trade unionists up against the problem of recognition. Little can be achieved in bargaining without it. Most big firms have had to accept trade unions as a fact of life, but many others still resist unionization. What rights does the law give the worker against the hostile employer?

The Trade Union and Labour Relations Act gives every employee legal protection if he has been sacked because of his membership of an independent trade union or because he has been taking part in the activities of that union.[9] 'Independent' means free from control by the employer; this would cover all TUC unions. The dismissed worker can go to an industrial tribunal where he can get cash compensation or a *recommendation* that he should be given his job back, but this cannot be enforced by the tribunal. The Employment Protection Act gives protection to a worker who is victimized on trade union grounds but not sacked.[10] Such protection can be helpful for workers trying to organize. But remember that you cannot get your job back through the tribunal if your employer stands firm. Picking on a key organizer can still be cheap at the price for an employer opposed to unions.

The Employment Protection Act says that a trade union has the right to take a recognition dispute to the Advisory, Conciliation and Arbitration Service,[11] which will make recommendations. If the employer still refuses to recognize the union then, the workers can take their claim about wages and conditions to the Central Arbitration Committee of the ACAS, which will make a binding arbitration award whose terms will become part of each worker's contract of employment. If the employer does not meet these terms, each worker can take him to court, which is very long-winded and time-consuming. In the end, the union may get arbitration but not recognition, and that's not what a union is there for. It shows how the law is limited in how far it can ensure that a company recognizes a union. An employer may 'recognize' a union but refuse to bargain realistically; you can take a horse to water but you can't make him drink. However, this doesn't mean that calling in the ACAS doesn't *sometimes* give you another lever, since many employers do not want the bad publicity of ignoring ACAS recommendations and will cave in at this stage. But will it crack a nut like D. C. Thomson, which has ruthlessly and successfully defeated every attempt at unionization since the Second World War? In the end, the only thing that can make recognition a fact is union strength on the ground.

If management is hostile you may have to accept halfway measures as a means of showing doubters that you can do something for them. You can then build up sufficient support and muscle to go further. Tread warily, plan carefully. You must win the members first and if you are victimized it can set things back for a long time.

When the employer is firmly opposed to the union and the workers are intimidated or only partly organized, you often find half the workers on the picket line and half inside breaking the strike. This is where the union is important, because it can use the resources of outside pressure, blacking all customers, suppliers, and other sources of the product. Here the help of fellow workers in subsidiaries, transport and the docks, is crucial. The lack of unity in the trade union movement often shows up here.

The recognition dispute at Fine Tubes, Plymouth, which involved the TGWU and AUEW, ended in failure in June 1973 after three years. The factory was still working with blackleg labour. It proved to be beyond the resources of the strike committee to successfully coordinate a blacking campaign of Fine Tubes products because this would have involved real solidarity among fellow unionists in Rolls-Royce, BAC, Henry Wiggins, etc. Management refused to accept the recommendation of a committee of inquiry which called for talks about recognition. In its final statement the members of the strike committee said: 'We cannot believe that the two biggest unions in the country have not got it in their power to break a small non-union employer. . . . In more than one case the unions officially stood aside while stewards refused to black Fine Tubes.'

Once recognition has been achieved, the next step is to try to get 100 per cent membership. People join unions to get results, so it is easier to recruit after recognition. While the union is rather weak, argument and persuasion may be the only weapons, but as it gets stronger, other sanctions can be used to build up membership. For instance, if someone won't join a union but is prepared to take the benefits won by his fellow workers, those workers are quite free to decide not to work with him. 'Mr Terry Webb, the Abingdon car worker who refused to rejoin a trade union, was sacked by British Leyland today when he returned to the MG works. Workers earlier told management they would not work with non-unionists. The workers made their demonstration and stopped the line for a few minutes when Mr Webb told stewards he was adamant and would not rejoin the GMWU.'[12]

Industrial tribunals are finding that it is reasonable for a company to dismiss in these circumstances. Cases such as that of Mr Langston at

Chrysler have shown that management will not look too kindly on someone who causes production losses by implementing his right not to join a union.

The vital artery is the point of entry. Management may recommend that all newcomers should join or may allow the steward to interview new entrants and even to take on labour. If you feel that you've got enough members amongst a group of workers or across a whole factory, office or department you can ask management to agree to a 'union membership agreement'. This is the closed shop allowed by the Trade Unions and Labour Relations Act.[13] It means that the employer will agree to *require* all workers in that particular group to join the union. If people refuse, the law says that the employer can sack them unless they have got religious grounds for objection. In the case above, British Leyland probably showed in practice that it sanctioned a union membership agreement.

At 1975 union conferences the NUJ declared its intention of establishing total membership amongst journalists, and the Civil and Public Services Association demanded a closed shop on behalf of its 220000 members. The Union of Post Office workers secured broad agreements with the Post Office about introducing a post-entry closed shop from October 1975 and the Bank Employees drew up similar plans.

Without a representative system at the work-place, recognition would not mean much. In bargaining the stewards are the key men. Victimization of stewards is still frequent. Any union which doesn't fight this to the last ditch is digging its own grave. 'The trouble started in January when a handful of militants began to reintroduce trade unionism into the firm. The response was fantastic. The workers, fed up with being pushed around, saw the union as a means of getting together to fight. Before long the membership in our department was nearly 100 per cent.'

Management declared the steward redundant although half his shop was on overtime. His members backed him.

'I argued that unless the notices were withdrawn management would have a strike on their hands. Management came back and announced that they had withdrawn the notices unconditionally. You can talk till the cows come home but it is rank and file action that gets results.'[14]

It does not always work like that. Linda Walsh was an USDAW steward at Northern Leather. Management refused to recognize the union and the workers struck. Management offered to take everybody back except Linda, and this was eventually accepted. A string of cases in the last twelve months tells the same story. Failure to accept a steward elected and duly appointed by the union challenges the reality of recognition. Yet in certain work-places management can veto the election. Any eligibility qualifications for becoming a shop steward should also be looked at very carefully. Are there any good reasons for them?

FACILITIES

Stewards need both time and channels to gather and present information, to plan work-place strategy, to communicate both inside and outside the work-place, to prepare and argue cases.

The Employment Protection Act provides a minimum entitlement to reasonable time off with pay for union activities which are a necessary part of the official's duties in connection with the employer's own organization; and the same, with or without pay, for wider union activities. For more detail on these matters we shall have to wait till ACAS publishes a new Code of Practice. If you feel that you have not sufficient time off your legal remedy would be to go to an industrial tribunal.[15] It can issue a declaration of right or award you compensation, but because situations vary so much officials would still have to bargain over *exactly what* facilities are needed, using the legal provisions as negotiating material.

The Government's present guidelines for good industrial relations, the 1971 'Code of Practice', are not legally enforceable, its recommendations are often vague enough to require interpretation; nevertheless, they may be useful as a bargaining prop in order to convince management about the need for facilities.

Trade union functions defined in the Code in para. 103 do not cover 'recruitment, maintaining membership and collecting contributions'. Yet facilities for these are essential. They *are* covered by the TUC.[16]

Stewards should assess their own situation to establish what can be achieved. In a recent survey by the Industrial Relations Review and Report of 168 companies,[17] 60 per cent said stewards were not entitled to collect dues in work time (not check-off); 10 per cent said stewards were not entitled to recruit new members in working hours; 41 per cent did not allow elections in working hours, and 35 per cent provided no typing facilities.

Meetings in working hours are obviously important in order to encourage participation. Alan Fisher of the National Union of Public Employees called for legislation to allow branch meetings in works time.[18] Many companies allow stewards to hold some meetings in working hours but expect mass meetings to be held at lunch time or after work. Suitable accommodation is also very important.

At Keith Blackman (GEC) there had been problems about holding meetings. A request for a joint office and shop-floor meeting was refused. When the stewards went ahead they were threatened with disciplinary action. After an occupation of $1\frac{1}{2}$ days, management agreed to withdraw the disciplinary letters and set up a meeting to discuss industrial relations in the company.[19]

Some companies still pay basic rates or do not pay night shift premia to stewards who have to attend special meetings. However, an Incomes Data survey said that Chrysler, Hoover, Dunlop, Gallaher and many other large companies now pay 'average, normal or anticipated' earnings. It is obviously preferable for senior stewards to have offices and their own telephones and the right to use clerical staff is obviously preferable to only having 'access'. Freedom to move around the work-place to handle problems and to report to members is usually covered in agreements by a clause requiring permission from the supervisor.

Conflicts will of course continue if stewards consider that facilities are essential rights and management regards them as privileges to be monitored and limited.

Should facilities be formalized in written agreements or left to be regulated by custom and practice? The I R R R survey showed only 51 per cent of their sample had jointly agreed written facilities; 40 per cent relied on custom and practice. In most places, custom and practice is still very important and written agreements tend to be very general, for instance: 'facilities adequate for the dispensing of the steward's responsibilities will be established and maintained' (Armstrong Patents Co.) or 'reasonable facilities will be afforded to staff representatives to allow them to deal with questions raised on behalf of those whom it is agreed they represent' (EEF–APEX, MATSA). Some agreements do go into more detail but still have to be filled out by custom and practice. Some stewards argue that written agreements involve a loss of flexibility and can narrow the scope of their activities. Others claim that they provide a better protected minimum which can be used as a basis for more informal extension.

Points to Note

1. If you have recognition problems, remember ACAS and the disclosure of information clause in the Employment Protection Act.

2. Are you 100 per cent unionized? Can 'union membership agreements' help? Discuss this with other unions.

3. Does your management encourage new workers to join? Try to get facilities to interview all newcomers about joining.

4. Stewards are *union* officials; management should not be allowed to pick their opponents.

5. Make sure you have a joint stewards' committee. Is there a combine committee? If not, make contact with stewards at other plants. Make sure you are represented on as many outside union bodies as possible.

6. Look at the Code of Practice and the TUC *Good Industrial Relations*. Don't feel limited by these documents, but you can quote them at management.

7. You should try to get: average earnings for your time off; accommodation for meetings; a stewards' room; clerical assistance and phone.

8. You should also try to get time off for training.

9. Written agreement or custom and practice? The key question is: does it help or restrict the steward?

10. There is a danger of getting separated from members: you should report back to them and involve them.

Redundancy

REDUNDANCY AND THE LAW

Management sees redundancy as an inevitable consequence of economic and technological change; it is essential to achieve better utilization of manpower, reduce overmanning, raise efficiency, increase profitability. For the unions, however, job security and satisfaction are important. Workers may not be opposed to greater efficiency, but may ask who benefits. A worker faced with the social and economic disruption of losing his job may well ask how he is benefiting from the greater efficiency. Management sees the problem as one of smoothly terminating employment and providing compensation, while the worker simply wants to continue in that job.

It has basically been the unions which have tried to establish rights and protect workers from the ups and downs of the economic system. The Redundancy Payments Act did not interfere with management's rights to reduce its labour force. It gives no more security to workers than the legal minimum periods of notice. It gives no property rights over the job; it merely set a price for compulsory purchase. It does not control the timing or extent of redundancy, nor does it set down the terms of selection of who is to be redundant.

The tribunals and the courts have found dismissal unfair where the redundancy guidelines of the Code of Practice are not followed.[20] However, many of these guidelines are limited and vague. Most principles are qualified 'as far as is consistent with operational efficiency and the success of the undertaking' (para. 40). In many ways the Code shores up managerial prerogative: 'Responsibility for deciding the size of the workforce rests with management' (para. 44).

The Employment Protection Act requires advance notification of redundancy and provides periods for consultation and time off to look for extra work.[21]

Redundancy and Bargaining

A redundancy can be swiftly and ruthlessly presented as a situation you can do nothing about. Management will claim that it is irrevocable, and an adamant statement of total closure can lead to fatalism. Those to be sacked and those to be kept on will be divided amongst themselves: it will be difficult because of their various economic and social circumstances to coordinate policy amongst those to be sacked, although immediate lump sums can reconcile people to the loss of their jobs. A study of the impact of the Redundancy Payments Act stated:[22] 'The Act had made it easier for many employers to discharge workers largely because it enabled them to dismiss men with an easier conscience and reduced costs and argument.'

Should unions negotiate in advance redundancy agreements and procedures? The argument is that if such an agreement leaves the final right to decide about redundancy in management's hands after consultation, then there is a built-in acceptance of sacking and a focus towards redundancy as inevitable. Thus bargaining will be about method and effect rather than the decision itself. A redundancy agreement ties your hands to a certain extent. Without one, you may be able to challenge the redundancy or at least achieve better terms. Some would argue that it is better to negotiate safeguards when you are stronger than when you are in the potentially weakening situation of a redundancy. The limitations of paper guarantee in relation to a changing balance of forces have also to be taken into account. A determined management can evade a written agreement, just as strongly organized workers may be able to determine decisions at the time at least as successfully as through a prior written agreement.

The best policy is total opposition to redundancy backed up by a demand that the company open its books to the workers. Then work sharing without loss of pay can be planned. Workers may be involved in planning production and schedules, and a working week can be calculated for the whole work force on the basis of the required cuts in production. How far a 'no redundancy' policy can be enforced depends on the circumstances, the balance of forces and the strength of organization and level of control.

In the 1970s workers have become determined to be involved in fighting redundancy decisions. The official union line still stresses negotiating procedures to cover future redundancies, with consultation and measures for avoidance (see TUC, *Job Security: A Guide For Negotiators*).

A survey in the Industrial Relations Review and Report[23] on redundancy procedure in 168 companies found that 102 of them had a written procedure. A survey conducted by the British Institute of Management found that 60 per cent had redundancy agreements and an Institute of Administrative Management survey of $1\frac{1}{2}$ million office staff in 939 different establishments found 44 per cent of them had formal redundancy schemes.

Union officials need as long a period of notice as possible to look at the options and inform the work force. BSC has agreed to give unions at least two years' notice of large-scale redundancies and six months' notice of others. One year's warning is increasingly common in the public sector. Most agreements in the private sector are vaguer, for instance Pirelli's with the T&G says: 'Where an abnormal situation occurs and management can foresee the possibility of redundancies occurring they will consult with the union and adopt methods to prevent redundancy as appropriate to the situation.' Similarly Firestone Tyre and Rubber Co.'s agreement states that 'the company accepts the principle of early consultation with representatives. As soon as the possibility of redundancy arises the IR Manager will inform the secretary and indicate the numbers likely to be affected.'

AVOIDING REDUNDANCY

Common measures in agreements are restrictions on recruitment, re-deployment, reduction of overtime, short-time working, re-training and an elimination of sub-contracted work (see Code of Practice, para. 45). The TUC's statement argues: 'the agreement should state categorically that no external recruitment in particular occupations should occur for which there are vacancies, until certain grades of existing employees have been given the chance to fill them after training.' The Pirelli agreement includes items such as the retirement of those over normal retirement age and termination of temporary and casual work, while the agreement between APEX and Dewrance Ltd specifies recruitment should be limited in departments not affected by redundancy but likely to provide substitute jobs.

In this first stage, bargaining over the decision, the first point is to get the company to justify its redundancy decision by opening its books.

The best situation is when workers have continuing access to information and can see redundancies coming. The options are then open and the workers can put forward alternative measures. Of course, a company can run itself down, transfer its assets, make it appear an uneconomic concern. Often it *will* be uneconomic in that it is not making a profit. While sometimes the books will show redundancies are avoidable, sometimes they will show that they are not. Here it is important to argue that the logic of the right to work comes before the logic of profit. Otherwise opening the books even under union control can simply lead to demoralization.

The Employment Protection Act provides for unions to be given information to aid them in collective bargaining. ACAS will publish a Code saying exactly what categories of information are to be made available. There is another procedure under the Industry Act.[24]

The most widely spread bargaining tactic and the best adapted to redundancies has been the 'sit-in': 'In a sit-down the workers' morale is heightened. They are inside and therefore know for certain that scabs are not operating the machines; they are really protecting their jobs. The men are protected from the weather. They are never scattered but always on call at a moment's notice.'[25]

Many companies in allegedly impossible markets have continued in business or kept on workers when faced with determined resistance. A growing demand from workers has been that the State should step in and nationalize companies declaring redundancies. Nationalization is in itself no panacea; but it can be a step forward if used by workers to extend control over all aspects of the work process. Recently employers have become less reluctant to use their legal rights.

Workers at Crosfield Electronics in North London called off an occupation which had lasted eight weeks when management agreed to restore seven of the original thirty-two redundant jobs. They found it difficult to get support in the rest of the De La Rue combine. Management tried to split those sections which were working normally, but paid a levy to the occupiers by imposing a three-day week; then secured a High Court order for repossession. One steward commented, 'It was the law of the land that defeated us.'[26]

Massey Ferguson also took legal action against strikers at its Coventry tractor plant. They had occupied the plant and forced management to operate from local hotels, but ultimately they accepted the writ.

Where there is a lack of will or bargaining power, unions will be limited to bargaining about selection and method. The two most common principles for selection are voluntary redundancy and 'last in first out'. This traditional union seniority rule often clashes with managerial 'efficiency'. Vauxhall specified that 'The last in first out approach is basically sound and fair and will be followed where other qualifications are equal.' Ford states: 'The company will depart from the practice where it is necessary to do so to maintain efficient operations and where it is possible to do so to avoid exceptional hardship.' A harder approach is taken in the ICL–ASTMS procedure: 'The efficiency of the department or unit is the most important factor in assessing individuals for redundancy. However in equal circumstances length of service will be taken into account.'

In April 1975, delegates from, for instance, Dunlop, Plessey and Hunts Engineering, attended a meeting sponsored by Evans Medical shop stewards' committee. They set up a committee to fight redundancies on Merseyside and passed a resolution opposing the employment in their

H

work-places of any worker who volunteered for redundancy. They thought that voluntary redundancy was a way of softening workers up for the real blow.[27]

Workers excluded from the provisions of the Redundancy Payments Act must be protected and the terms of the Act generally improved on. Some company schemes are as follows: Perkins Engines, $1\frac{1}{2}$ weeks' basic pay for each year's work for those over eighteen, with no maximum on the number of years; Spicers, roughly double the Act's requirements; United Glass, additional 2–17 weeks' wages, depending on age; International Harvester, 33 per cent above statutory requirements.

Most company schemes provide for lump sum payments. TASS's document 'The Right to Work' suggests that unions should seek to obtain for someone made redundant weekly benefits continuing until he or she gets a new job or for twenty-six weeks after dismissal; together with State benefits these weekly payments should be 75 per cent of the final week's pay. British Steel pays weekly redundancy payments calculated as a percentage of average earnings and varying according to whether the redundant worker has found a new job or not.

A real problem is often the lack of notice of redundancy. After six months of negotiation over redundancy plans and wage rises the thirty-nine workers at the litho plate-making firm of Mabbutt and Johnson in Islington received letters by post one weekend saying that the company was being closed down. The workers had to elude security men and break in through the roof in order to occupy. The same kind of thing happened at Imperial Typewriters, where the decision to close was taken abruptly without prior consultation. The Employment Protection Act may help here. It increases the periods of contractual notice so that after twelve years' service a worker is entitled to twelve weeks' notice, and provides for consultation periods of up to ninety days which have to be given to the union. In mid-1975 the TUC called for a ban on all redundancies of more than four hundred in development areas and two hundred elsewhere.

Points to Note

1. Do you want a redundancy agreement or are you stronger without one?

2. What is your union's policy on redundancy?

3. How does it measure up to the points discussed?

4. Remember the stronger you are *now*, the better you can tackle redundancy if it comes. You need support from other plants.

5. The more information you have about the company *now* the better you can see the future and assess the threat.

6. Remember to deal with redundancy on a broader level. You need to argue for a 35-hour week, extensions of holidays and restrictions on overtime.

Lay-Off and Short Time

The TUC *Economic Review*, 1975, claimed that 'At present it appears that companies are laying off clerical, part time and female staff, while production workers are tending to be put on short time rather than being made redundant.' In early 1975, there were about 250 000 workers temporarily laid off or on short time.

THE LAW

The legal protection of workers temporarily laid off or on short time is uncertain and inconsistent.[28] Where nothing is specifically laid down a company can probably lay off without pay in the event of machine breakdown, power failure, shortage of orders, circumstances beyond its control. The lack of cases makes it difficult to know exactly what situations this last category would cover. The courts have said that a business recession is not beyond an employer's control, though unsafe working conditions are. An employer may be able to prove an all-embracing customary right to lay off without pay, but this has not been established in any case. (A worker also has certain rights under the Redundancy Payments Act to leave and claim redundancy when on temporary lay-off or short time.)

In one case a colliery had to close down for a period so that repairs could be done. Conditions were unsafe through no fault of the employer. The workers who were on piecework were laid off with no wages. They took the company to court. The judge, arguing from the premise that there were two equal parties to the contract, said it was only fair that losses owing to unexpected events like this should be shared. The company lost its profits, the workers their wages (*Browing* v. *Crumlin Valley Collieries Ltd.*, 1926). Laws like these make it hardly surprising that workers have attempted to protect themselves more directly against the capitalist system.

The idea now embodied in the Employment Protection Act is to make the employer and not the State pay the bill for short-term periods of unemployment. The worker can claim unemployment benefit in certain circumstances, however, and this should be taken into account.[29]

LAY-OFF AGREEMENTS

The objective of negotiators is to ensure that workers temporarily prevented from working by circumstances beyond their control should suffer no economic loss. In recent years, with developments like the three-day week, this problem has hit most workers. Workers can start getting used to short time; then we are back to casual employment. Is a specific lay-off agreement necessary, or can you enforce a custom and practice of work or full pay, obviously the best solution? Remember, again, that there is nothing sacred about a written agreement. During the three-day week many employers tried to throw away their lay-off agreements.

Management and indirect workers at British Leyland Cowley operated a customary arrangement by which these workers would not be laid off. In the recession in the car industry, Leyland wanted to introduce an agreement similar to the one made with production workers. Leyland argued that it could operate the basic engineering industry guaranteed week. When management attempted to lay some indirect workers off at Pressed Steel Fisher, all the indirect workers walked out. They decided on a 'one out, all out' policy to safeguard their custom and practice.

There are great disparities in the protection agreements give. The first problem is how much money the worker is guaranteed when laid off. Agreements range from average earnings to basic rates. Most provide for payment of less than a full week's pay. Many agreements guarantee only the basic hourly rate (BP, Birds Eye Foods), some provide for even less. At industry level, the agreement in silk spinning with the T&G, G&M and Dyers and Bleachers provides appropriate time rates for 80 per cent of the normal working week; in papermaking it is 75 per cent of the basic rate per shift or day. However, in tobacco manufacturing, employees with three years' service receive their normal weekly wage. Within industries there are variations: Vauxhall pays 70 per cent of the personal day shift basic rate, British Leyland at Cowley 80 per cent of the grade hourly rate with a maximum of eight days a quarter because workers can carry over three unused days from one quarter to another.

Often no service qualifications are specified, but it may be four weeks or longer. In nearly all the agreements a worker must be ready to undertake reasonable alternative work in order to qualify. A worker liable to disciplinary action is usually excluded from benefit.

Another important weakness of agreements is the time that guarantees last for. Vauxhall has a twenty-five-day maximum a year with up to ten days in one situation; British Leyland 28 days; Chrysler 28 days on a quarterly basis. Dunlop allows six days in a six month period. At national level the building industries working rule No. 2A allows an employer to require the worker to register as unemployed after one week's lay-off; in civil engineering the worker must register for unemployment benefit after one week.

A suspension clause can be found in most agreements. It may be limited to industrial action within the plant, within the company or even within the industry. A strike in an EEF engineering firm entitles any federated employer whose production is affected to lay off. In the Cotton Spinning and Weaving and the Rubber Manufacturing Agreement suspension is permitted even if there has been no actual dislocation of production as a result of the strike. Massey Ferguson manual workers are guaranteed thirty-two hours a week at average earnings provided they are not laid off owing to disputes among manual grades.

Whereas in the agreements at BP or Dunlop industrial action will be the only opportunity for suspension, other agreements are wider and allow suspension in the event of shortage of supplies, lack of business, circumstances beyond the employer's control. Some agreements provide for notice to suspend; some make it automatic.

If management in, say, the car industry knows a lay-off is coming in one section, it is easy to provoke a dispute in another section and then refuse to pay anyone lay-off pay. If the people in the section in dispute take this into account – and they may feel a great responsibility – or if other sections pressurize them not to come out, it weakens their bargaining power and means that management can force concessions. If a whole factory comes out, the other parts of the combine may give no support but instead wait until they are laid off. If they keep their right to pay like this, in the short term, they may weaken the other workers. Thus the present system maximizes sectionalism amongst workers, so an essential objective must be to put a stop to penalty clauses.

The strike in December 1974 of eight hundred assemblers at Triumph, Coventry, was important as it was the first time British Leyland had conceded the principle of lay-off pay for internal disputes in any circumstances.[30] In the public sector, the Electricity and Gas Councils, the Post Office and BAC have no agreement in writing about a guaranteed week; they claim that in practice workers would be found other work even if the cause of lay-off was a strike by employees of the organization. Elsewhere in the public sector written guarantees do exist.

Given the important restrictions embodied in these agreements, only a tiny minority of workers possesses any meaningful protection from large variations of income because of events over which they have no control. The Employment Protection Act does not make any significant difference. Employers are required to make payments at a guaranteed rate arrived at by dividing a week's pay (as defined for the Redundancy Payments Act) by the employee's normal hours. There would be a limit of five days at a maximum of £6 a day in any period of thirteen weeks. The right does not apply if the reason for the lay-off or short time is 'an industrial dispute in any establishment of the employer concerned'.[31] This leaves the ball very much in the court of the bargainers.

Points to Note

1. Do you need a lay-off agreement or can you enforce work or full pay?
2. An agreement should apply to all workers regardless of the number of their years of service.
3. Can you improve on an industry or company agreement at plant level?
4. Lay-off on basic rates is no good. Go for earnings including overtime and all premia.
5. The period for calculating average earnings should make an allowance for seasonal fluctuations, holidays and sickness.
6. Limit the suspension clauses. Try to get coverage for *any* stoppage. The employer's interference with the right to strike of other workers must be stopped.
7. Extend the time limits as far as you can, since 15–20 days soon go.
8. Organize a walk-out policy with other unions in order to avoid sectional problems. Can you limit flexibility arrangements, the mobility of labour and overtime if there are any lay-offs?
9. Have a look at unemployment pay.
10. Does the legal right to lay off help?

Dismissal

Mr Clapton had a good record for over thirteen years with his firm. He was also involved in union activities. One Thursday he took the day off without permission and then stayed away all the following week. The company sacked him. When he took the case to an industrial tribunal they found he had been unfairly dismissed. He had been involved in negotiating a pay claim, his wife was sick and things had got on top of him. He had no previous misconduct. No explanation had been asked of him and he had not been given a warning. This conduct was not bad enough to merit instant dismissal (*Clapton* v. *Ketton Foundry*).

An employer has to show a tribunal that he has acted *reasonably* in dismissing a worker. He has to show that his conduct warranted dismissal, that he had had a chance to explain, been given a warning and a chance to improve and the right to an appeal. A worker should not get the idea that this is a watertight protection. Mr Clapton did not get his job back. A tribunal can only ask; it cannot insist. Mr Clapton didn't win the pools, he got £200, reduced to £150 because of *his* conduct. The decision to go to a tribunal needs a lot of thought. If fellow workers are taking action in support they might return to work relying on the tribunal to provide a solution. The tribunal, however, unlike the workers themselves, cannot enforce reinstatement.

A NUPE shop steward was picked on and sacked. His members were raw, inexperienced, new to trade unionism. They came out on strike but they were not very firm. The officer played down a suggestion that they go to law. The strike achieved the steward's reinstatement. Afterwards the officer said, 'We couldn't have got reinstatement at the tribunal. Direct action gave us a fighting chance. But if we'd have gone to the tribunal as well, many members would have said, "What's the point of continuing to lose money, let's go back and let the tribunal decide." '

In the case of a strike or industrial action the employer can sack everybody but he cannot pick out individuals because of their union membership or activities.[32] The Employment Protection Act makes selection even more difficult.[33] In one case, *Khan* v. *Perivale Guteman*, a tribunal held that it was fair for the employer to sack fifty-seven workers who were operating an overtime ban.

So you can't rely on the law here: you've still got to bargain. You can fall back on the law when all else fails; it is no substitute for organized strength for getting the job done.

PROCEDURES

Mr Clapton's company suffered because it did not operate a reasonable procedure. Because tribunals are saying that managements must follow a suitable procedure before sacking people, managements are making sure that their procedures are good enough to meet the tribunals' standards. Unions should ask if they are good enough to meet the workers' standards, as companies are now getting their procedures written down in detail, which they did not bother much about before.[34] The standards the law asks for are basically those laid down in the Code of Practice.

The Code asks for a specific disciplinary procedure. Until recently it was usual for discipline and dismissal matters to be dealt with as part of the general disputes procedure. This is now changing in order to meet the need for speed and efficiency. Union members cannot afford to loiter in these types of cases. Nor can you have 'ghost' stages, where management deals with problems it lacks either the will or authority to settle.

The Code also states that 'procedures should be agreed with employees' representatives or trade unions concerned'. A steward can argue the strongest case when the procedures are on his side.

Some procedures are jointly agreed and provide for union involvement not merely as representative but as judge at the appeal stage. At Firestone Tyre and Rubber, the convenor and two stewards sit with the department head on a misconduct committee in which there is provision for appeal to the union district officer. 'The process is less that of adjudication than of joint bargaining and decision-making.'[35] In the docks, the system of appeals tribunals with two wingmen dealing with dismissal has worked well in the National Dock Labour Board. This kind of participation may be justifiable where workers control a wide range of other decisions, but otherwise it can place a great strain on the trade union.

The Code also argues that management should make known to each employee its disciplinary rules and agreed procedure; the type of circumstances which can lead to suspension or dismissal. The advantages of being specific are clarity, knowledge and understanding. Others would argue that it is best to participate in decisions about penalties afterwards rather than before.

Points to Note

1. If somebody is sacked unfairly, act fast. Remember the limitations of the law.

2. Have you a special discipline procedure? Does it work speedily? Are there time limits? Are any stages redundant?

3. Make sure supervisors have no authority to sack or suspend.

4. The steward should be informed when warnings are given and be entitled to represent his members at each stage.

5. There should be a right of appeal to higher levels of management.

6. Nobody should be dismissed until procedure is exhausted.

7. Warnings should be wiped off a worker's record after as short a period as you can negotiate has elapsed.

8. Check your procedure against the Code.

Safety and Health at Work

THE PROBLEM

The Report of the Royal Commission on safety began: 'Every year something like 1,100 people are killed at their work in this country. Every year about half a million suffer injuries in varying degrees of severity. 23 million working days are lost annually on account of industrial injury and disease.' There appears to be much agreement that the situation is unacceptable; that legal rules and collective bargaining have not successfully dealt with the problem.

The criminal law on health, safety and welfare is contained in some thirty different Acts of Parliament, supported by more than five hundred statutory instruments. It is fragmented, unwieldy and restrictively interpreted. With only just over a thousand inspectors in all, the average workplace is routinely inspected once every four years. The International Labour Organization says that once a year is necessary. In the 1970s the average fine under the Factories Act was about £40; many would claim that enforcement has been crippled by the inspectorate's philosophy of advice and persuasion.

The new Health and Safety at Work Act does not revolutionize this. The penalties are only slightly increased (the average fine is just over £100), the standard of care imposed is weak[36] and in spite of increasing the coverage of 5 million workers there are question marks over plans to increase the size of the inspectorate which will weaken the utilization of the new improvement and prohibition notices. Compensation in the civil courts is very much a lottery, and workers often lose the right to industrial injuries benefits for accidents at work owing to the restrictive interpretation of the tribunals.[37]

The way things work can be graphically illustrated by two examples given by Kinnersley.[38]

Mr. E. Peel for the company (W. & C. French) said that if the regulations regarding shoring up of trenches were rigidly enforced there would be a thousand such prosecutions a day. There would have been no prosecution now had there not been an accident. He added that contractors would find jobs economically impractical if they shored earth works as thoroughly as the regulations demanded. Report in *Colchester Evening Gazette* of magistrates court case after a man was injured in a trench collapse. The company was fined £50.

We have the knowledge and apparatus for absorbing gases, arresting grit, dust and fumes and preventing smoke formation. The only reason we still permit the escape of pollutants is because economics play such an important part in the word 'practicable', in the expression 'best practicable means' and most of our problems are cheque book rather than technical. (Chief Alkali Inspector addressing International Air Pollution Conference, December 1970)

Kinnersley concludes: 'They can get away with it because the law is soft and not intended to present any fundamental challenge to profit.'

UNIONS AND SAFETY

What has been the record of trade unions? The failure to achieve better legislation than the new Act speaks volumes. For years unionists have had to rely on one TUC doctor and the limited services of the TUC Centenary

Institute of Occupational Health. Only three unions, AUEW, EEPTU and NUM, have full-time safety officers. Unions have done very useful work in compensation cases but have not sufficiently focused on prevention. Problems are many. Pressures from management wage systems which encourage safety short cuts, attitudes which equate dangerous conditions with virility, cause divisions amongst the unions. Yet a working man's capital is his health and a fight for safety and welfare guarantees should be an intrinsic part of trade unionism. When you consider safety at work, you will find that you cannot rely on law and outside agencies, but you can use them. You've got to do most of the hard slog yourselves. Because of this, the union safety representative elected by the shop floor is a kingpin. One of the advantages of the new Act is that it places a duty on employers to *consult* safety representatives and to allow the establishment of safety committees.[39] Regulations give more detail on their functions. The Act gives four issues on which management must consult with the safety representative: the making of safety arrangements; the maintaining of safety arrangements; the checking of the effectiveness of these arrangements; other functions to be laid down in future regulations. Remember that it is a criminal offence not to consult safety representatives. If you don't think you are getting a fair deal, call in the inspector.

When the Industrial Relations Code of Practice talks of 'consultation', it means that management discusses matters with the representatives, exchanges views and gives information. This is all well and good, but it is important that safety committees should not be merely meetings at which management tells safety representatives what it is going to do (or not going to do), or asks their advice and keeps the right to make the decisions itself. Safety can be a matter of conflict and management has no more right to make unilateral decisions here than it has on wages or discipline. In the United States the National Labour Relations Board has made health and safety matters mandatory subjects for union bargaining. Here, too, unions should *negotiate* agreement on safety committees, not merely be 'involved' in the decisions made by others.

In the past workers have complained that joint safety committees tended to be Friday afternoon talking shops, with a lot of piety but little follow-up. If each area or department has its own safety steward he is working on the job and is in an ideal position to evaluate hazards and get things done. The union side of a committee will then consist of activists who can report back, argue decisions which should be binding on management, monitor them and involve the workers in their implementation. Regular meetings, chairmen alternately from union and management, speedy carrying out of decisions and full information about safety can make a committee work.

It is important to ensure that the workers' side consists of *union* representatives elected by and responsible to the members.[40]

Insist that safety representation is a union function. You cannot ignore non-members, but you can use safety in order to recruit people. How many workers should each representative look after? That depends on the layout of the work, the hazards, the size of the work force and the amount of initial interest. The regulations have more to say on this. The advantage of having a separate safety steward is that he will give a second opinion in a conflict between money and safety but it will depend who the steward is, his attitudes, how many he represents, and so on. If you do have a separate safety representative it is important to integrate him in the work-place organization through, say, a safety sub-committee of the works committee. You may need departmental committees as well as a central committee.

A safety representative will need facilities. He should be involved in all negotiations which affect safety: bonus, manning and job evaluation in particular. The job of the representative is to build up his knowledge and skill about safety, and thus his authority with those he represents. Like an ordinary steward, the more he does this and the more time he spends on the job the more business he will generate and the more respect, support and involvement he will get from the members. The law can be used as a jumping-off point: how far you can jump depends on you and your members.

Many workers handling safety problems feel that their representatives should have the right to stop the job. In the United States, workers' safety representatives can apply directly for court orders requiring inspectors to enforce regulations and can stop a process or machine they consider to be dangerous (Occupation, Safety and Health Act, 1970).[41] This right is not contained in the new British Act.

When workers believe that there is a safety hazard but management disagrees, safety stewards can exercise this right in practice, if they have the support of their members. An industrial tribunal decided, in 1972, that a worker had the right to refuse an order which put him in physical danger. In such circumstances stopping work is the only answer. Anybody can call in the inspector and in a dispute of this type doing so can give strength to your arm, although you may find it difficult to get him quickly. Should safety problems be taken through procedure? Yes, if the procedure is fast enough and nobody is going to get hurt in the meantime. If procedure is too slow and you're in the situation above, then action works wonders.

Inspectors now have a legal duty to give the representatives information they have received from management and details of any recommendations they have made. The safety representatives should be there when the inspector comes in and should go round with him on his inspection. They should ensure that he sees everyday life in the work-place, not a cover-up that would do justice to a visit by the Queen.

Companies are now legally obliged to produce and to publicize a written safety policy.[42] This can be used by workers to launch their own safety analysis. All hazards, danger areas, unsafe processes, all chemical and toxic substances in use, should be listed. Accident and sickness records should be obtained from management. Methods of change or eradication can be investigated and priorities for action worked out.

Finally, there is the vexed question of accepting money for safety, that is, hazard allowances. The acceptance of this money really erodes the principle that you should not have to work in unsafe situations. And it can cause other problems.

In a soap factory, people were anxious about the dangers to workers directly handling an enzyme-based washing powder. The advice of union doctors was that there was a real hazard and production should be discontinued. This did not impress the company. There was a growing and lucrative market for the product and their medical advisers claimed that the danger was being exaggerated. After negotiations, an extra allowance was agreed for the group of workers directly involved with the powder as an interim measure, without prejudice to the union position, that production should be discontinued. Within weeks the union branch looked like disintegrating into warring factions as groups of workers involved in later stages of the production of the powder demanded extra allowances.

If you call for production to be stopped, then you have to insist on re-allocation of workers to other jobs. With an important product this can cause difficulties. But once workers accept extra cash they have a vested interest in the dangerous conditions.

Points to Note

1. Safety representatives should be elected by union members and be part of the work-place organization. Get the Regulations; see if they help.

2. Safety representatives should have the right of access to records and safety equipment; freedom of movement; the right to inspect plant at any time, to call meetings, to be involved in training.

3. Elected decision-making safety committees should meet regularly.

4. Get hold of the literature: the Codes of Practice; technical notes; regulations from the inspectorate and the Commission which relate to hazards at your work-place. Make yourself an expert. Be in touch with your union and the TUC on safety.

5. Know your company's safety policy. Is it implemented by management? Do your own safety analysis and draw up a plan of action.

6. When you have a good case, urge workers not to work in unsafe conditions.

7. Relate safety to speeding up, manning cuts, long hours, shift work and payment schemes.

8. Build up good relations with the inspectors – and phone them about your problems.

9. Watch the money for safety situation like a hawk.

Women's Rights

Women now constitute 36 per cent of the labour force and 27 per cent of all trade unionists, and these percentages are increasing. Women's problems must be taken up by the unions. And what problems! Women work in badly organized, badly paid areas. Compared with men they occupy subordinate or unskilled positions concentrated in lower grades. Often they have three burdens: those of worker, housewife and mother. Collective bargaining and legislation have not yet greatly helped women at work.

Since 1968 most women's basic minimum rates moved up to 90 per cent or more of male rates. By the end of 1975 they had to be the same as male rates. The week's earnings of women manual workers were 49·9 per cent of men's in 1970, and their hourly earnings were 60·1 per cent of men's. By 1974 women's weekly earnings were 55·5 per cent of men's and their hourly earnings 67 per cent of men's. In non-manual work in 1974 women's average weekly earnings were 52 per cent of men's and their hourly rate 55 per cent. Men manual workers do an average seven hours a week more then women so this must be taken into consideration. In non-manual work men tend to do similar hours to women, so average weekly earnings figures provide a realistic picture. Overall there has been no real change in the picture since the Second World War.[43]

BARGAINING ABOUT EQUAL PAY

Why has the Equal Pay Act not been more successful? The first problem is the nature of the Act: it can only touch on the problem. Most women do not come within its brief of equal pay for similar work because their jobs are not comparable to men's. What they are getting is low pay for the worst jobs. The second problem is the implementation of the Act.

Anything to be got out of this Act has to be bargained for, and employers have not been slow in taking up positions which can ensure the Act just remains a piece of paper. Because of the type of jobs women do, there may be no men to compare with. Where there are men to compare with, an employer may be able to reduce the number of jobs done by both men and women, or make sure the terms and conditions of employment are not the same elsewhere in the combine so that women cannot compare themselves with men doing similar jobs; for example, an employer can change hours or holidays. Levelling up to lowest male rates means that employers will fight to keep this rate as low as possible For certain jobs they may decide to bring in contract labour, since as these women are employed by someone else they will not be able to claim equal pay with the men they work with.

As long as grades are not termed 'male' and 'female' and are technically open to men and women, an employer can pay a grade containing nearly all or all women less than an all-male grade. All he has to do is change the sex basis of the grading: women's work becomes light work and men's work becomes heavy work. In a recent laundry agreement four grades appeared: A, transport; B, washroom operatives (heavy); C, process operatives (light); D, others. Not surprisingly, 90 per cent of the women were graded into C, though the jobs done by C and D were basically the same.

Job content can be slightly changed and the job reclassified. A factory paid male toilet attendants and cleaners £26 and females £17. To avoid raising the female rate to £26, women were reclassified as attendants. Job evaluation is a major problem. This system is really a rationalization of prejudices about how jobs should be ranked. The factors chosen and their weighting can be based on social prejudices about women's work and so confirm its low status. Skills like manual dexterity or conditions of work for women have been given low weightings compared with physical effort or conditions of work for men. Other factors such as length of training can be heavily weighted against women. If you get involved, *negotiate* over factors and weightings and get a committee of women to supervise.

The British Paper Box Federation lists four factors which can be used to reintroduce wage discrimination: long service; merit payments; attendance bonus; willingness to work overtime. Women are likely to have had breaks in service, for instance for pregnancy, and to have changed jobs on returning to work. Similarly, women may take time off to look after children or husbands and if they have families they will not want to work long overtime. On these factors men obviously get the best deal.

Some employers have simply considered stopping employing women or cutting down on absenteeism and time off for domestic reasons.

In the face of this attitude only a determined offensive by the unions can ensure that women get any benefit from the legislation. Yet the social subordination of women is reflected in the unions.

WOMEN AND THE UNIONS

The Office of Manpower Economics stated in its report on equal pay: 'About a quarter of the companies visited had experienced union pressure for equal pay . . . but about one in ten contended that its introduction had been blocked by the attitudes of male members . . . the men had resisted changes which would have narrowed the differentials.'[44] In 1973 APEX supported a vigorous campaign of strike action to achieve equal pay. On the other hand it was one of the first demands to be dropped by the AUEW in their 1972 strikes. For many years the Union of Post Office Workers opposed permanent status for women in the Post Office.

Women participate less than men at every level in the unions. NUPE with 63 per cent female membership had an all male executive until recently. APEX with half its membership female had only two women at this level and COHSE with an even higher female membership had only one woman executive member. Women must get involved in their unions and fight for themselves. There are signs that this is happening. There should be discrimination in favour of women on committees so that they are directly represented and start getting involved. Meetings should be held at times suitable for women and arrangements made for children. It is most important that men trade unionists change their attitudes about the role of women.

In July 1973 women at GEC Spon Street, Coventry, earning a basic rate of £13, believed that the introduction of new materials would bring piece-rate earnings down. The AUEW convenor, Albert Beardmore, told drivers to please themselves about crossing the picket lines. He did so himself, saying, 'I'm not going to have my men laid off by a bunch of silly girls.' When his deputy, Elsie Noles, supported the women he tried to take away her card and had to be overruled by the district committee.

Support from other workers, particularly better organized men, is crucial for women. The women on strike in 1975 at Wingrove and Rogers, Liverpool, won in the end, after three months, because of support from other factories, and the docks Liverpool Trades Council organized picket support. At SEI Heywood an equal pay strike was defeated. No support was forthcoming from the Eccles Factory. The union did not succeed in getting intensive blacking and the workers were isolated. It cuts both ways: men need the support of their wives, otherwise there are the strike breaking attitudes as at Cowley and Chrysler. Women have the *right* to the rate for the job like any other wage earner, but it is clear that it will not be handed out on a plate; it needs unions' vigilance, involvement and strength.

The TUC women's conference earlier this year gave overwhelming support to an ASTMS resolution calling for free contraception and abortion facilities for all women. Many trade union bodies including the ATTI and ASTMS annual conferences have opposed James White's Abortion Act Amendment Bill. This restrictive measure would hit working-class women who cannot afford private abortions.

Equal pay, equal opportunities, participation in the trade union movement can only become a reality for women if they can be freed from the sole responsibility for the care of the family and given the right to control their own fertility.[45]

Equal pay is no good unless women have equal opportunities to get jobs. The Sex Discrimination Act tries to deal with this problem.

NURSERIES

A fifth of all married women in the country with at least one child under five works. But there are only 493 local authority day nurseries providing 23 838 places in England and Wales. The Industrial Relations Review and Report[46] did a survey of 25 organizations which ran day nurseries. Nearly every one had been set up unilaterally by management to overcome a female labour shortage. Other reasons given were the desire to improve their image and the need to cut training costs. Other companies such as Vitality Bulbs in Bury St Edmunds reserve and pay for twenty places at the local authority nursery. Most of the companies felt it had been a good experience and were thinking of extending it. The cost to the employee per week in the firms surveyed varied from 50p per week at Church and Co., Northampton, to £5·50 per week at BBC Pebble Mill. The highest number of places was 120, at John Bright, Rochdale.

Obviously, this type of scheme is attractive if the standard of care is high, the cost is reasonable and the children are near at hand. However, many unionists have pointed out that this type of welfare facilities can divert people from noticing their low pay and can tie the worker to the job. Obviously the basic aim of unions should be a comprehensive state system which will involve a hard fight against the Labour Government's attempt to cut back on nursery facilities. Company nurseries can only be a short-term palliative.

The Inland Revenue nursery, Cardiff, is run by the local authority, although it is paid for by the Civil Service; a joint committee of local employers and staff representatives is responsible for admissions.

MATERNITY LEAVE

Collective bargaining on maternity leave has had erratic successes. One study[47] in 1973 of seventy-four private companies in a wide range of industries and seventeen public sector authorities found that in the public sector there was an almost complete coverage of maternity leave schemes with detailed policies allowing full pay or half pay in most cases. In the private sector only eighteen companies had written policies, six of which provided maternity pay for varying lengths of time. Big firms like Express Dairies, Ford, Heinz, Kellogg and Shell, had no formal policy, and these were the majority, although many had informal discretionary policies. Time off to attend the clinic during pregnancy was often covered and between 1973 and 1975 more and more policies extended to both married and single women. Here are some more facts from this study.

The British Printing Corporation allowed women up to eighteen weeks' maternity leave on half pay plus national insurance benefits. Continuity of employment was maintained. The qualification was twelve months' continuous service. Ever-Ready Battery gave unpaid absence up to thirteen weeks without loss of continuity after a year's service: 'The company will endeavour to provide the same or a similar job on return to work.' Penguin Books gave twenty weeks' maximum maternity leave after a year's service if the worker said she would return and work for at least five months and repay on a proportional basis any benefit received for part of this guaranteed period not worked. The basis was twelve weeks at full pay less state benefit, and a further eight weeks at half pay.

An example from the public sector is British Railways which gave up to thirteen weeks without pay. An established or permanent unestablished woman civil servant was entitled to three months' paid leave; the first two months' money to be issued on normal pay days and the last month's to be withheld until the woman had returned and worked three months. Unestablished women with five years' service were entitled to six weeks' paid leave which would count against their normal sick leave.

Paternity leave clauses have also been included in a number of agreements recently, either as a short period to help at birth or as an alternative to maternity leave if the mother wants to work instead. The Association of University Teachers have a policy that the husband should have the option of twelve months' unpaid leave if he looks after the baby while the mother works.

Here collective bargaining has not made great inroads. It has largely been left to employers to develop policies which often leave much to be desired. There are new rights in the Employment Protection Act. This entitles a woman to be paid by her employer six weeks' wages when on maternity leave minus the State maternity allowance. She is also entitled to reinstatement in the same or a similar job for a period of up to twenty-nine weeks. The qualification is a year's service. She must tell the employer she is going to exercise her right and give him a week's notice when she does. If he does not take her back her remedy is procedure for unfair dismissal. If a woman is sacked because she is pregnant that is unfair dismissal also.

At the TUC's women's conference in March 1975 the delegates voted to ask the TUC to support paid maternity leave of eighteen weeks; they also asked that either the father or mother of the child should have the right to a year off work after its birth.

Women need special attention because of the raw deal they have had in the past. They *are* part of the workers' movement. Everything that's been said before holds. For example, it is no good winning equal pay and being put on short time the next day. When public services are cut and unemployment grows, women are the first to be thrown on the dole, and only strong organization, unity and support from men can fight this.

Many of the points listed below are contained in the Working Women's Charter adopted by many union branches and Trades Councils. It has been accepted by the annual conference of TASS, CPSA, NUJ and the ATTI.

Points to Note

1. What progress has been made towards equal pay at your work-place? Know the Act. Use contacts at other work-places to see if women can compare with workers there.

2. Are there any discriminatory practices in recruitment, promotion conditions, dismissal or lay-off? Can the Sex Discrimination Act help? Make sure that women are not laid off or made redundant because of equal pay. Make sure the Act does not encourage the employer to try to intensify the pace of work for women or clamp down on time off for domestic reasons.

3. Watch out for gradings being fiddled. Avoid discriminatory and derisive allowances as part of the wage structure.

4. Job evaluation: factor weightings and points allocation should be mutually agreed. Final gradings should be agreed and *then* money should be negotiated. The process should be supervised by committees with women representatives.

5. Do you need a work-place nursery? What are the obstacles? Do you need more flexible hours for men *and* women to look after the children or do the shopping?

6. Maternity leave: try to get:

Full pay for as long as possible; the target should be eighteen weeks.

Sickness or holiday entitlement should not be affected.

As short a qualification period as possible.

No loss of continuity, pension or promotion prospects.

Maternity leave should be seen as a right which goes with the job, not something dependent on future service. Try to remove conditions such as working out a period on return or giving back the money.

Manual workers should demand the superior standards on these matters which staff workers often have. *All* women have similar problems.

7. Unions should work out a work-place and combine strategy to fight for equal pay and opportunities. Equal pay can mean *high* equal pay for both men and women.

There should be women on all committees.

Meetings should be held at convenient times, and arrangements should be made for child care.

Special meetings of women at all levels may be useful to discuss their specific problems and in order to give them confidence in speaking.

Unions should investigate the pattern of inequality in their own areas, as ACTT did and NUBE were doing in 1975.

In a dispute mobilize the housewives.

8. Union policy should include these wider demands:

Free contraception and abortion.

Extension of state nurseries.

Removal of remaining pension schemes, taxation, etc., having legal impediments.

Conclusion

Perhaps you would like to go back to Table 7 (pp. 212–13) and add a fourth category, 'Bargaining'? Make some notes on what you think of the new rights, what improvements could be made, and what bargaining you think is needed about them.

Here we have only had a chance to look briefly at a few things. What about hours, holidays and sickness benefit? Where have British workers fallen behind workers in Europe and the USA? If the law hasn't kept pace, what are *you* doing in bargaining terms?

Manna doesn't fall from heaven. The laws are the product of trade union strength on the ground and also, as we have seen, more control is not necessarily gained by laws being passed. But muscle can help in using the new legal framework. It can jack up the platform an inch or so. If you haven't got the muscle you may be able to use the new rights to build on. But we always have to look at the wider issues and try to control them. The law may help with trade union recognition or equal pay, but these mean different things if we accept in return wage restraint policies and 1½ million unemployed.

But don't get starry-eyed! Without union strength these laws are like a balloon with no air. Our strength must rely on organized shop-floor encroachment on managerial rights, more control over hiring and firing, more control over the allocation and pace of work, more control over financial decisions.

Remember two things. First, it's no good controlling decisions in your factory if you don't control decisions about the society in which your factory operates. Secondly, you don't get 'owt for nowt'. It's hard work, and those with the power and privilege will also fight right along the line to keep what they've got.

Notes

1. Trade Union and Labour Relations Act (TULRA), Sch. 1.6 (4).
2. Employment Protection Act (EPA), Ss. 11–16.
3. TULRA, Sch. 1.
4. Quoted in Wedderburn, K. W., *The Worker and The Law* (Pelican, 1971).
5. Taken from Abel Smith, B., and Stevens, B., *Lawyers and The Courts* (Heinemann, 1967).
6. Kahn-Freund, O., *Labour and the Law* (Sweet & Maxwell, 1972), p. 12.
7. Chamberlain, N., *Labor* (McGraw Hill, 1958), p. 76.
8. Fox, A., *Man Mismanagement* (Hutchinson, 1974), p. 16.
9. TULRA, Sch. 1.6 (4).
10. EPA, Ss. 53–6, 78–80.
11. EPA, Ss. 11–16.
12. *Oxford Mail*, 1 June 1975.
13. TULRA, Sch. 1.6 (5).
14. *Socialist Worker* (March 1975).
15. EPA, Ss. 57–8.
16. *Good Industrial Relations* (TUC, 1971); Topham, A., *The Organized Worker* (in this series), Chapters 2, 3, 8.
17. Industrial Relations Review and Report (IRRR) No. 53. Biased, as most of these surveys are, to the more 'progressive' company.
18. *Financial Times*, 2 June 1975.
19. *Socialist Worker* (May 1975).
20. O'Higgins, P., *Workers' Rights* (in this series), Chapter 6.
21. EPA, Ss. 61, Ss. 99–107. Most of the examples of agreements here are from Incomes Data Studies (IDS) Nos 13, 17, 36, 61, and IRRR No. 55.
22. Parker, S. R., *et al.*, *Effects of the Redundancy Payments Act* (HMSO, 1971).
23. IRRR No. 55.
24. Industry Act, 1975, Ss. 27–36. See Barratt Brown, M., *Information at Work*, in this series.
25. Linder, P., *The Great Flint Sit Down* (Solidarity pamphlet).
26. *Guardian*, 29 May 1975.
27. *Socialist Worker* (February 1975).
28. O'Higgins, P., and Hepple, B. A., *Individual Employment Law* (Sweet & Maxwell, 1972), pp. 80ff.; Aiken, O., and Reid, J., *Employment Welfare and Safety at Work* (Penguin, 1971), pp. 178–9.
29. Look at H. Calvert's *Social Security Law* (Sweet & Maxwell, 1974) and his article 'Lay-Offs and the Three-Day Week' in *Current Legal Problems* (1974); Ogus, A.,

'Unemployment Benefit for Workers on Short Time', *Industrial Law Journal* (March 1975).

30. *Guardian* and *Financial Times* reports, December 1974. Most of the agreements mentioned are taken from IDS Nos 20, 22, 81.

31. EPA, Ss. 23–33.

32. TULRA, Sch. 1 (8).

33. EPA, Sch. 1.

34. National Joint Advisory Council, 'Unfair Dismissal'; Anderman, S. D., *Unfair Dismissal and the Law* (IPM, 1973) is a good survey.

35. Wedderburn, K. W., *Employment Grievances and Disputes Procedure in Britain* (University of California Press, 1969).

36. The Factories Act imposes absolute duties. Here they are only duties to be reasonably practicable.

37. Wedderburn, K. W., *The Worker and The Law*, Chapter 6.

38. Kinnersley, P., *The Hazards of Work* (Pluto Press, 1973).

39. Health and Safety at Work Act (HWSA), S. 2 (iv-vii).

40. The Employment Protection Act makes the appointment of the legal safety representative a union function.

41. Lewis, D., *Industrial Law Journal* (March 1974).

42. HWSA, S. 2 (iii).

43. Figures from the Department of Employment *Gazette*.

44. *Women and Work*, Department of Employment Manpower Paper No. 10 (HMSO, 1974).

45. On equal pay: National Council for Civil Liberties, *Equal Pay and How to Get It* (1974); TUC, *Your Job and the Equal Pay Act* (1974). Also, Patterson, P., and Armstrong, M., *Employers' Guide to Equal Pay* (Kogan Page, 1972).

46. IRRR No. 95.

47. IDS No. 58.

Picketing and the Law
by Paul O'Higgins

This essay takes one particular union weapon used in bargaining, and gives a detailed account of the confused position of the law, and of the obstacle race which unions have to run when picketing. The author suggests some actions which are necessary in order to remove these obstacles, underlining the claim that 'the basic answer to how workers get their rights is by organization: through union negotiation and action'. (Eds.)

The Right to Picket

Although, or perhaps because, picketing is one of the most important weapons available to workers and unions in the course of industrial action, there is no 'right to picket' in British law. Consider the following examples taken from the decisions of the courts.

There was a strike at a factory but some of the workers remained at work. Groups of strikers stood at the entrances to the work-place in order to persuade those still at work to join the strike. One striker wished to join a small group of workers who were already engaged in picketing. The situation was quite peaceful. There was no violence or threat of violence. A policeman forbade the worker from joining his comrades already engaged in picketing. The worker pushed gently past the policeman and was arrested. He was subsequently convicted of the crime of obstructing a policeman in the execution of his duty. This was in a case called *Piddington* v. *Bates*.

Broome, a picket standing in the street at a construction site in 1972, flagged down a lorry driver making deliveries to the site and endeavoured to persuade him not to cross the picket line. When the driver did not respond Broome stood in front of the lorry and continued to try to persuade him not to make the delivery to the site. Broome was arrested and convicted of the crime of obstructing the highway, contrary to the Highways Act, 1959. This was in a case called *Hunt* v. *Broome*.

Pickets were standing outside a hospital where the electricians were on strike. When workers who had taken the place of striking electricians left the hospital by bus the police formed cordons to prevent the pickets stopping the bus and shouting abuse at the strike breakers. One of the pickets tried to push his way through the police cordon to persuade the bus driver not to pass the pickets. He was arrested and later convicted of obstructing and assaulting the police in the execution of their duty. This was in a case called *Kavanagh* v. *Hiscock*.

These and many other cases illustrate the simple fact that however peaceful picketing may be it can lawfully occur only so long as the police decide to allow it to. In order to understand this extraordinary situation there are certain basic facts about the British legal system that need to be borne in mind.

Firstly, British judges enjoy an unusually wide authority not only to interpret the rules laid down by Parliament in statutes, but also, in the past at least, to create new legal wrongs. Where judges had formerly invented new legal wrongs, later judges involved in a case could easily extend their ambit to cover working-class action. The set of rules created in this way by judges is what is sometimes called the 'common law'.

Secondly, given that judges have wide discretionary powers, their class background and sympathies have inevitably meant that when interpreting vague areas of criminal liability they have tended to adopt interpretations that have restricted freedom of action by workers.

Thirdly, since it has been usual in labour relations to recognize the legitimacy of trade union action by conferring *immunities* upon trade unions and workers from judicially created or extended legal liabilities, there are few positive *rights*. The very existence of trade unions is unlawful under the rules of the common law, the rules made by the judges. It has been necessary to pass legislation to enable trade unions lawfully to exist. The first statute to do this was the Trade Union Act, 1871. This has been repealed, but the Trade Union and Labour Relations Act, 1974, now protects trade unions from the application of the judge-made rules which would make them unlawful. This method of passing statutes to enable trade unions to exist is a way of conferring *immunities* on trade unions from the application of judge-made rules. It should be explained that some judge-made rules made trade unions and their activities *civilly* unlawful. That means that trade unions could not own property or employ officials. Some judge-made rules make union activity *criminal*. This means, for example, that someone who continues to picket after being told to stop by a policeman is guilty of a criminal offence and may be sent to prison.

The result of the development of rules by the judges about labour conflict is that workers taking industrial action find it virtually impossible to organize effectively without breaking them. Because of union pressure, therefore, Parliament has passed legislation which provides that some of the judge-made rules shall not apply to union action. Thus, although workers taking industrial action may sometimes be immune from legal proceedings, they have not been given a positive right to strike or to picket which would enable them to call upon the courts to prevent others, in particular the police, from interfering with the exercise of those 'rights'. This is because where a *right* exists in the full sense it implies a legal obligation upon others not to interfere with the exercise of that right.

Lastly, it would indeed be surprising if Governments in this country had been willing to establish a right for workers to take action which might decisively improve their chances of success in industrial conflict, for instance by recognizing a *right* to picket.

It is a reflection of a century or more of working-class struggle that workers believe that they have a right to picket, but their true position in law does not correspond with this. Of course, though, trade union strength often enables workers in practice to enjoy what is tantamount to a right to picket.

Legal Hurdles Confronting Pickets

Amongst the myriad of legal wrongs which may be committed by pickets there are four principal ones. Two of them are civil: private nuisance and trespass. Two of them are criminal: public nuisance and obstructing the highway contrary to the Highways Act, 1959. However peaceful, quiet and unobjectionable, not to say ineffective, a picket may be, he will not find it easy to avoid committing at least one of these wrongs.

Private nuisance involves interference with another's enjoyment of his property, so that a successful or prolonged picket may make a factory owner enjoy his property less.

Private trespass: assuming that picketing occurs on the highway (if it occurs anywhere else without the consent of the private landowner it is always a private trespass) it is generally believed to be a trespass against the owner of the subsoil on which the roadway rests. In urban areas this is normally the local authority.

Crimes: as regards the crimes of public nuisance and obstruction under the Highways Act, liability for the first occurs where there is unreasonable interference with the rights or freedoms of others, and the latter occurs where anyone stands still on the highway.

IS PICKETING UNREASONABLE?

Of course, peaceful picketing ought to be accepted as a perfectly normal and reasonable activity in a democratic society. It is not clear, however, that the fact that what is being done is a reasonable form of behaviour will prevent one from being liable for some of the four legal wrongs described above. For private nuisance it must be shown that what is being done is an unreasonable activity. However, the courts have so far taken the view that trespass on the highway is committed whether or not what is being done is a reasonable form of activity, although in some cases judges have suggested that this activity is reasonable. It has clearly been established that to be liable for the crime of public nuisance one must be behaving in an unreasonable way. As regards obstructing the highway under the Highways Act, there is a conflict amongst the cases decided by the courts as to whether reasonable behaviour can make one liable.

We have talked about whether it is necessary, in respect of the four principal wrongs which may be committed by pickets, to show that the pickets have been behaving in an unreasonable way. Why?

Because in a democratic society picketing is a form of demonstration combining the exercise of the liberty to communicate information and opinions to other people with the exercise of the freedom of meeting or assembly. In any democratic society freedom of expression and freedom of assembly are supposed to be basic liberties, and the peaceful exercise of these liberties is obviously a reasonable form of behaviour.

The paradox in Britain is that there does not exist any legal recognition of a *right* to freedom of expression or of assembly, or of the combined exercise of both, that is, a right to picket. Therefore the legality of the exercise of these basic 'rights' turns upon the technical issue whether or not certain legal wrongs may be committed when the persons involved are behaving in a perfectly reasonable way. In the case of private nuisance and public nuisance there must be unreasonable conduct. The position under the Highways Act is uncertain. But in the case of private trespass against the owner of the subsoil on which the highway stands most judges think that there need be no evidence that the pickets have behaved unreasonably.

The recognition of this simple fact, that British law may make picketing unlawful however peaceful it may be, has occasionally led a liberally minded judge, who sees the absurdity of the law not recognizing the basic rights essential in a democratic society, to avoid the application in a particular case of the letter of the law. Lord Denning is a very good example. However, a liberally minded judge has little practical impact for two reasons. First of all, most judges do not share this view, so that in most cases peaceful picketing will be found to be unlawful. Secondly, quite irrespective of whether picketing is peaceful or not, the police have the power to forbid the continuance of all picketing. This is the result of a case called *Duncan* v. *Jones*. In 1933 a member of the Unemployed Workers' Movement planned to hold a meeting outside a Government Training Centre in a Welsh town. The speaker was about to mount a box on the street outside the Centre when a policeman ordered her to hold her meeting some distance away. She refused, thinking that she had a right to express her views at a public meeting, but was arrested. She was subsequently convicted of the crime of obstructing the police in the execution of their duty. Such a crime already existed, but it was believed to be concerned with people who resisted arrest, or acted similarly, when the police were performing some duty. The court, however, took a different view and extended the scope of the crime so as to include anyone who disobeys an instruction issued by a policeman whenever he believes it necessary to issue such an instruction to lessen the chances of a breach of the peace occurring. The grounds which the court held in *Duncan* v. *Jones* that made it all right for the policeman to prevent the meeting taking place outside the Training Centre was that *fourteen months* previously, when the speaker had held a meeting outside the centre, a disturbance had occurred in the Training Centre on the same day. No evidence was given to suggest that there had been any connection between the meeting and the disturbance. The 'disturbance' was that someone had stood on a table and sung the 'Red Flag'. This case shows the simple fact that the courts will always uphold the instructions issued by a policeman however slight the evidence is that a breach of the peace might occur which would make it necessary for him to take steps to prevent it. The result of this case is that wherever a policeman reasonably believes that a breach of the peace may occur, he may take steps to lessen the chances of it doing so. Wherever there is a difference of opinion, whether it be at a football match or a strike or a lock-out, it will always be reasonable for a policeman to believe that a breach of the peace may occur. In these cases liberally minded judges have failed so far to undermine in any way the principles laid down in *Duncan* v. *Jones*.

Statute Law

We have been talking so far mainly of common law wrongs, like private trespass and public and private nuisance, and of the common law power to take action to prevent a breach of the peace occurring. But what about Parliament? Has Parliament remained unaffected by working-class pressure demanding a right to picket?

There has in fact been a whole series of Acts passed by Parliament seeking to give some recognition, usually in the form of immunity from legal wrongs like private trespass and public and private nuisance. The first of these Acts was in 1859. The most important ones still in force include the Conspiracy and Protection of Property Act, 1875. In 1873 there was a strike of gas stokers in London; the strikers were prosecuted and it was suggested during the legal proceedings that they could be liable for the crime of conspiracy if what they had agreed to do interfered with their employer's freedom of action, as a strike must necessarily do, or caused him annoyance. In other words, where strikers did something which was quite lawful, but which annoyed or interfered with their employer, it made them liable for a crime. Section 3 of the 1875 Act, which was passed as a result of trade union pressure, provided that workers should only be liable for the crime of conspiracy if the action agreed to by the workers was itself a crime. This Section of the 1875 Act is essential to lawful strike action and to lawful picketing by workers, because in practice it is virtually impossible for pickets to avoid committing some form of criminal conspiracy. The same Act in its Section 7 said that certain actions, already unlawful at common law, could give rise to additional criminal proceedings if they could be shown to fall under the following heads:

Every person who, with a view to compel any other person to abstain from doing or to do any act which such other person has a legal right to do or abstain from doing, wrongfully and without legal authority, –
1. Uses violence to or intimidates such other person or his wife or children, or injures his property;
   or,
2. Persistently follows such other person about from place to place; or
3. Hides any tools, clothes, or other property owned or used by such other person, or deprives him of or hinders him in the use thereof; or,
4. Watches or besets the house or other place where such other person resides, or works, or carries on business, or happens to be, or the approach to such house or place; or,
5. Follows such other person with two or more other persons in a disorderly manner in or through any street or road. . . .

Liability under Section 7 exists only when the action taken by the workers is itself unlawful and is taken for the purpose of compelling somebody to do or not to do something. In so far as picketing falls short of compulsion, it does not cause liability under Section 7 even if the pickets are behaving unlawfully in that they are committing a trespass to the highway or obstructing it contrary to the Highways Act, 1959. However, Section 7 clearly is a deterrent to pickets and it was used in many prosecutions of pickets after the General Strike in 1926.

In spite of the statutory recognition of the legitimacy of industrial picketing in the 1875 Act, some courts still found pickets liable for private nuisance if they tried to persuade people not to 'scab', as opposed to merely giving them the information that there was a strike on. As a result, Parliament passed the Trade Disputes Act, 1906, Section 2 of which gave better protection to pickets by permitting them not only to give information but also to seek to persuade scabs not to go to work. The Trade Disputes Act remained in force until 1971, when it was replaced by the Industrial Relations Act. When that Act was replaced by the Trade Union and Labour Relations Act, 1974, the provisions of the Trade Disputes Act of 1906 were largely re-enacted. Section 15 of the 1974 Act reads:

It shall be lawful for one or more persons in contemplation or furtherance of a trade dispute to attend at or near –
  (a) a place where another person works or carries on business; or
  (b) any other place where another person happens to be, not being a place where he resides,
for the purpose only of peacefully obtaining or communicating information or peacefully persuading any person to work or abstain from working.

There has been a considerable amount of judicial interpretation of these provisions, and as a result the courts have narrowed very much the protection for pickets. First of all, the courts have said that – in so far as it may be possible to picket at all without committing some technical offence like obstruction – the number of pickets permitted by the Act is limited to the smallest number necessary to fulfil the objects of picketing, namely to give information or persuade people. Secondly, it is now generally established that if pickets are peaceful but numerous, their mere numbers show that they cannot all be there for the purpose of giving information or persuasion, and therefore none of them are protected by the statute. Thirdly, although this has still not been finally decided, the term 'It shall be lawful' does not confer a *right* to picket, only an immunity from the basic legal wrongs that the smallest number of pickets must inevitably commit. Therefore, since there is no right involved, the police have no corresponding duty to refrain from interfering with peaceful pickets by using the powers given them by the decision in *Duncan* v. *Jones*. Fourthly, although the permitted purposes of picketing are to give information and to persuade, it does not include stopping workers in order to persuade, and above all stopping vehicles is not permitted.

In other words, the courts have taken away the 'right' which Parliament might appear to have conceded to workers, namely the right to picket. But no government is willing to admit this, and so they seek to give the impression that they have given a 'right'.

Some of the things we have said so far may be qualified. First of all, the statutes we have discussed do not apply to picketing for non-industrial purposes. Thus picketing as part of a political protest over American nuclear submarines in British waters is not covered by the statutes. Secondly, industrial picketing to persuade members of the public not to buy goods from a 'struck' employer, that is, 'consumer picketing', is not protected.

When picketing does occur without interference or legal proceedings it is a result of police inaction, which reflects both the strength of trade unions and, sometimes, the instructions given to the police by those in authority. It is strange that picketing is almost always unlawful, but it can take place because the police choose not to enforce the law. It is patently not a 'right to picket'.

Home Office Instructions to the Police

One of the basic facts of life in this country is that the Home Office issues instructions in the form of circulars to police forces. Formally, of course, these circulars are merely advisory, but in practice it would be a bold Chief Constable who made a practice of ignoring them. The legal powers of the police are so wide that it is vital to know what precisely are the instructions issued by the Home Office about police behaviour in trade disputes, above all picketing. The circulars are confidential and are rarely made public. However, one of them, issued by the Home Secretary, Sir John Anderson, on 30 December 1925, on the eve of the General Strike, was in fact published. It is worth reproducing part of it here, *if only because it gets the law wrong*. This circular advised the police that picketing outside the scope of the Trade Disputes Act, 1906, broke Section 7 of the Conspiracy and Protection of Property Act, 1875. It also took a narrow view of the Trade Disputes Act, which if it gave anything at all to pickets must have enabled them to obstruct the highway, because it is difficult to see how picketing can occur without obstruction. Police in 1976 no doubt are governed by more up-to-date circulars, but it would be a criminal offence to publish such a circular here, even if we had a copy!

This is the most important part of the 1925 Circular:

The Secretary of State desires to emphasise the point that all that is made lawful by the later enactment is picketing *for the purpose of peacefully obtaining or communicating information, or of peacefully persuading any person to work or abstain from working*; the offences described in section 7 of the Act of 1875, as quoted above, remain criminal offences.

The only effect of section 2 of the Act of 1906 is that 'attending at or near a house or place' is not criminal if it is done merely for the purpose of peacefully obtaining or communicating information, or of peacefully persuading any person to work or abstain from working; but it remains a

254 Industrial Studies 2

criminal offence under the Act of 1875 if it goes beyond these peaceful purposes and is carried on for purposes of compulsion. The Act of 1906 gives no protection to a person who attends at or near a house or place with a view to compulsion or who intimidates or uses threats of violence, actual or implied, and the duty of the police in dealing with these offences is not in any way affected by that Act.

The chief difficulties, however, which confront the police in dealing with trade disputes arise, no doubt, in the enforcement of the law rather than in the interpretation of it, expecially where acts which are complained of were not observed by the Police and witnesses are reluctant to come forward to give evidence in Court. Occasionally there may also be doubt whether picketing which is being carried on is merely for the purpose of peacefully persuading a person to cease from work or to abstain from working or amounts to intimidation. In endeavouring to deal with this question, the number composing the picket is often a material point. The Act has not laid down any limit to the number of a picket, but it is clear that where a crowd watching or besetting any works is so disproportionate in size to what is needed for lawful purposes as to exclude the idea of peaceful persuasion, the Act of 1906 may cease to apply, and the persons taking part in the demonstration would then become liable to be charged with watching or besetting under the Act of 1875.[1]

In this connection the Secretary of State would also point out that the Trade Disputes Act confers no right to hold meetings upon or *otherwise to obstruct the highway*[2] and occasions may arise where the police should take action on this account and disperse a crowd which has assembled in connection with a trades dispute, even though there is at the time no actual evidence of intimidation.[3]

The police's different attitudes to picketing in different strikes are certainly often due to the instructions issued to them by the Home Office.

The Shrewsbury Case

In 1974 some workers were convicted because of events arising out of a strike in the building industry which was largely directed against lump labour. This case has caused widespread criticism of the law on picketing, including demands for the repeal of the 1875 Act. Total repeal would make all picketing once more a criminal conspiracy. Repeal of Section 7 would not alter the fact that at common law, and in some cases under other statutes, the acts described in Section 7 would remain unlawful. However, the main criticism that ought to be made of the Shrewsbury case is that the pickets were found *guilty of conspiring to commit the Section 7 offence of intimidation*. Conviction on this charge means firstly that it is not necessary to prove that actual intimidation occurred; secondly, that it is not necessary even to establish an agreement to commit the crime of intimidation, but it is sufficient to establish a common course of conduct; thirdly, that although the Section 7 offence of intimidation carries a maximum fine of £20 or three months' imprisonment, because it was a conspiracy the pickets were found guilty of, and not the actual crime of intimidation, there are no upper limits to the sentence which can be imposed upon them. The campaign arising from the case of the Shrewsbury pickets should demand the abolition of the crime of conspiracy, or that the sentence for conspiring to do an act should not be more severe than the sentence which can be imposed for doing the act itself.

Reform of the Law

Apart from altering the law so as to limit the use of conspiracy charges in picketing cases, there are other reforms that would help and might be won with trade union pressure. It is unlikely, of course, that any Government would agree to legislation which would guarantee in effect that picketing would always lead to a victory of the trade union in any particular industrial dispute. There are, however, quite sensible reforms which would prevent the practice of picketing being dependent on the whim of the police.

Firstly, the power of the police to interfere with or prevent picketing by acting under the powers given them by *Duncan* v. *Jones* could be abolished by Act of Parliament. This would leave the police the power to interfere only when some crime was actually being committed or was just about to be committed. Where picketing was peaceful the mere possibility that a breach of the peace might occur would not entitle them to interfere.

Secondly, it could be made clear by Act of Parliament that there is a right to picket and so peaceful picketing is always to be regarded as a reasonable activity, so that in picketing it would not be enough to make people liable for those legal wrongs which are committed by people acting unreasonably. This would apply to the civil wrong of private nuisance and the criminal wrong of public nuisance.

Thirdly, an Act of Parliament could provide that there should be no liability for obstructing the highway contrary to the Highways Act, 1959, or for private trespass against the owner of the subsoil on which the highway stands, unless the action of the persons involved is unreasonable.

Fourthly, the TUC has recommended that pickets should be given a limited right to stop vehicles in order to try to persuade anyone inside them to respect the picket line.

Fifthly, an Act of Parliament should permit consumer picketing.

Sixthly, the law about the place of picketing could be changed. At present protection for pickets is confined to the street, on the highway. Picketing in other places is always unlawful unless the owner has given permission. Thus picketing in many places where the public has free access is unlawful, for instance in a station forecourt or in one of the wide open spaces in shopping precincts. A statute to enable picketing to lawfully occur in these public places would be desirable. The greater understanding of judges in other countries of the realities and necessities of industrial relations can be illustrated by the fact that in Canada in 1974 a court refused to help the owner of a shopping precinct to evict peaceful pickets. It is inconceivable that any English judge would adopt such a liberal approach.

Seventhly, the crime of conspiracy should be abolished, or its application restricted to an agreement to commit a crime.

Lastly, the law should be altered so as to extend the 'right to picket' to all demonstrators instead of being confined, as at present, to pickets acting 'in contemplation or furtherance of a trade dispute', for instance picketing to protest at Government policies generally, or to protest at the sale of South African fruit by a grocer.

Practical Advice on Picketing

Because of the legal difficulties encountered by pickets it may be of interest to print here the advice given by the National Union of Mineworkers to their pickets in the course of their national strike in 1974. Although the Industrial Relations Act, 1971, which was in force then, has now been replaced by the Trade Union and Labour Relations Act, 1974, this advice remains essentially the kind of advice which still has to be given in the light of the current state of the law. It should be added that the NUM also made the point to its members that 'the leader of the picket line will be clearly identified, and any problems should be raised with him. The object of the picket lines is to prevent the movement of coal and extraordinary movement of oil *not* to prevent other workers from attending at their normal place of work. . . .'

The Purpose of Picketing

The purpose of picketing may be to persuade other employees to join in the withdrawal of labour; to dissuade workers recruited by the employer during the Strike from entering the strike-bound premises; or to establish check-points to ensure that no strikers return prematurely. Picketing may also be aimed at deflecting supplies of custom from the employer in dispute.

The Law on Picketing

It is lawful for persons to picket a workplace or any other place (except a person's home), provided they do no more than peacefully obtain or communicate information or peacefully persuade workers to abstain from work. The right to picket is subject to the following legal restrictions:

(i) if pickets enter private property without permission and damage ensues, they are liable to be sued individually for trespass or collectively for conspiracy;

(ii) pickets may communicate or obtain information 'peacefully' but may not 'interfere' with persons entering or leaving premises. 'Interference' has been defined as including the use of such methods as lying down in the road, linking arms to prevent the entry of lorries to premises, jostling or detaining persons entering or leaving the premises, and making threats of violence or engaging in acts of violence;

(iii) it is unlawful for any person to use violence or to intimidate a person or his family, or to injure his property or to deprive him of it; to watch or beset the premises where a person works or the approach to such premises; or to follow him in the street with two or more other persons in a disorderly manner. [See text of Conspiracy and Protection of Property Act, 1875, above.]

In addition any abuse of the right to picket or any wrong other than trespass may constitute a 'Nuisance' at common law;

(iv) Since 1875, protection has been available to Trade Unions against actions for 'simple conspiracy' provided they were acting in contemplation or furtherance of a 'trade' or 'industrial' dispute. (The concept of a 'trade dispute' was replaced by 'industrial dispute' in the Industrial Relations Act 1971.) The three Shrewsbury building workers were not found guilty of 'simple conspiracy' but of conspiring to commit a criminal act (i.e. intimidation). Intimidation is a criminal offence under the Conspiracy and Protection of Property Act 1875, and it carries a maximum sentence of three months, However, the use of conspiracy charges allows unlimited sentences to be passed.

(v) Hunt v. Broome established that Section 134 of the Industrial Relations Act conferred no right on a picket to stop a vehicle against the driver's will. Lawful methods of persuasion were limited to 'oral or visual methods' and did not permit pickets to commit acts such as physical obstruction of a vehicle or person.

(vi) The law gives the police considerable discretionary powers to decide whether the methods used by pickets are lawful. This has led to anomalies and uncertainties. In 1960 the courts supported a police officer who decided that a picket of two persons was adequate and arrested a third man who joined the picket line. However, on other occasions, mass pickets have been permitted by the police. In 1966, the courts ruled that where pickets walked in a continuous circle around a factory and refused to obey a police officer's order for them to stop, the police officer had been obstructed in the course of his duty. Sensible police officers often take no action as long as there is no violence or serious obstruction.

I

Support from Other Unions

It is important that any request for members of another union not to cross picket lines should be directed to the appropriate official or body of the other union, so that proper instructions can be issued to the members concerned.

Identification

Badges should be carried by pickets so that they are clearly identifiable as official pickets. If it has been agreed that members of other unions should have access to the premises – for instance those engaged in essential safety or maintenance work – this should be made clear to the pickets.

Discipline

Impress on pickets that they must behave in a disciplined and peaceful manner even if they are provoked by non-unionists or others. It will help to ensure that picketing is peaceful if an experienced member, preferably a union official, is in charge of the picket line. He should have a letter of authority which he can if necessary show to police officers or to workers attempting to cross the picket line.

Advice should also be given on what can be said because it is an offence to use insulting words or behaviour whilst on picket duty. Statements should always be factual, and not directed in a derogatory manner at individuals. Any talking or direct appeals to individuals should be done by official pickets.

Offers of help are normally welcome, but it should be made clear to outsiders who join a picket line that they must undertake to behave in a lawful and disciplined manner, otherwise their offer of assistance should be refused.

Mass Picketing

The effect of a large body of pickets brings home the depth of feeling that exists among the strikers and also constitutes an effective appeal for solidarity. However, the police may regard a large body of workers as obstructing entry to premises or as intimidation towards those who wish to enter.

Moreover, in any situation where large numbers of people with strong feelings are involved, there is a danger that things can get out of control. It is, therefore, particularly important for pickets to be conducted in a well-organised and disciplined manner.

Summary

Peaceful picketing is the conveying of information or verbally persuading people not to work or enter premises.

It is unlawful to obstruct a person or a vehicle.

The picket must not touch a person or a vehicle to prevent free passage.

Persuading a vehicle driver to turn back could be construed as inciting a breach of contract and is an offence.[4]

Too many pickets in one place can be causing an obstruction and be in danger of creating a breach of the peace, therefore, the police can move the pickets or restrict the numbers on the line.[5]

Notes

1. This is, and was in 1925, untrue.
2. Author's italics. This is again untrue.
3. The author is grateful to the Controller of the Stationery Office for permission to quote from this Circular.
4. Incorrect.
5. The author is grateful to Lawrence Daly, Secretary of the NUM, for permission to quote the NUM's advice on picketing.

Section VI
Reading Guide and Useful Sources

There is very little published material on bargaining skills as such. But if 'bargaining' is defined in its widest sense, as it is throughout this volume, then the whole of the literature of industrial relations might be included, and the problem becomes one of selection rather than one of scarcity. We would, however, draw the reader's attention to *Industrial Studies 1*, which contains more general bibliographies. Here we give: a general list of sources; main references for the material covered in the four books linked to this volume; further references for the material covered by the essays in this volume. We also give on pp. 267 ff. some guidance for tutors without legal training on the problems of teaching the law of industrial relations. (Eds.)

General List

BIBLIOGRAPHIES

GOTTSCHALK, A., *Workplace Industrial Relations and Bargaining Behaviour: A Behavioural Approach: A Select Bibliography* (University of Nottingham Department of Adult Education, 1973). Available from the Society of Industrial Tutors.

Although much of this bibliography is drawn from American sources, there are many references to books and articles published in Britain.

WALTON, R. E., and MCKERSIE, R. B., *A Behavioral Theory of Labor Negotiations* (*New York*: McGraw Hill, 1965).

This is not strictly speaking a bibliography, but it is the major theoretical work on bargaining behaviour. It also contains many practical examples to support its theoretical arguments. The bibliography and notes at the back of the book contain some two hundred references to other books and articles on the subject. Most of the sources quoted refer to American experience.

GENERAL WORKS

BBC, *Trade Union Studies* (1975).

This book accompanies the BBC/TUC/WEA series of the same name. It is a veritable mine of information on many different aspects of collective bargaining. It gives references to further reading material in each of its ten sections which deal with a wide range of bargaining issues.

BLACKBURN, R., and COCKBURN, A. (eds.), *The Incompatibles* (Penguin Special, 1967).

A useful and illuminating source of the kinds of ideas and attitudes which sometimes underlie trade union bargaining.

FISHER, R., *Basic Negotiating Strategy* (Allen Lane, 1969).

This book discusses the kind of negotiations undertaken by diplomats. But it has some usefulness because it provides insights into the thought processes of bureaucrats who are constantly involved in negotiations.

ILO, *Collective Bargaining – A Workers' Education Manual* (Geneva, 1960).

A somewhat dated descriptive account of the various aspects of collective bargaining.

Labour Research Department

LRD publishes a number of useful booklets and their Fact Service will provide information on companies. A recent publication is *How to Get the Facts About Profits and Prices*.

Trade Union Industrial Studies series (Hutchinson/Arrow).

The books in this series, both those published and those to come, contain much that is useful to the student of collective bargaining.

WARR, P. *Psychology and Collective Bargaining* (Hutchinson, 1973).

A not very convincing psychological view of collective bargaining; it contains some ideas from Walton and McKersie's book (see above) put in a much simpler way.

TRADE UNION PUBLICATIONS

APEX Training Texts

APEX, the white-collar union, has produced two booklets which are aimed at the union's members and which deal with subjects of importance to bargainers:

Statistics for Negotiators (1974).

Deals with the techniques necessary for handling statistical data.

Company Information for Negotiators (1974).
Analyses the various sources of financial information available to the union negotiator.

Transport and General Workers' Union

Plant Level Bargaining
A useful booklet giving the T&GWU's attitude and arguments on a number of issues facing negotiators at plant level.

The TUC

The TUC publishes a number of other useful publications which deal with the more practical aspects of bargaining, e.g. *Good Industrial Relations*, the TUC's answer to the Conservative Government's Code of Industrial Relations Practice; *Costs and Profits*; *Threshold Agreements*, etc. Lists are available from the TUC. Also, the Post-Donovan Conference Reports contain much useful material but it must be sifted from the usual conference-style oratory.

Trade Unionism (1967).
The TUC's evidence to the Donovan Commission, and a much underrated explanation of the need for collective bargaining and of the various forms it takes. Very suitable as a simple text for trade union students.

TEACHING NEGOTIATING SKILLS

There is a dearth of well written and well researched material on this subject, mainly because little research has been done and because negotiators seldom commit their thoughts and experiences to paper. Nevertheless the bibliography by Andrew Gottschalk (see above, p. 261) and the sources mentioned in the following two articles will set the reader off on the right tracks:

KNIVETON, B. H., 'Industrial Negotiating: Some Training Implications', *Industrial Relations* (autumn 1974).

PEDLER, M., 'The Training Implications of the Shop Steward's Leadership Role', *Industrial Relations* (spring 1974).

FILM AND TV RESOURCES

These were covered adequately in *Industrial Studies 1: the key skills* (in this series), and we refer the reader to pp. 145–9 for a selection of films and distributors. Many of the films listed there deal with negotiating

situations; we particularly recommend the film *The Space Between Words –
Work* (distributed by BBC Enterprises) as an authentic example of real-
life negotiations between management and unions.

STUDIES OF NEGOTIATIONS AND STRIKES

All of the following look at a particular dispute or use as case studies
negotiations which have actually taken place:

ARNISON, J., *The Million Pound Strike* (Lawrence & Wishart, 1970).
BECK, A., *The Fine Tubes Strike* (Stage 1, 1974).
BEYNON, H., *Working for Ford* (Allen Lane, 1973).
CLEGG, H. A., and ADAMS, R., *The Employers' Challenge* (Blackwell, 1957).
HUGHES, J., and MOORE, R., *A Special Case: Social Justice and the Miners*
    (Penguin, 1972).
HYMAN, R., *Disputes Procedure in Action* (Heinemann, 1972).
LANE, A., and ROBERTS, K., *Strike at Pilkingtons* (Fontana, 1971).
MCCARTHY, W. E. J., and COLLIER, A. S., *Coming to Terms with Trade
    Unions* (IPM, 1973).
MATHEWS, J., *The Ford Strike* (Panther, 1972).
THOMAS, R. (ed.), *An Exercise in Redeployment* (Pergamon Press, 1969).

Useful Books Recommended by Bill Conboy, author of *Pay at Work*

Good basic reading about pay systems is hard to find. Most available
material has resulted from Government-sponsored research, such as PIB
or OME pamphlets, or has been essentially academic research work.
Although unions spend a lot of their time talking about pay very few of
them have published anything in writing to help their members, apart
from a few lines in a shop steward's handbook.

The following books cover the field surveyed in *Pay at Work*. Where
possible paperbacks have been chosen, most of which contain references to
or lists of other books and articles that will be of interest to anyone who
would like further reading.

PAY SYSTEMS

Payment-By-Results

1. ILO, *Payment by Results* (Geneva, 1965).
    In spite of its date, this is still a very useful book on PBR. In fact it was
first published in 1951, but it explains most of the various systems clearly
and asks the right questions. Best value will be gained by reading the first

two chapters on the main features of the schemes and the procedures used in introducing and applying them, followed by Chapters 5, 6 and 7: the effects, advantages, disadvantages and principles.

2. National Board for Prices and Incomes, *Payment by Results*, Report No. 65 and Supplement (HMSO, 1968).

The PIB was not a popular body with many trade unionists but many of its reports provide extremely useful information. Report No. 65 looks at various pay schemes with particular reference to wage drift and its effect on the operation of the incomes policy then in force. Its main value, apart from description of the schemes, lies in the case studies from various firms.

3. BROWN, W., *Piecework Bargaining* (Warwick University, 1973).

This book is one of a series from the Industrial Relations Research Unit at Warwick University. Based on research at Coventry firms, it deals first with the basic principles of piecework and the sources of its instability and then with bargaining factors. It has very useful sections on wage structures and differentials in various firms and the importance of custom and practice in piecework. It also examines the role of shop stewards.

Measured-Day-Work

4. Office of Manpower Economics (OME), *Measured Daywork* (HMSO, 1973).

This is the most comprehensive published study of MDW in this country carried out by the OME as part of its initial research programme. It deals with recent trends in payment systems, the extent and distribution of MDW, reasons for its introduction, how it operates, as well as the implications of the system for management, employees and union organizations.

The report is based on a statistical survey (to find out where MDW was worked) backed up by information from thirty case studies. It has much useful descriptive material, but unfortunately the statistical material was based on a sample of establishments where MDW was worked instead of a sample of employees working MDW in various industries. Hence we still do not know how many workers are under this scheme of pay.

OTHER SYSTEMS

5. LUPTON, T. (ed.), *Payment Systems*, Penguin Modern Management Readings (Penguin, 1972).

This book of readings has useful chapters on time span by its designer

I*

Elliot Jaques (Chapters 17 and 18) and a powerful critique by Alan Fox (Chapter 20) as well as sections on Scanlon plans, MDW and incentive-based pay systems. Taken in small doses it provides valuable information for anyone interested in pay systems.

WAGE STRUCTURES AND DIFFERENTIALS

6. National Board for Prices and Incomes, *Job Evaluation*, Report No. 83 (HMSO, 1967).

If we are interested in wage structures then we compare the wages paid for different jobs. Job evaluation is a systematic and formal method of comparing jobs. This report by the PIB is a useful introduction to the procedures used and links up with the report on PBR.

7. ROBINSON, D. (ed.), *Local Labour Markets and Wage Structures* (Gower Press, 1970).

This book presents some of the findings of research into wage structures, wage systems and local labour markets carried out by different groups at Glasgow, Manchester and Oxford Universities. Its main value is to relate the operation of wage systems to internal wage structures and from there to make comparisons with other firms in the same locality.

8. MACKAY, D. I., BODDY, D., BROCK, J., DIACK, J. A., and JONES, N., *Labour Markets under Different Employment Conditions* (George Allen & Unwin, 1971).

This book attempts to describe and explain the behaviour in labour markets in five separate areas through an analysis of the personnel records of 75 000 manual workers from 66 different engineering plants and comparisons with wage and employment data for the period studied. Much of the work was based on Birmingham and Glasgow firms. Its main value lies in the excellent introduction in Part I, the information on wages in Part II and the conclusions in Part VI.

9. LERNER, S. W., CABLE, J. R., and GUPTA, S. (eds.), *Workshop Wage Determination* (Pergamon Press, 1969).

Wages research in this country is heavily concentrated on the engineering industry. The reason is simple. The information is obtainable more easily in engineering than in other industries. The value of this book is that it has, in addition to a chapter on engineering, other chapters on the chemical, soap and baking industries. The wage information is now dated but many of the issues raised, such as formal works level bargaining, are still relevant.

Income Distribution

10. Royal Commission on the Distribution of Income and Wealth, *Initial*

Report, Report No. 1 (HMSO, 1975); *Income from Companies and its Distribution*, Report No. 2 (HMSO, 1975).

Views about the distribution of income and wealth are often highly contentious and reliable information is hard to find. These two reports from the Royal Commission set up in 1974 are useful because they clear the ground. Report No. 1 analyses and evaluates statistics on income and wealth and introduces the controversial notion that accrued pension rights held by individuals might be considered when measuring the distribution of wealth.

Low Pay

11. FIELD, F. (ed.), *Low Pay* (Arrow Books, 1973).

This is a useful introduction to the problems of low pay. It is a readable book written by those who want to see changes carried out and who use sensible documentation from this country and abroad to buttress their arguments.

12. FISHER, A., and DIX, B., *Low Pay and How to End It* (Pitman Publishing, 1974).

This book is worth reading if only because it is written by trade unionists. Some of their ideas, particularly those involving trade union action, are worth thinking about.

Apart from these books, much valuable information about current pay systems and rates of pay is available from the *New Earning Survey, 1974*, published by the HMSO; from the Incomes Data Services and from Industrial Relations Review and Report. These sources tend to be expensive for the individual, but it should be possible to gain access to them through the union.

Another useful source of information is the Trade Union Research Unit at Ruskin College which regularly produces reports on matters of interest to trade union bargainers in general and for those interested in pay questions in particular. Copies of these reports can be obtained either through the union or directly from the Unit at Ruskin College, Oxford.

Recommendations by Paul O'Higgins, author of *Workers' Rights*

SUGGESTIONS FOR TUTORS

To a large extent teaching in the area of the law and labour relations is bound to be expository, drawing on the materials in *Workers' Rights* and other suggested reading in this volume. However, this should be qualified in two respects. First of all it is desirable that the role of the law should be brought out in any general course in labour relations, for instance on collective bargaining. If it is at all relevant, the role of the law should be included on any course. When doing any case study in a class it is always relevant to ask, 'What role does the law have to play in this problem?' In other words, it is often easier to illustrate some of the general themes suggested above in classes other than those specifically devoted to labour law, although it may be desirable to have classes on the general theme of 'workers' rights'. Secondly, it is often a useful exercise to try to establish what are the rules which operate inside the work-place. Students should be encouraged to bring copies of company handbooks, works rules, texts of collective agreements, etc., to class. These are worth discussing in class, paying particular attention to the extent to which the rules laid down in these documents are ignored in practice by mutual agreement between workers and management. Sometimes the agreement is explicit, sometimes merely tacit. Quite apart from the rules contained in bits of paper, what other rules or informal practices have grown up in the work-place which regulate relations between workers and management? How are both formal and informal rules enforced by workers and management? How often are rules laid down by the law or legislation relied upon or acted upon in the work-place? Is the employer's policy over dismissals affected by the law on unfair dismissals? What difference has the Health and Safety at Work Act made to working conditions?

It may be useful to examine collective agreements applicable in a particular industry to find out how far the minimum standards established by legislation, such as the Employment Protection Act, have been improved upon by collective bargaining.

The basic thing to remember is that the object of discussing the role of law in labour relations is not to educate workers to be lawyers, but to show the limited role which the law plays in the actual conduct of labour relations. There are a number of general themes to be borne in mind.

Basic Reading

1. WEDDERBURN, K. W., *The Worker and the Law* (Penguin, 1971), 2nd edn.
2. KAHN-FREUND, O., *Labour and the Law* (Sweet & Maxwell, 1977), 2nd edn.

This discusses basic problems in a very stimulating way. In particular it brings out the general theme that for a variety of reasons the law can play only a very limited role in British labour relations. The collapse of the Industrial Relations Act, 1971, illustrates this.

The Failure of the Industrial Relations Act, 1971

3. WEEKES, B., *et al.*, *Industrial Relations and the Limits of the Law* (Blackwell, 1975).
4. THOMSON, A. W. J., and ENGLEMAN, S. R., *The Industrial Relations Act: A Review and Analysis* (Martin Robertson, 1975).

The Role of the Judges and the Courts

5. WEDDERBURN, K. W., *The Worker and the Law* (Penguin, 1971), 2nd edn.
   Deals particularly well with the subject.
6. SIMON, D., 'Master and Servant' in Saville, J. (ed.), *Democracy and the Labour Movement* (Macmillan, 1954), pp. 160–200.
   Brings out very clearly the inequality of the legal rules applicable to workers in the nineteenth century.
7. PELLING, H., *Popular Politics and Society in Late Victorian England* (Macmillan, 1968).
   The most useful part of this book is Chapter 4 which discusses the development of working-class attitudes to the law in some detail.

The Role of Legislation

Legislation has embodied concessions made to the working class as well as often being the result of working-class agitation to obtain improvement in their conditions by legislative means.
   K. W. Wedderburn's book (detailed above) illustrates this.

The Theme of Collective Bargaining

The theme is that in Britain collective bargaining is the traditional method of establishing acceptable minimum standards in labour relations, instead of reliance on legislation as a means of establishing minimum working conditions.
   K. W. Wedderburn's book develops this theme. See also:
8. O'HIGGINS, P., 'Collective Bargaining in Britain', in Mayer-Maly, T. (ed.), *Kollektivverträge in Europa* (Munich; Fink Verlag, 1972).

Allied to this is the need to discuss the extent to which this tradition is being changed by legislation such as the Employment Protection Act, 1975, and whether the establishment by law of minimum labour standards is a desirable trend. One should distinguish between legislation establishing minimum standards for all workers, unionized and non-unionized, like the Employment Protection Act, and legislation designed to establish minimum standards for some groups of workers who are industrially weak, for example those in the wages council system.

Redundancy

Do rights to redundancy compensation, established by the Redundancy Payments Act, help workers or management? On this last issue useful material can be found in:

9. PARKER, S. R., THOMAS, C. G., ELLIS, N. D., and MCCARTHY, W. E. J., *Effects of the Redundancy Payments Act* (HMSO, 1971).
10. FRYER, R. H., 'Myths of the Redundancy Payments Act', *Industrial Law Journal,* Vol. 2 (1973), pp. 1–16.

Foreign Systems

A special problem arises about the discussion of foreign systems of labour relations and labour law. The fact that there are very different rules in other systems may be interesting in itself: it may illustrate the fact that for any one problem in labour relations there may be very different solutions in various countries. These can help to illuminate the significance of what happens in Britain. Equally they can sometimes show that there may be better ways of doing things than the way they are done in this country. However, it is important to bear in mind that rules and institutions are not readily transferable from one country to another. Each country's system of labour relations and the rules governing it are the product of that country's own social and historical development and the strength of trade unionism there, not to mention its own cultural and political traditions. There is unfortunately no very adequate book on foreign labour relations systems, although useful material can be found in the monthly *European Industrial Relations Review.*

Note

There is one problem of terminology in discussing labour law which gives rise to much confusion. As explained in *Workers' Rights,* the term 'contract of employment' describes the agreement between a worker and an employer whereby the former agrees to work for the latter. In practice, however, the term is nowadays widely used to describe the document given by every employer under the Contracts of Employment Act, 1972, to his workers describing the principal terms of the contract. This document is *not* itself the contract of employment.

USEFUL BOOKS

Bibliographies

11. HEPPLE, B. A., NEESON, J. M., and O'HIGGINS, P., *A Bibliography of the Literature on British and Irish Labour Law* (Mansell, 1975).
This is a comprehensive bibliography of labour law, listing books, pamphlets and articles, which will be kept up to date by occasional supplements.

12. *Industrial Law Journal*, quarterly (see below).
Publishes regular lists of articles on labour law published in British and Irish periodicals.
Any general bibliography devoted to labour relations is likely to contain many items of relevance to the impact of the law on labour relations.

Reference

13. HEPPLE, B. A., and O'HIGGINS, P., *Encyclopaedia of Labour Relations Law* (Sweet & Maxwell, 1972), 2 vols. (kept up to date by six annual supplements).
This is the basic reference book. It contains the texts of all relevant statutes and delegated rules, summarizes decisions of courts, gives a detailed introduction to individual employment law, etc.

14. HARVEY, R. J., *Industrial Relations* (Butterworth, 1971) (kept up to date by occasional supplements).
This has a much more limited scope than the *Encyclopaedia*.

Periodicals

15. *Industrial Law Journal* (Sweet & Maxwell), quarterly. The principal periodical devoted to labour law published in this country.

16. *Industrial Relations Review and Report,* monthly. Much material on labour law.

17. IDS *Briefs*, published by Incomes Data Service. IDS also publish guids to various aspects of labour law from time to time.

18. *European Industrial Relations Review*, monthly. Gives developments inside EEC.

Reports of Decisions of Courts and Tribunals

There are four series of law reports specializing in labour law:

19. *Managerial Law*
20. *Industrial Tribunal Reports* (HMSO).
21. *Industrial Cases Reports* (Incorporated Council of Law Reporting).
22. *Industrial Relations Law Reports.*

It should be emphasized that industrial tribunal decisions are interesting, but do not establish legal principles which must be applied in similar cases decided by other industrial tribunals.

23. WEDDERBURN, K. W., *Cases and Materials on Labour Law* (Cambridge University Press, 1967).
   This contains extracts from many of the most important decisions on labour law, and from the chief statutes. It is now somewhat out-of-date but is still very useful.

Works Discussing General Principles

24. WEDDERBURN, K. W., *The Worker and the Law* (for details, see above, no. 1).
   This is the best overall view, although a little out-of-date. It is a really excellent work illuminating the whole area.

25. KAHN-FREUND, O., *Labour and the Law* (for details, see above, no. 2).
   Professor Kahn-Freund's works, especially this book, are of great importance, on a more theoretical level.

General Textbooks

At the moment there are few up-to-date textbooks of labour law, although Part I of the *Encyclopaedia of Labour Relations Law* (for details, see above no. 13) *is* kept up-to-date and gives a general account of most aspects, paying particular attention to the rights of individual workers.
   Reference should also be made to the following textbooks:

26. HEPPLE, B. A., and O'HIGGINS, P., *Employment Law* (Sweet & Maxwell, 1976).
27. RIDEOUT, R. W., *Principles of Labour Law* (Sweet & Maxwell, 1976), 2nd edn.

Industrial Conflict

28. GRUNFELD, C., *Modern Trade Union Law* (Sweet & Maxwell, 1966).
This is much less out-of-date than the date of publication might suggest. It contains a good overall view of the problems.

29. KAHN-FREUND, O., and HEPPLE, B. A., *Laws Against Strikes*, Fabian Research Series No. 305 (Fabian Society, 1972).
Discusses the issues raised by the 'right to strike' from the point of view of general principle.

30. AARON, B., and WEDDERBURN, K. W., *Industrial Conflict: A Comparative Legal Survey* (Longman, 1972).
A very stimulating work.

Machinery for the Settlement of Disputes

The leading work is:

31. WEDDERBURN, L. W., and DAVIES, P. L., *Employment Grievances and Disputes in Britain* (University of California Press, 1969).

32. GREENHALGH, R. M., *Industrial Tribunals – A Practical Guide* (IPM, 1973).
A special study of tribunals.

Public Employees

The rules governing workers in the public sector are often very different from those in private industry. An account of these rules can be found in:

33. HEPPLE, B. A., and O'HIGGINS, P., *Public Employee Trade Unionism in the United Kingdom: The Legal Framework* (Institute of Labor and Industrial Relations, University of Michigan and Wayne State University, 1971).

Race

The most important book is:

34. HEPPLE B. A., *Race, Jobs and the Law in Britain* (Penguin, 1970), 2nd edn.

Redundancy

The standard work is:

35. GRUNFELD, C., *The Law of Redundancy* (Sweet & Maxwell, 1971).

36. FARNDALE, W. A. J., and COOPER, A. J., *The Law on Redundancy with Special Reference to the National Health Service* (Ravenswood Publications, 1971).
A special study of redundancy in the Health Service.

Safety at Work

The best textbook is:

37. MUNKMAN, J. H., *The Employer's Liability at Common Law* (Butterworth, 1975), 8th edn.

38. WILLIAMS, J. L., *Accidents and Ill-Health at Work* (Staples Press, 1960).
This is the classic work of criticism on this topic. It brings out most aspects of the problem of reducing the incidence of accidents and diseases at work.

39. KINNERSLEY, P., *The Hazards of Work: How to Fight Them*, Workers' Handbook No. 1 (Pluto Press, 1973).
This book relates problems of safety at work to action taken by workers themselves. It is full of useful information.

Trade Unions

The best is still C. Grunfeld's *Modern Trade Union Law* (for details see no. 28 above).

Unfair Dismissal

This topic is often quite well dealt with in the general textbooks. Two will be found useful in discussing current trends:

40. ANDERMAN, S. D., *Unfair Dismissals and the Law* (IPM, 1973).

41. JACKSON, D., *Unfair Dismissal: How and Why the Law Works* (Cambridge University Press, 1975).

Women

There is not a good book on the position of women in employment. Two, however, contain an explanation from the point of view of management of the Equal Pay Act, 1970:

42. PATERSON, P., and ARMSTRONG, M., *An Employer's Guide to Equal Pay* (Kogan Page Associates, 1972).

43. BUCKINGHAM, G. L., *What to Do about Equal Pay for Women* (Gower Press, 1974).

Useful Books to Accompany Ernie Johnston's *Industrial Action*

Industrial Action, unlike most of the other books in the present series, contains details of the sources used. Here for the reader's convenience we list the main ones and draw attention to other relevant material. The reader should also note the works contained in the section above entitled *Studies of Negotiations and Strikes* (p. 264).

1. BEEVER, C., 'Sitting It Out', *Industrial Society*, Vol. 55 (May 1973).

2. *Cameron Report*, Cmnd. 3396 (HMSO, 1967).

3. CHADWICK, G., 'The Manchester Sit-Ins', in Barratt Brown, M., and Coates, K. (eds.), *Trade Union Register*, No. 3 (Spokesman Books, 1973).

4. CLARKE, TOM, 'Sit-In at Fisher Bendix', Institute of Workers' Control Pamphlet No. 42 (1975).

5. Institute of Workers' Control Bulletins: November 1973; December 1973; No. 7, January 1974; No. 9, February 1974; No. 13, March 1974.

6. 'The Social Audit', Institute of Workers' Control Pamphlet No. 26.

7. THOMPSON, W., and HART, F., *The UCS Work-In* (Lawrence & Wishart, 1972).

Books Relating to *Work Study* by Jim Powell

In suggesting a book list for further reading on this subject you will note that the word 'recommended' has been excluded. It would be wrong to write a criticism of the system and then recommend books which totally contradict my views.

Many of the authors listed are devotees of work study and they present the system as a panacea which will solve industry's production problems.

Of all the authors I researched none was prepared to identify the cost in terms of job loss, and there was little criticism of the system, except perhaps by B. W. Niebel, who comes near it since he highlights the United States Government's investigation of the 'Taylor system'. Nevertheless, for those who wish to read other books, the following list is given.

METHOD STUDY

GILBRETH, F. B., *Motion Study* (New York: D. van Nostrand & Co., 1911).

Describes the early days of Gilbreth as a bricklayer and his discovery of the different methods of bricklaying used then. Also deals with the development of micromotion study and chronocyclegraph techniques. It also identifies method study as a labour-saving device.

2. GILBRETH, F. B. and I. M., *Applied Motion Study* (New York: Sturgis & Walton, 1917).
A joint venture by husband and wife, showing the development of method study and its application to work situations.

3. SHAW, A., *The Purpose and Practice of Motion Study* (Harlequin, 1952).
A devotee of Gilbreth – and it shows!

WORK MEASUREMENT

4. TAYLOR, F. W., *The Principles of Scientific Management* (New York: Harper & Brothers, 1929).
Taylor at his best. He identifies management difficulties and their need for his system.

5. TAYLOR, F. W., *Shop Management* (New York: Harper & Brothers, 1910).
Taylor's testimony before a special committee from the House of Representatives. A Watergate type of investigation in which the truth about the system and Taylor's purpose in applying it to work is drawn out by probing Congressmen. Worth reading since it condemns the application of time study to work.

6. BARNES, R. M., *Motion and Time Study* (New York: Wiley, 1963).
Possibly the most prolific writer on the subject. Ideal for potential industrial engineers. Barnes believes in the system, and it certainly sounds that way, especially when he is discussing allowances.

7. FARMER, E., *Time and Motion Study*, Industry Fatigue Research Board Report No. 5 (HMSO, 1923).

8. NIEBEL, B. W., *Motion and Time Study* (Homewood, Illinois: Richard D. Irwin, Inc., 1972).
Quite a critical view of the system. Sometimes writes like a trade unionist.

WORK STUDY

9. CURRIE, R. M., *Outline of Work Study* (BIM, Pitman, 1963).
Currie is recognized as the British master of the American system. He

is also a leading exponent of its application in ICI. But even ICI will admit work study has its faults.

10. WHITMORE, D., *Work Study and Related Management Services* (Heinemann, 1968).
  A modern look at an old system. Dennis Whitmore is convincing and does not fault anything.

11. LOWRY, S. M., MAYNARD, H. B., and STEGEMERTEN, G. J., *Time and Motion Study and Formulas for Wage Incentives* (New York: McGraw-Hill, 1940).
  The team responsible for MTM. It is not difficult to see why management are devotees of this system.

CLERICAL

12. NANCE, H. W., and NOLAN, R. E., *Office Work Measurement* (New York: McGraw-Hill, 1971).
  Ideal for clerical staff who are complacent enough to believe that work measurement is only for industrial workers. Identifies a need for measurement within the clerical industry.

Useful Books Relating to Essay Subjects

PRINCIPLES IN WORK-PLACE BARGAINING

A more detailed discussion of many points raised in this essay can be found in Batstone, Boraston and Frenkel's forthcoming publications, the first of which is:

1. *Shop Stewards in Action* (Blackwell, 1976).

Other useful books are:

2. BROWN, W., *Piecework Bargaining* (Heinemann, 1973).
  Looks at steward organization and bargaining relationships.

3. BENYON, H., *Working for Ford* (Penguin, 1973).
  Stresses the importance of good organization.

4. LANE, T., *The Union Makes Us Strong* (Arrow Books, 1974).
  Contains useful warnings for shop stewards.

BARGAINING IN PRACTICE AND THEORY

Ron Bean's essay 'Industrial Reactions' in the present volume with its extensive notes provides the best bibliography for this section. Here we select a few key works and follow them with a list of best buys for learning to negotiate by Mike Pedler.

General

Both the following from their different sociological viewpoints provide a view of conflict in industry.

1. FOX, A., *Beyond Contract: Work Power and Trust Relations* (Faber, 1974).

2. BLUMBERG, P., *Industrial Democracy* (Constable, 1968).

The following two give in turn a classic and detailed study of the causes of strikes in the motor industry and an examination of strikes and other manifestations of conflict in industry.

3. TURNER, H. A., CLACK, G., and ROBERTS, G., *Labour Relations in the Motor Industry* (Allen & Unwin, 1967).

4. BEAN, R., 'The Relationship Between Strikes and Unorganised Conflict in Manufacturing Industries', *British Journal of Industrial Relations*, Vol. 13 (1975).

Some Best Buys for Learning to Negotiate

The following books contain both theory and exercises for developing skills such as influencing, changing, communicating, negotiating.

5. JOHNSON, D. W., *Reaching Out – Interpersonal Effectiveness and Self-Actualization* (Englewood Cliffs, New Jersey: Prentice Hall, 1972). Paperback.
   This book was originally written for young people, but in fact is an excellent collection of theory, exercises and checklists to measure your understanding. The material works well with adults and young people alike. Areas covered include developing trust, communication skills, confrontation and conflict resolution.

6. FORDYCE, J. K., and WEIL, R., *Managing with People – A Manager's Handbook of Organisation Development Methods* (Addison Wesley, 1971). Paperback.
   A clear yet terse book covering techniques and methods being used in organization development. The methods are particularly aimed at bringing about change in interpersonal relationships, groups and organizations. Also includes some case studies and loads of ideas and examples.

7. PFEIFFER, J. W., and JONES, J. E., *Handbooks of Structured Experiences for Human Relations Training* (University Associates Press, 1969, 1970, 1971, 1973).

Together with their companion volumes *Annual Handbooks for Group Facilitators*, 1972, 1973 and 1974, the Pfeiffer and Jones collections have become almost a bible for experiential exercises of all types. These are loose-leaf books containing over a hundred exercises. The *Annuals* contain little lectures, instruments and bibliographies as well. Very good stuff but fairly expensive. They are available in England through various suppliers, one of whom is Tom Boyce, Department of Economics, University of Wales, Cardiff.

THE FRAMEWORK OF COLLECTIVE BARGAINING

The Growth and Development of Trade Unions and Collective Bargaining

1. PHELPS BROWN, E. H., *The Growth of British Industrial Relations* (Macmillan, 1965).

2. RODGER, C., *The Development of Industrial Relations in Britain 1911–1939* (Hutchinson, 1973).

3. Report of the Royal Commission on Trade Unions and Employers' Associations (HMSO, 1968), Cmnd. 3623.

4. CLEGG, H. A., *The System of Industrial Relations in Great Britain* (Blackwell, 1972), Chapters 2, 4, 6.

5. HUGHES, J., *Trade Union Structure and Government*, Research Paper No. 5 (Parts 1 and 2), Royal Commission on Trade Unions and Employers' Associations (1968).

6. TUC, *Trade Unionism* (TUC, 1967).

7. TUC, *Good Industrial Relations: A Guide for Negotiators* (TUC, 1971).

The reader is also referred to the General List (pp. 261–4).

Employers' Associations

8. BRADLEY, J. F., *The Role of Trade Associations and Professional Business Societies in America* (Pennsylvania State University Press, 1965).

A useful if somewhat uncritical view, including 'the contributions of these various associations to the aspirations of a free society and the growth and development of the individual in that society'.

9. BULL, G., *Industrial Relations: The Boardroom Viewpoint* (Bodley Head, 1972).

Although somewhat dated, with many references to the Industrial Relations Act, 1971, this book by an editor of *The Director* gives an insight into management thinking.

10. CLEGG, H. A., and ADAMS, R., *The Employers' Challenge* (Blackwell, 1957).

A case study of the confrontation between the EEF and the engineering unions in 1957.

11. PEP, *Industrial Trade Associations; Activities and Organisation* (Allen & Unwin, 1957).

12. MILLERSON, G., *The Qualifying Associations: A Study in Professionalism* (Routledge & Kegan Paul, 1964).

13. GRANT, W. P., and MARSH, D., 'The Confederation of British Industry', *Political Studies*, Vol. 19, No. 4 (1971).

An interesting summary of the formation of the CBI from its constituent members and an insight into some of the issues of the early years of its existence.

Government Intervention in Collective Bargaining

14. CLEGG, H. A., *How to Run an Incomes Policy and Why We Made Such a Mess Of the Last One* (Heinemann, 1971).

15. BALFOUR, C., *Incomes Policy and the Public Sector* (Routledge & Kegan Paul, 1972).

16. BLACKABY, F., *An Incomes Policy for Britain* (Heinemann, 1972).

17. FELS, A., *The Prices and Incomes Board* (Cambridge University Press, 1972).

18. ULMAN, L., and FLANAGAN, R. J., *Wage Restraints* (California University Press, 1971).

19. ROBINSON, D., 'Differentials and Incomes Policy', *Industrial Relations Journal* (spring 1973).

20. TURNER, H. A., 'Collective Bargaining and the Eclipse of Incomes Policy', *British Journal of Industrial Relations*, Vol. 2 (1970).

21. TURNER, H. A., and WILKINSON, F., *Do Trade Unions Cause Inflation?* (Cambridge University Press, 1972).

BARGAINING AND WORKERS' RIGHTS

John McIlroy's notes to his essay *Bargaining for Rights* provide complete references to the main Acts and commentaries on labour law, as also does Paul O'Higgins' bibliography above (pp. 267–75). But for the specialist subject of picketing we give below a bibliography produced by Paul O'Higgins.

It has not been possible for him to give an adequate account of this extremely complicated branch of the law in the space available, and in fact no such account exists. However, most of the articles listed below include those points which are omitted from the numerous discussions of the picketing problem.

Bibliographies

1. HEPPLE, B. A., NEESON, J. M., and O'HIGGINS, P., *A Bibliography of the Literature Relating to British and Irish Labour Law* (Mansell, 1975).
   Contains extensive references to books, pamphlets and articles.

Basic accounts

2. WEDDERBURN, K. W., *The Worker and the Law* (Penguin, 1971), 2nd edn.

3. GRUNFELD, C., *Modern Trade Union Law* (Sweet & Maxwell, 1966).

4. LABOUR RESEARCH DEPARTMENT, *Picketing: A Trade Unionist's Guide* (LRD, 1972).

Articles

5. KIDNER, R., 'Picketing and the Criminal Law', *Criminal Law Review* (1975), pp. 256–70.

6. TRICE, J. E., 'Methods of an Attitude to Picketing', *ibid.*, pp. 271–82.

7. WALLINGTON, P., 'The Case of the Longannett Miners and the Criminal Liability of Pickets', *Industrial Law Journal*, Vol. 1, No. 4 (1972), pp. 219–28.

8. DRAKE, C., 'The Right to Picket Peacefully: Section 134', *ibid.*, pp. 214–18.

9. WALLINGTON, P., 'Picketing', *Industrial Law Journal*, Vol. 3, No. 2 (1974), pp. 109–12.

10. KAY, M., 'Picketing and the Law', *The Industrial Tutor*, Vol. 2 (1975), pp. 49–56.

History

11. HEDGES, R. Y., and WINTERBOTTOM, A., *The Legal History of Trade Unionism* (London, 1930).
Traces the history of the law on picketing up to 1927.

Cases

There are innumerable court decisions on picketing.

12. WEDDERBURN, K. W., *Cases and Materials on Labour Law* (Cambridge University Press, 1967).
Gives the older cases.

The more important cases decided since 1967, or not in Wedderburn's book, include the following:

Duncan v. *Jones* [1936] KB 218.
Piddington v. *Bates* [1961] 3 All ER 660.
Tynan v. *Balmer* [1967] 1 QB 91.
R. v. *Jones* [1974] ICR 310 (the Shrewsbury case).
Hunt v. *Broome* [1974] ICR 84.
Kavanagh v. *Hiscock* [1974] ICR 282.
Hubbard v. *Pitt* [1975] ICR 77 and 308 (a case of non-industrial picketing).
(KB—King's Bench Reports; QB—Queen's Bench Reports; All ER—All England Reports; ICR—Industrial Court Reports.)

Political assessment

13. ARNISON, J., *The Shrewsbury Three* (Lawrence & Wishart, 1974).

Industrial Action

Ernie Johnston

Industrial action is conflict. Faced with an overtime
ban, a strike or a sit-in, employers will bring up all the
power they have.

Trade unionists have to get mobilized too, if they hope
to win. This book has grown out of a lifetime struggle.
It shows the active trade unionist

*how to organise a disciplined and effective strike
committee

*how – and when – to negotiate with management

*how to avert possible splits within the factory

Ernie Johnston has been an active trade unionist for over
twenty years, as convenor, divisional and national
committee delegate. He is currently a trade unionist
research worker.

Pay at Work
Bill Conboy

You may think that the size of your wage packet is what counts – but that may depend on how you get paid. Do you understand how your own system of payment works? Would it pay you to change it? Or do you leave it to management to make the running?

You should know the best system for your situation. This book can help you. It looks at

*time rated systems

*payment by results

*measured day work

*some alternative pay schemes

and relates them to pay structures inside and outside the place of work.

Bill Conboy is staff tutor in economics and industrial relations at Oxford University Department for External Studies.

Work Study
Jim Powell

Work study isn't a science in the real sense of the word. But it is the kind of science that managers try to blind their workers with. This book shows you how to take the blindfolds off. It shows you how to test and understand

*method study and work measurement

*time study

*job evaluation

Jim Powell, a former convenor and currently a free-lance tutor, learned about 'scientific management' the hard way – but this book makes it look easy.

Workers' Rights
Paul O'Higgins

Do you know what rights you've got at your place of work? And how you can set about getting what the law has provided? Many rights have been won by trade union action over the years. You should know how to exercise them for yourself and your fellow trade unionists.

This book tells you

*which rules and regulations at the work place have the force of law

*what legal status the contract of employment has

*the law on dismissal and redundancy

*your rights on health and safety

*what the new Acts say on Trade Unions and Labour Relations, and on Employment Protection

Paul O'Higgins lectures in labour law at Cambridge University. He has considerable experience of teaching labour law to extra-mural, WEA and trade union courses.

Statistics for Bargainers
Karl Hedderwick

Are you losing out in the wage-price battle?

Statistics are a vital part in the complex world of modern industrial relations. If today's trade unionist is to bargain effectively he must match management's statistical sources and techniques.

This introduction to statistics – specially written to fit the needs of bargainers – covers areas such as

*What is an average?

*How are wages rates and earnings linked?

*What is the Retail Price Index?

*How do you measure productivity?

*How to understand the unemployment figures

Karl Hedderwick is lecturer in Economics and Industrial Studies in the Extra-Mural Department of Sheffield University.

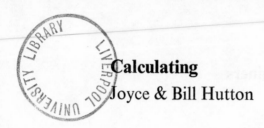

Calculating

Joyce & Bill Hutton

Isn't it strange that people who can work out in their heads betting odds or the price of a round still feel at sea when it comes to more systematic calculations?

This workbook – specially geared towards practical calculations – makes mathematics easier. It deals with

*Fractions and decimals

*Ratios, percentages and interest

*Formulae and graphs

*Slide rules and calcuiators

This book gives trade unionists the confidence and techniques they need at work and in their daily lives.

Joyce Hutton is a former mathematics teacher who served on the Schools Council Mathematics Advisory Committee.

Bill Hutton is a former investment analyst with experience of teaching adults.

Both have had long service in the trade union movement.